Louis Althusser was born in Algeria, at Birmandreïs, in 1918. After schooling in Algeria, Marseille, and Lyon he went to the École Normale Supérieure where in 1948 he took his degree in philosophy. Since then he has taught there and is now the Secrétaire of the School. During his youth he was active in the Catholic student movement as a member of the Jeunes Étudiants Catholiques. In 1948 he joined the French Communist Party. He has published the following books: *For Marx* (Allen Lane 1970); *Reading Capital* (NLB 1970); *Lenin and Philosophy and Other Essays* (NLB 1971); *Politics and History* (NLB 1972).

Louis Althusser

NLB

Essays in Self-Criticism

Translated by Grahame Lock

Réponse à John Lewis was published by François Maspero, 1973
© Louis Althusser, 1973

Eléments d'Autocritique was published by Librairie Hachette, 1974
© Librairie Hachette, 1974

Est-Il Simple d'Etre Marxiste en Philosophie? was published in
La Pensée, October 1975
© Louis Althusser, 1975

This edition, *Essays in Self-Criticism*, first published 1976
© NLB, 1976

NLB, 7 Carlisle Street, London W1
ISBN No 902308 87 4

Printed in Great Britain by
Lowe & Brydone Printers Limited, Thetford, Norfolk

Contents

Preface   vii

Introduction   1

1. Reply to John Lewis   33

Reply to John Lewis   35
Note on "The Critique of the Personality Cult"   78
Remark on the Category : "Process without a
Subject or Goal(s)"   94

2. Elements of Self-Criticism   101

Elements of Self-Criticism   105
On the Evolution of the Young Marx   151

3. Is it Simple to be a Marxist in Philosophy?   163

"Something New"   208

Bibliography   217

Index   222

Preface

In 1970 I was invited to lecture at Marx House in London on the work of Althusser. John Lewis was sitting in the front row of the audience. In the discussion he expressed his disagreement with what he had heard, and, later, his intention to combat it. Early in 1972 he published his article on "The Althusser Case" in *Marxism Today*. James Klugmann, the editor of the journal, asked Althusser to reply, and this reply appeared in October and November of the same year.

This latter text was then rewritten and expanded, and appeared in a French edition in 1973, together with two other pieces. The French edition is translated in its entirety in the present volume, which also includes a translation of *Eléments d'autocritique*, published in France in 1974, and of the text "Est-Il Simple d'Etre Marxiste en Philosophie?", published in *La Pensée*, October 1975. In total, then, this volume contains some five times the volume of material contained in the original *Marxism Today* article.

It is preceded by an Introduction in which I attempt to show something about the political inspiration behind Althusser's writings by applying certain of his concepts to a specific and controversial political question.

The bibliography of works by and on Althusser to be found at the end of the book builds on that provided by Saül Karsz in his *Théorie et Politique* (Paris, 1974), but adds more than twenty new titles.

For helpful discussions in the preparation of this Introduction I must thank Althusser himself, together with Etienne Balibar. For help with the translation I am grateful to Ann,

Jean-Jacques and François Lecercle, and for the typing, to Maria Peine.

Grahame Lock,
Leyden, Holland, 1975.

Introduction

Louis Althusser became a controversial figure in France with the publication of his essay "Contradiction and Over-determination" in 1962. He became a politically controversial figure when the essay "Marxism and Humanism" appeared in 1964.[1] The reason was his attack on the notion of *humanism*. "Ten years ago", he wrote at the time, "socialist humanism only existed in one form: that of class humanism. Today it exists in two forms: class humanism, where the dictatorship of the proletariat is still in force (China, etc.), and (socialist) personal humanism where it has been superseded (the USSR)". But while "the concept 'socialism' is indeed a scientific concept ... the concept 'humanism' is no more than an *ideological* one". His purpose at this time was thus, *first*, to distinguish between the sciences and the ideologies; and *second*, to show that while Marxism is a science, all forms of humanism must be classed among the ideologies.

This was the basis of what he called "theoretical anti-humanism". (Althusser's use of the term "humanism" is specific, and it has of course nothing to do with "humanitarianism".) The reaction to his arguments, however, went far beyond the realms of theory, and into the political world itself. I will try to outline this political reaction and Althusser's response to it, because this is one of the best ways of approaching his philosophical work, and also of learning something about a man whom the French weekly *Le Nouvel Observateur* thought it useful

1. Both articles are reprinted in *For Marx* (Allen Lane, 1969).

to describe as "one of the most mysterious and least 'public' figures in the world"!

It was clearly impossible for the French Communist Party, of which Althusser has been a member since 1948, to endorse all of his writings as they appeared, since on certain points they put its own positions in question. Nevertheless, these writings were intended as an intervention in the debate within the party, and the enormous interest which they raised did not remain without an echo there. Articles, some of them hesitantly favourable, began to appear in Party journals.[2] Lucien Sève, in some ways the Party's senior philosopher, devoted a long note to Althusser in his work *La Théorie marxiste de la personnalité*, outlining certain points of disagreement. But Althusser stuck to his position.[3] Waldeck Rochet, Party General Secretary at the time, gave encouragement to his research work, while distancing the Central Committee from its conclusions.

Meanwhile the row between the philosopher Roger Garaudy and the Party of which he had so long been a member was blowing up. The situation was already changing. An article by Jacques Milhau for example, published in the Party journal *La Nouvelle Critique* in 1969, made it clear, referring to Garaudy and Althusser, that "there can be no suggestion of putting on the same level [Garaudy's] out-and-out revisionism, whose theoretical premises go back ten years, and what can be considered as temporary mistakes [*gauchissements*] made in the course of research work which always involves risks". The lecture-article "Lenin and Philosophy" (1968) seems to have been quite well received in the Party, but the article "Ideology and Ideological State Apparatuses" (1970) caused anxiety in some circles, which misinterpreted it as implying a simplistic condemnation of the ideological role of the education system in the service of the ruling class.

When the *Reply to John Lewis* appeared in a French edition in 1973, it provoked some excitement. One news journal ran a story (though without any foundation) to

2. See for example Christine Glucksmann, "La Pratique léniniste de la philosophie", in *La Nouvelle Critique*, April 1969.

3. Sève has replied to Athusser in the third edition of the same work.

the effect that a copy of the book was being sent to every Party Central Committee member and official so that they could prepare their answers. A review by Joe Metzger in the Party weekly *France Nouvelle* (October 9, 1973) praised Althusser for having "raised the essential questions", but argued that he had supported the "dangerous" thesis of the sharpening of the class struggle under socialism, a thesis which "justifies priority being given to administrative and repressive measures over ideological confrontation". This remark, however, seems to be in contradiction with the sense of the text.

The reaction to Althusser's writings in the International Communist Movement was also mixed. A critical (but not over-critical) article by T.A. Sakharova appeared in the Soviet magazine *Voprosy Filosofii*, following the debate carried by *La Nouvelle Critique* in 1965–66. But the Bulgarian S. Angelov took a much harsher line in an article in *World Marxist Review* in 1972, characterizing Althusser's anti-humanism as an "extreme" view, and implying (though indirectly) its connexion with "barracks communism", a term used to describe the line of the Chinese Communist Party. The Yugoslav Veljko Korać, writing in the journal *Praxis* in 1969 on "The Phenomenon of 'Theoretical Anti-humanism'", went even further: Althusser's book *For Marx*, he said, was written "in the name of inherited Stalinist schemes"; it was "Stalinist dogmatism" to reject as "abstract" humanism everything that could not be used as an ideological tool.

On a more serious level, André Glucksmann attempted in 1967 to "demonstrate the weakness" of Althusser's work from a rather traditional philosophical standpoint (see *New Left Review* no. 72), while in Britain Norman Geras offered a serious if limited critique of *For Marx* and *Reading Capital* (*New Left Review* no. 71; see also John Mepham's reply in *Radical Philosophy* no. 6). But these articles contained little politics. It seems that the reaction to Althusser was, in general, either a real but rather narrow theoretical interest, or political hysteria.[4] The article by Leszek

4. See for example the article by Althusser's ex-collaborator Jacques

Kolakowski in *Socialist Register 1971* ("Althusser's Marx") might seem to be an exception; its length at least would suit it for a serious treatment. But his misunderstanding of the subject is so severe that Kolakowski never comes near to constructive criticism. He accuses Althusser of "religious thinking", and attacks him for "failing to remember" how long ago it was discovered that knowledge "has nothing to do with pure, immediate, singular objects, but always with abstractions", so long ago that it had become "a commonplace in contemporary philosophy of science" (Kolakowski, p. 125). But Althusser had pointed out, in black and white (*Reading Capital*, p. 184) that the theses according to which "an object cannot be defined by its immediately visible or sensuous appearance", so that a detour must be made *via* its concept in order to grasp it, "have a familiar ring to them—at least they are the lesson of the whole history of modern science, more or less reflected in classical philosophy, even if this reflection took place in the element of an empiricism, whether transcendent (as in Descartes), transcendental (Kant and Husserl) or 'objective'-idealist (Hegel)". This is just one example of the kind of criticism levelled at Althusser.

The unfortunate failure of Althusser's critics to produce reasoned arguments must have its *political* causes, whether or not these are explicit. Sometimes the motives are rather clear, as in I.Mészáros' comment that the category of symptomatic reading is a veil for "the sterile dogmatism of bureaucratic-conservative wishful thinking" (*Marx's Theory of Alienation*, p. 96). At other times the lack of a serious approach seems to be based on a simple lack of ability to understand his work, as in the case of David McLellan, who comments that *For Marx* "may well be profound, but is certainly obscure" (*Encounter*, November 1970, "Marx and the Missing Link"). On occasion even the background facts are wrongly reported, as in the case of Maurice

Rancière, "Sur la théorie politique d'Althusser", in *L'Homme et la Société*, no. 27, January-March 1973. His critique was expanded to book length as *La Leçon d'Althusser* (Gallimard, 1974). According to Rancière, Althusser's philosophy performs a "police" function. Rancière prefers the standpoint of "anti-authoritarianism", "anti-State subversion", etc.

Cranston's article in the United States Information Service journal *Problems of Communism* (March-April 1973), which mistakenly promotes Althusser to the Central Committee of the French Communist Party! Cranston also attributes some strange philosophical positions to him: "For Althusser", he says, "membership of the proletariat is determined by the existence of certain attitudes in the minds of individuals .... The external economic situation (whether a person is in the lower-, middle-, or upper-class income group) hardly matters." But whether or not Cranston's study can be counted a useful contribution to the debate, it must have flattered Althusser to find himself the subject of a full-length article in a US Government journal.

From the other side of the political spectrum, the "ultra-left", come the attacks of the novelist Philippe Sollers and the *Tel Quel* group, inspired by their own interpretation of "Mao Tse-Tung thought". An article in the journal's Spring 1972 issue ("*Le Dogmatisme à la rescousse du révisionnisme*") accuses Althusser of evading and suppressing the notion of struggle, and in an interview with the journal *Peinture* Sollers describes his thesis that philosophy has no object as "ultra-revisionist" and "hyper-revisionist" ("Tac au tac", *Peinture* nos. 2/3).

In the middle of this ferment, the *Reply to John Lewis* appeared. In a review in the daily paper *Combat* (June 19, 1973), Bernard-Henri Lévy summed up the situation: "There has been a lot of speculation in the *salons* about Althusser's 'commitments'. Is he a Maoist or an orthodox Communist? Is he a product of Stalinism or a consistent anti-Stalinist?" At last Althusser intervenes on these questions—"he puts his cards on the table, in order to clarify the political meaning of his philosophical interventions". First: *For Marx* and *Reading Capital* are placed in their historical context—the Twentieth Congress of the Soviet Communist Party and "de-Stalinization"; in a sense, Khrushchev's de-Stalinization came *from the right*. And it led, as might have been expected, to a shift to the right in the theoretical work of Communist intellectuals.

It also left the Communist Parties open to attack from those, either to the right or left, who wanted to claim that their Marxism was *more consistently humanist*. This would presumably be true of figures otherwise as different as Garaudy, Marcuse, Kolakowski, and even Mandel with his "Marxist theory of alienation".[5]

But Althusser's critique goes back further than 1956, back to Stalin himself. The Stalin period does indeed haunt the Communist movement, and not only because anti-communism will always evoke the spectre of "Stalinism". It will continue to haunt the movement, says Althusser, until a left critique of the period replaces the "rightist" analysis dominant in certain circles. And he suggests that such a critique must treat it as an example of a deviation characterized by the terms *economism* and *humanism*. He *suggests* as much, but could not in the space available go on to spell the matter out.

II

How then are we to understand the enigmatic references to Stalin which occur in Althusser's *Reply to John Lewis*? It is true that he says little enough on the subject, and this has led certain commentators to claim that the function of his remarks is purely political. Rancière, for example, thinks that their role is to allow him to adapt to his own use—or rather, to the profit of "orthodox Communism"— some "currently fashionable ideas about Stalinism"[6] (above all, presumably, those of certain "pro-Chinese" writers, including Charles Bettelheim[7]). But Rancière's arguments are themselves all too obviously motivated by directly political considerations. In my opinion, what Althusser says in this text, together with what he has said elsewhere, allows us to constitute a genuinely new theory of the Stalin period.

5. It may even explain the fact that a recent collection of Trotskyist essays against Althusser resurrects Karl Korsch and Georg Lukács as sources for its theoretical critique (*Contre Althusser*, J.-M. Vincent and others; 10/18, 1974).

6. Rancière, *La Leçon d'Althusser*, p. 11.

7. *Cf.* especially Bettelheim's *Luttes de classes en URSS* (Seuil/Maspero, 1974).

It therefore seemed useful to devote this Introduction to just this question, so that the reader can at least get an idea of what kind of politics lies behind Althusser's "philosophy".

Simple as the following scenario may be, and incomplete as it is (it only attempts to provide some elements of an explanation), it contradicts alternative accounts. That is enough to be going on with.

According to the *Reply to John Lewis*, "the Stalinian deviation can be considered as *a form* ... of the posthumous *revenge of the Second International*: as a revival of its main tendency"; it is based on "an economistic conception and line ... hidden by declarations which were in their own way cruelly 'humanist'".[8] To talk about Stalin's *humanism* is not to talk about a simple philosophical or theoretical mistake. It is to talk about something with political causes and political effects. These can be more easily understood if we glance at certain aspects of Soviet history.

When the working class and peasantry took power in Russia in 1917, great hopes were raised among exploited peoples throughout the world. Perhaps they expected too much, too soon. At any rate, when the euphoria had given way to practical tasks, and especially to the Civil War and to the New Economic Policy, it became clear that there could be no straight, unsullied path to Communism. There would have to be detours, sometimes steps back; there would be mistakes and even disasters.

The Soviet Union faced two major problems on the economic front: industrialization and the resolution of the agrarian question. These were not simply economic, but also ideological and political problems. The peasant question, for example, following the relatively short NEP period, was handled by the introduction of collectivization, but at an enormous cost. This cost was of course not the result of purely "technical" economic mistakes. The rich peasants, for example, resisted collectivization. No amount of agitation or of socialist propoganda could convince them that they

---

8. In the "Note on 'The Critique of the Personality Cult'".

should *voluntarily* hand over their lands and property.

Industrialization was vital. The machinery had to be provided to accompany the development of agriculture, and weapons had to be made available to enable the army to resist any further attempt at capitalist intervention. It was in general a question of generating the surplus necessary for investment in a country where the most basic services were still lacking in many areas, where a large part of the population was illiterate, and where the towns and industrial regions contained only a very small proportion of that population.

During the NEP period the resolution of certain *political* and *ideological* problems was postponed in the interest of survival. The new economic system represented a retreat. The economy was decentralized; enterprises were given financial and commercial independence; certain small enterprises were denationalized; foreign companies were granted concessions; private shops appeared, together with private merchants; the links between agriculture and industry became market-oriented once again. Lenin called this a "transitional mixed system"—that is, not something stable in itself, but a state of affairs to be superseded *either* (it was hoped) by a development towards communism, *or*—and this was a real possibility—by a reversion to capitalism, if the *kulaks* and *Nepmen* grew too powerful.

The possibility of counter-revolution was thus recognized. The danger was seen as two-fold: on the one hand, the capitalist states might attempt an intervention; on the other hand, the old and new capitalist and *kulak* classes might attempt to overthrow the régime from within. These were indeed the immediate dangers. But another, deeper threat was not clearly recognized. To understand why, we can usefully begin by looking at *one particular problem* faced by the Soviet state, which then throws light on a *more general contradiction*.

It was very quickly realized, following the October Revolution, that industry and agriculture urgently required the services of workers of all levels of knowledge and skill, *and also* of managers, technical experts, etc. These latter groups—which on the one hand obviously did not constitute a capitalist class, but on the other hand could not be said to form part of the working class—presented special problems. Even in the mid-twenties, before the first Five-Year Plan was put into effect, these specialist groups numbered some tens of thousands of persons, totalling perhaps 100,000.

One problem about the specialists (I use the term in a general sense, to include managers) was that many of them were opponents of the régime. In 1925, Kalinin, President of the Central Executive Committee of the Soviet Union, explained that "Communism is being created in the provinces by the man who says: 'I am against Communism'". Moreover, these groups were not particularly popular among the working class. E.H. Carr reports for example in his *Foundations of a Planned Economy* that a number of "excesses" were said to have taken place in this period against engineers and technicians, for which ordinary workers were responsible.[9] Several attempts were actually made against the lives of specialists in the Ukrainian mines during the summer of 1927. What kind of contradictions were at work here?

The government's policy towards the specialists, at least up to 1928 or so, was not based on the use of repressive measures. Even after the Shakhty trial of 1928, when numbers of technical personnel were executed and imprisoned for alleged "sabotage" in the mines of the Donbass region, official pronouncements continued to be made against "baiting the specialists". At this time it seems that monetary incentives were the main instrument used in keeping them in line. There was a serious shortage of specialists, of course, and many had to be imported from America, Germany and Britain. Of the existing native specialists, moreover, less than one per cent were Party members.

The first and second Five-Year Plans did require and provide an enormously increased pool of experts and skilled workers of all kinds. Those in the population equipped with at least secondary technical school education were estimated to have increased by two and a half times during the life of the first Plan, and specific figures for teaching, medicine, etc. show similar advances. From 1928–29 on, we can in

9. *Foundations of a Planned Economy*, Part I, C, ch. 21: "The Specialists".

fact talk of an enormous effort to train a new generation of "red experts". The problem was, however, not only that this could not be done all at once, but also that the new generation had to be educated by the old, with all the ideological consequences that this implied. In fact there was, during the Plans, a tendency for wage differentials in general to rise, and in particular for the salaries of the experts to rise disproportionately when compared with those of manual workers. This phenomenon seems to reflect the fact that the new generation of specialists was not prepared to work for primarily ideological rewards. The new Soviet man was not to be born in a single generation.

Let me halt there for a moment. I have raised certain problems posed by the role of the specialists in the early years of the Soviet state. I wanted to make it clear that these problems were not simply "technical", but also *political* and *ideological*—that is, in fact, problems of *class struggle*. But, secondly, these particular problems make up only one aspect of a *more general question*: that of the *continued operation under socialism of the wage system*.

We must therefore go back for a moment and look at the wage system *in capitalism*. We know that the very existence of this system is linked to distinctions in the degrees of skill or qualification of labour power. We also know that the difference between the price of skilled and unskilled labour power rests on the fact that the former "has cost more time and labour, and ... therefore has a higher value" (Marx in *Capital*, vol. I). But it *also rests* on something else, because this value must be realized. The difference in price (that is, the existence of wage differentials) *also rests* on the *ideological and political conditions* which enable and cause the skilled worker to demand—normally with success—that he be paid *more* than the unskilled worker. The same holds for the differentials which separate the expert on the one hand and the worker (including the skilled worker) on the other.

These ideological and political conditions are actually among the conditions of the reproduction of capitalist relations of production, therefore of (capitalist) exploitation—that is, of the extraction of surplus-value. They are fulfilled by the operation of the Ideological State Apparatuses.[10] These apparatuses help to guarantee the continuing domination of one class, the capitalist class, *over* another class, the working class. But, as we shall see, this they do—and can only do—in a contradictory manner, by also reproducing *class struggle*. Thus, finally, we can say that the existence of the wage-system in capitalism is linked to the existence both of exploitation and of class struggle.

We can go further, however. The process of the creation of value in general (what Marx calls *Wertbildung*) is itself bound up with the process of the realization of surplus-value (*Verwertung*); indeed, the latter is nothing but the former, says Marx, continued "beyond a certain point" (*Capital*, vol. I, Part III, ch. VII). It is therefore not only the wage system (the production and exchange of labour power as a commodity) but *commodity production in general* (*i.e.*, the value-creating process) which is bound up with the process of the realization of surplus-value, that is, with *exploitation*.

The creation of value takes place within the labour process, which is both "technical" (a process of the production of use-values) and "social" (a process of the production of commodities). Thus the socio-technical division of labour is at the heart of the process of exploitation.

This process in fact depends on the fact that labour power itself functions as a commodity, with of course the special characteristic that its use-value is a source of more (exchange) value than it has itself. Thus the socio-technical division of labour is linked to the system of differentiation between the prices of more or less complex forms of labour power.

We can in this way establish a number of *general* connexions: between commodity production, the wage system, the socio-economic division of labour, and the extraction of surplus-value.

We ought finally to glance at the special situation in capitalism of what are often referred to as the "middle

10. See Althusser's "Ideology and Ideological State Apparatuses", in *Lenin and Philosophy and Other Essays* (NLB, 1971).

strata". The various groups which are aggregated under this heading are in fact of very different character.[11] It is true that, in general, they are distinguished from the working class by the fact that the reproduction of their labour power takes place separately from that of the working class (its members compete on a different labour market). In the course of the development of capitalism, certain of these groups—especially the so-called "employees"—*tend* to become "proletarianized", that is, thrown onto the same labour market as the workers. But *not all* are in this position: far from it. Some remain quite outside of the process of proletarianization. Moreover, while the "employees", though not productive workers, tend to become subject to exploitation, other groups not only are not so exploited, but actually combine their productive function with the task of managing the process of production and circulation—*i.e.*, of exploitation.[12]

The above detour through capitalism was necessary to our understanding of socialism. We shall see later more exactly why. Meanwhile, however, we are at least in a position to pose a few questions. For example: why does the wage-system continue to operate *after* the proletarian revolution? Why does commodity production continue—in a different form—to take place? Does the persistence of commodity production imply the continued operation, in socialism,

11. The "middle strata" do not constitute a social *class*. The development of capitalism tends to reduce the existing social classes to *two* only, the bourgeoisie and the proletariat. (*Cf*. E. Balibar, *Cinq Etudes du matérialisme historique*, p. 134.) The antagonism between them is an element of the *definition* of the capitalist mode of production, whereas the character of the relations between the "middle strata" on the one hand, and the bourgeoisie and proletariat respectively on the other, are *not* so given. In particular, the question of whether an "alliance" between the proletariat and middle strata is possible in any given situation can only be answered in concrete political practice, and not by a formal definition of a new "middle class" or "petty-bourgeoisie". See also Lenin's comments on the Draft Programme of the RSDLP, 1902: "*In the first place* it is essential to *draw a line of demarcation* between ourselves and all others, to single out the proletariat *alone and exclusively*, and only then declare that the proletariat will emancipate all, that is call on all, invite all" (*Collected Works*, vol. 6, p. 73).

12. *Cf*. E. Balibar, *Cinq Etudes du matérialisme historique*, pp. 144, 150.

of a value-creating process, and therefore, indeed, *also* of a process of production of surplus-value? Finally: we know that, after the proletarian revolution, the working class must take over from the bourgeoisie the function of organizing production. But, on the one hand, must it not also, at the same time, struggle continuously *against* the forms in which it is forced to organize production, since its goal is the complete elimination of the conditions of exploitation (therefore the elimination of the wage-system, commodity production, etc.)? And, on the other hand, must it not at one and the same time *make use* of the old bourgeois specialists, and yet *struggle against* them?

These were some of the questions facing the young Soviet state. But, of course, they did not present themselves spontaneously in this form. Stalin, for example, formulated the questions rather differently. And, curiously enough, he often changed his mind about the answers. For example, he was apparently unable to make up his mind about the internal class struggle in the USSR. In 1925 he was talking about the need to struggle against a "new bourgeoisie". In 1936, on the occasion of the introduction of the New Constitution, he considered the class struggle to be at an end. But in 1937 he was again talking about the need to combat "sharper forms of struggle" by the old exploiting classes. Then, in 1939 he was once again speaking of the USSR as "free of all class conflicts".

Stalin in fact recognized two threats to the development of socialism. He recognized a struggle between the Soviet state and the imperialist states; and he recognized (though it disappeared sporadically from his speeches) a struggle between the Soviet working class and peasantry on the one hand and the *former* exploiting classes on the other. But he did not (or rarely, and in distorted form—for example in 1952) recognize a threat which might be formulated in terms of the questions which I posed. In particular, he tended to displace the problems resulting from the contradictory development of class relations within the USSR *onto* the two forms of class struggle which he did recognize, thus explaining them as effects either of the international class struggle or of the struggle against the former exploiting classes. This perhaps explains his vacillations: whenever the class struggle between the various classes and groups inside the Soviet Union became intense, Stalin would pull "imperialism" or the "old exploiting classes" out of the bag.

We have said that the "Stalin deviation" may be characterized by the terms *economic* and *humanism*. Why? And what is the link between these two forms of a single deviation? In order to answer these questions we must make use of a number of theoretical concepts of Marxism, including those of the *mode of production* and of the *social formation*. A mode of production is characterized *primarily* by a given system of production relations, and *secondarily* by the "level of the material productive forces". The reproduction of a system of production relations is not a function of the operation of the mode of production alone, but of the social formation as a whole, including its "superstructural forms".

To "forget about" the role of the "superstructure" in the reproduction of production relations, to want to explain everything (for example, crises in capitalism or the transition to communism) by reference to the economic infrastructure alone, is of course *economism*. But to "forget about" the role of the superstructure is also to forget how the superstructure operates. It operates through apparatuses which maintain the domination of the ruling class, but at the cost of continuously reproducing *class struggle*. To fall into economism is therefore also to forget about class struggle, and to forget about class struggle is *humanism*. Stalin fell into both economism and humanism when he argued, for example, that the problem of the transition to socialism was primarily a problem of the development of the productive forces. Etienne Balibar has pointed out that "this interpretation of Marxism was already dominant among certain Socialist leaders of the Second International (like Kautsky), and was developed and plainly stated by Stalin on several occasions".[13]

Stalin, in fact, did tend to "forget about" class struggle.

13. In *Les Sciences de l'économie* (eds. A. Vanoli and J.-P. Januard), article on "Les Formations sociales capitalistes", p. 287.

This claim may surprise some readers, since, after all, he is known for the thesis that the class struggle sharpens as socialism develops. Indeed, it is precisely this thesis which is often held responsible for the "excesses" and "crimes" of the Stalin period. But the class struggle which he recognized was, as we have seen, either the struggle against international capitalism or the struggle against the old exploiting classes. There is a logic to his position. For example, if these classes have been defeated, if only *remnants* still exist, then the obvious course of action for them would be to resort to terrorism, sabotage, etc. in collaboration with their natural ally, imperialism. The obvious way of dealing with such acts of terrorism would be to use the Repressive State Apparatus (police, courts, and so on). Thus the importance for Stalin of the show trial, in which the accused are treated as criminals, and in particular as foreign agents.

A scientific treatment of the Stalin period will, in my opinion, show that the events which characterized it (trials, purges, etc.) were, in spite of "appearances", effects of (a specific) class struggle fought out in the economic, political and ideological spheres. It is of course true that—for example—the great trials of 1936–38 were not, legally speaking, directed against the representatives of a particular class, but against certain senior Party members. Again from a legal point of view, they contained many absurd allegations. But that does not mean that they can be explained—and written off—as simple "violations of socialist legality". The trials and purges played a role *determined in the last instance by the class struggle inside the USSR*, even if in practice their victims were the "wrong" ones. But this was inevitable, since the methods used were the "wrong" ones, too: they were *bourgeois methods* used against the bourgeoisie, and they backfired disastrously. This too, however, is not surprising, since "Stalinism"—the deviation from Leninism—is, after all, a consequence of the penetration of Marxism by bourgeois theory (economism/humanism) and bourgeois practice.

To illustrate the argument, let us compare the Soviet situation with its "opposite": the case in which the *capitalist* class resorts, for whatever reasons, to the use of large-scale physical repression. Such a policy is of course never the result of a "decision" on the part of some "executive committee of the bourgeoisie" as a whole. On the contrary: in practice it tends to result in large-scale splits inside bourgeois political organizations. The Nazi régime, for example, suppressed not only the organizations of the working class (Communists, Social-Democrats, trades unions) but also the old bourgeois and "petty-bourgeois" parties, together with cultural, artistic and scientific institutions and of course racial groups. The millions which it murdered came *from all classes*. It is precisely this fact which makes it easy to *misunderstand* the Nazi régime, even to suppose that there is some essential resemblance between it and Stalin's government. One can have lived through fascism, fought for years against it, even died in the fight, without knowing that its roots lay in the *class struggle between labour and capital*.

This example is not intended, let me repeat, to imply a similarity between the Stalin and Nazi régimes (one of the tricks of anti-communism), nor any mirror relation between them. On the contrary: it is intended as a warning against empiricism, against the temptation of assuming that in order to locate the cause of an event one need not look much further than the effects. Hitler killed and imprisoned the leaders of the capitalist parties. Was he therefore an anti-capitalist, a traitor to the capitalist class? Is the case of Stalin so much simpler?

I argued that behind Stalin's "crimes" was hidden a specific class struggle. But what were its *roots*? Why do we claim that *in spite of* the disappearance of the old exploiting classes, such a struggle continued to exist in the USSR? The answer to this question demands further theoretical clarification.

We arrive here at a critical point in the argument. We know that the Marxist orthodoxy of the Stalin period conceived of the relation between *base* and *superstructure* under socialism by analogy with capitalism: whereas capitalism is based on the capitalist mode of production, which is of course socially determinant in the last instance, socialism is based on the *socialist mode of production* (state ownership, and so on). This too is ultimately determinant, in that it tends, perhaps slowly but still inexorably, to produce a population steeped in the "socialist ideology" whose development is a necessary superstructural condition for the transition to communism. The infrastructural condition is of course satisfied by the development of the productive forces, a consequence of the efficiency of the socialist economy.

Now this picture—which effectively eliminates the question of class struggle under socialism—is organized around one key concept, precisely that of the *socialist mode of production*. It is however this concept which unfortunately constitutes the principal obstacle to understanding socialism. Because *there is no socialist mode of production*.[14]

The neatest way of formulating this point is perhaps to say that social formations of the transition period called socialism are based not on a single, socialist mode of production (stamped perhaps with the birth marks of the old, capitalist society), but on a *contradictory combination of two modes of production, the capitalist and communist*.[15] We must however not forget that these modes of production do not (co)exist in a "pure" form, and that no concrete revolutionary transition can be explained by reference to the contradictory presence of the general form of two modes of production. What we find in any given *socialist system* is in fact a specific combination of a concrete, determinate form of the capitalist mode of production, transformed and "emasculated" by the proletarian revolution, and a similar form of the communist mode of production, as it emerges and develops on the basis of the victories of that revolution and of the continuing class struggle.[16]

But what characterizes the capitalist mode of production (Lenin's "capitalist form of social economy")? According

14. "There is no socialist mode of production"—thesis advanced by Althusser in a course on Marx's *Zur Kritik der politischen Oekonomie*, given at the Ecole Normale Supérieure, rue d'Ulm, Paris in June 1973.

15. *Cf.* the interesting Section 1 of Lenin's *Economics and Politics in the Era of the Dictatorship of the Proletariat* (1919); *Collected Works*, vol. 30.

16. *Cf.* Balibar, *op. cit.*, p. 305: "In all existing 'socialist countries', capitalist relations of production—and thus the structure of classes themselves— have been profoundly transformed. But in no case have they totally dis-

to Marx and Lenin, it is the extraction of surplus-value. But to obtain surplus-value you need not simply a system of commodity production and exchange, but "a commodity whose process of consumption is at the same time a process of the creation of value. Such a commodity exists—human labour power".[17] The capitalist mode of production cannot exist except where labour power itself is produced and exchanged as a commodity.

We know however that the wage system—precisely, the production and exchange of labour power as a commodity—continues to operate after the proletarian revolution, and that general commodity production in Marx's Department I (production of means of production) and Department II (production of means of consumption) also continues to take place.

Let us now look at Stalin's attempt to deal with the question of the role of the commodity under socialism (in his *Economic Problems of Socialism*, 1952). He argues very clearly that "commodity circulation is incompatible with the prospective transition to communism". And he concludes that "the transition from socialism to communism and the communist principle of distribution of products according to needs preclude all commodity exchange" (in the "Reply to Sanina and Venzher"). But how does Stalin understand the abolition of commodity exchange? Essentially in terms of the abolition of collective-farm (socialist, but non-public) property, in terms of its conversion into state—or, more exactly public—property. Thus, "when instead of two basic production sectors, the state sector and the collective-farm sector, there will be only one all-embracing production sector, with the right to dispose of all the consumer goods produced in the country, commodity circulation, with its 'money economy', will disappear" (ch. 2).

Two things can be said against Stalin here. *First*, the

---

appeared". Naturally, the reproduction of these relations of production also depends on the existence of corresponding superstructural forms. The contradictory coexistence of two modes of production under socialism thus also implies contradictory superstructural relations (for example, at the level of the *State*, as we shall see).

17. Lenin, "Karl Marx", *Selected Works* (Moscow, 1967), vol. 1, p. 18.

abolition of the role of the commodity is certainly not simply a question of bringing all sectors of production into public ownership. Centralized state control and planning can itself be a form of commodity circulation. *Second*, the sale of means of consumption to the public implies its ability to buy them. But the fact that the public can buy such products—even from a single "all-embracing" publicly-owned production sector—implies that it can pay, *i.e.*, that it earns wages. It implies, in other words, the existence of a *wage system*.

Stalin, however, specifically argues that (in the USSR of 1952) "the system of wage labour no longer exists and labour power is no longer a commodity" (*ibid.*)—a rather curious claim. His reasoning is that talk of labour power being a commodity "sounds rather absurd", as though the working class "sells its labour power to itself". But in that case why was it—if *not* because of the operation of the "law of value"—that those members of the working population whose training had been relatively lengthy and costly were able to command a higher income?[18]

For Stalin the socialist commodity is not "of the ordinary [capitalist] type", but "designed to serve . . . socialist production". The socialist commodity is a remnant of capitalism, but "essentially" not a "capitalist category".[19] For him, indeed, the link between the process of the creation of value (*Wertbildung*) and that of the realization of surplus-value (*Verwertung*) is broken. He believes in socialist commodity production, a distinct form, though it is a *remnant of* capitalism, just as some economists believe in a *mode of production* called "simple commodity production" distinguished from capitalism *because it preceded it*.[20]

Stalin's political positions are consistent with his theoretical

18. With some exceptions (relatively low rewards for doctors, relatively high rewards for miners, and so on). These exceptions are *indices* of the strength of the working class, and of the development of communist relations of production. But we should add that the transition to communism is by no means equivalent to a simple process of wage equalization!

19. In the "Reply to A.I. Notkin".

20. *Cf.* Balibar, *Cinq Etudes*, p. 125; also Marx, *Pre-Capitalist Economic Formations* (International Publishers, 1972), p. 114: "The rule of exchange-

standpoint. His attempt to solve the problem of the specialists is an example. Because he had no theory of class struggle under socialism with which to orient his policy, it was always decided on an *ad hoc* basis. Thus it vacillated constantly between the use of monetary incentives and political repression.[21]

Another example is the primacy which he attributed to the question of the development of the productive forces. "Why", he asks (in his *Problems of Leninism*), "can socialism, must socialism, will socialism necessarily vanquish the capitalist economic system? Because ... it can make society richer than the capitalist economic system can do."[22] Such economic progress would of course be possible only on the basis of *socialism*; but socialism, here, means above all public ownership and *planning*. Like many another Marxist, he simply contrasts capitalist *commodity* production with socialist *planned* production, forgetting that commodity production and planning are in principle compatible, and that the required distinction therefore cannot lie *there*.

The common belief in a fundamental incompatibility between commodity production and planning has in fact distinct *humanist* connotations. In Paul Sweezy's formula-

---

values, and of production producing exchange-values *presupposes* alien labour power as itself an exchange-value. That is, it presupposes the separation of living labour power from its objective conditions; a relationship ... to them *as capital*."

21. By 1939—when, as we saw, Stalin was (again) claiming that the USSR was "free of all class conflicts"—he could also speak of a "new, socialist intelligentsia" which was "ready to serve the interests of the peoples of the USSR faithfully and devotedly" (*Report to the 18th Party Congress*).

22. Khrushchev took over this position as his own. It is dangerous—not for any "moral" reason (because it "alienates", "reifies", etc.), but because of its political effects. Some of the proposals for economic reform in the socialist world are influenced by this standpoint. One example is Wlodzimierz Brus' proposed rectification of Stalin's economic policies. He says that Stalin's picture of a "complete conformity" between socialist production relations and productive forces is false. In fact, he argues, socialist production relations may cease to *meet the needs* of the development of the productive forces. The theoretical framework here is identical with that of Stalin (primacy of the *productive forces*). Only its application is different: growth now demands of course, the extension of market (commodity) relations. See Brus, *The Market in a Socialist Economy* (Routledge, 1972).

tion, for instance, when the law of value is king, the economy is regulated only by that law, while planning means that "the allocation of productive activity is brought under conscious control" (*The Theory of Capitalist Development*, p. 53). In his *Reply to John Lewis* Althusser contrasts the humanist thesis, *man makes history*, with the (Marxist) thesis: *the motor of history is class struggle*. We can contrast the humanist thesis on socialism: *man makes socialism*—by conscious planning, and so on—with the (Marxist) thesis: *the motor of socialism is class struggle*.

If the progress of socialism cannot be measured (simply) in terms of the development of the productive forces; if it must be measured instead in terms of the development of the contradiction between specific forms of the capitalist and communist modes of production, then it becomes clear that it depends on the development of the class struggle. It may therefore be that, in the case of two socialist states, the one which is *behind* in building its productive forces is *ahead* in building communism. I think, for instance, that undue optimism was originally placed in some of the People's Democracies of Eastern Europe, at least as far as the tempo of the advance to communism was concerned, an optimism based on their relatively developed economic infrastructure. But it is quite likely that Cuba (to take an example), which did not contain such a strong—and ideologically formed— educated "middle class" as, say, Czechoslovakia, is neverthe-less at least equally advanced *politically*.

The thesis that *there is no socialist mode of production*, that socialism rests on the contradictory combination of specific forms of two modes of production, capitalist and communist, allows us to understand the *roots* of the class struggle under socialism. It also allows us to deal with the inevitable question: if there is class struggle under socialism, where are the classes in struggle? Where, in particular, is the *capitalist class*?

We could of course answer the question (answering that there is no capitalist class) and leave it at that. But we have not yet reached the heart of the matter. The reason is that social classes do not *precede* the class struggle: on the contrary, *the class struggle creates the classes*. We must therefore rephrase the question. The problem is not to find a capitalist class, but to find out under what conditions a capitalist class is *generated*.

That is not such a curious way of posing the problem. Lenin, after all, had argued that "even in Russia capitalist commodity production is alive, operating, developing and *giving rise to a bourgeoisie*" (my emphasis).[23] The difficulty is that Lenin thought that this new bourgeoisie was emerging *mainly* from among the peasants and handicraftsmen. Thus Stalin, following the *letter* of Lenin, was able to claim that collectivization and nationalization had at the same time put a stop to the process by which the new bourgeoisie was being produced.

But we must go further. We must add that the capitalist class does not *precede* the production of surplus-value; on the contrary, *it is the production of surplus-value which creates the capitalist class*. The consequence should be obvious. If socialism rests on a contradictory combination of specific forms of the capitalist and communist modes of production, it follows that certain conditions for the generation of a new bourgeoisie are fulfilled, and that only class struggle on the part of the proletariat can prevent it. The modalities of its generation (out of which social groups does it emerge? and so on) cannot be dealt with here. What we can say, however, is that just as the Ideological State Apparatuses of the *capitalist* State reproduce the domination of the capitalist class only at the cost of reproducing class struggle, so too, in the same way the Ideological State Apparatuses of the *proletarian* State only reproduce the domination of the proletariat at the cost of reproducing class struggle—a class struggle whose stake is the generation of a new bourgeoisie, and ultimately counter-revolution and the restoration of capitalism. That is why Lenin was right when he claimed that "the transition from capitalism to communism takes an entire historical epoch". But Lenin

23. At the 8th Congress of the RCP(B). Lenin, *Collected Works*, vol. 29, p. 189. *Cf.* his *Theses Presented to the First Congress of the Comintern:* "The entire content of Marxism ... reveals the economic inevitability, wherever commodity economy prevails, of the dictatorship of the bourgeoisie" (*Collected Works*, vol. 28, p. 464).

was most concerned with the threat from the old exploiting classes, and it is not clear how he would otherwise have wanted to establish his claim.

It should now be rather clearer why Althusser characterizes the Stalin period in terms of a deviation from Marxism which took the form of *economism* and *humanism*. It is not of course that the events of this period were the simple consequence of a theoretical mistake. The deviation was itself not only theoretical, but also political. But in any case its roots lay in the class struggle—in the class struggle under capitalism, which had allowed bourgeois ideology to penetrate deeply into the Marxism of the early Social-Democratic Parties, and in the class struggle under socialism, which prevented Stalin from casting off that influence.

I ought to say a few words at this point about alternative conceptions of the Stalin period.[24] *First*, it should by now be evident that what I have said conflicts in the sharpest possible way with every explanation couched either in terms of legal ideology (Stalinism is essentially a "violation of socialist legality") or psychology (Stalin was mad, a criminal, or both).

Secondly, it is incompatible with Trotsky's accounts. I agree with Charles Bettelheim that in spite of the political struggles which he waged against Stalin, Trotsky's *theoretical* positions coincide with those of Stalin in two important respects: on the one hand he too thought that the disappearance of "private property" excluded the development of a new capitalist class; and on the other hand he too affirmed that "the root of all social organization is in the productive forces".[25] As a consequence, his account of the so-called "degeneration" of socialism in the USSR

24. I will not mention the many "bourgeois" accounts here. What they naturally cannot see is that Stalinism was a result, first, of the penetration of *bourgeois* theory and *bourgeois* methods into internal Soviet politics, and second, of the isolation of the new and still extremely weak socialist state in a capitalist world. "Stalinism" is not the price of communism; it is a price *paid* by the Soviet people, but *extorted, ultimately*, by imperialism.

25. Bettelheim, *Luttes de classes en URSS*, pp. 25–27. According to the author, "the two theses (on the disappearance of antagonistic classes in the USSR and on the primacy of the development of the productive forces) were a kind of '*commonplace*' for 'European Marxism' in the 1930s".

is in any case unilaterally *political*, especially as far as his comments on the role of the "bureaucracy" are concerned.[26]

But, *thirdly*, what I have said also conflicts with Bettelheim's positions. This becomes clear if one considers his account not only of the Stalin but also of the post-Stalin period.

It is true that Bettelheim correctly cites Stalin's economism and his belief in the disappearance of the objective basis for the existence of classes. But he adds that these doctrinal weaknesses led not only the existence of class struggle but also the rise of a new class, the *State Bourgeoisie*, to be overlooked.

It is this category of the State Bourgeoisie which presents the first difficulty (I speak only of *theoretical* difficulties here). It is that the category is not sufficiently specific. *Every* bourgeoisie, after all, is a "state bourgeoisie" in the sense that the action of the state is integral to the process of its constitution and reproduction as a unified ruling class.[27] Bettelheim means of course that this bourgeoisie is constituted by a body of functionaries and administrators "which become in effect the *proprietors* (in the sense of a relation of production) of the means of production".[28] Since he is convinced that the emergence of this new class has, at some time since Stalin's death, resulted in the restoration of capitalism in the USSR, we know that it must now be not simply a bourgeoisie but a capitalist class in the strict sense (the two things are not exactly the same).

One reason for Bettelheim's conclusion (a theoretical reason—I say nothing of the political reason) may lie in his treatment of the distinction between the legal and real appropriation of the means of production. His version of this distinction contrasts *property* (in the legal sense) and *possession*. He uses it, however, in such a way that property sometimes appears to be little more than an illusion. For example, it appears that the new capitalist class establishes

26. *Cf.* Nicos Poulantzas' argument that the problems of bureaucracy "always concern the state apparatus and not the state power" (*Political Power and Social Classes*, p. 333.) On this distinction, see below.

27. *Cf.* Balibar, *Cinq Etudes*, p. 177.

28. Bettelheim, *Calcul économique et formes de propriété*, p. 87.

its *possession* of the means of production not so much by creating new legal relations—by constituting its *property* in the means of production—but rather by reducing state property to "a merely legal relation", therefore a fiction.

The consequence is that it becomes rather easier for Bettelheim to conclude—like the Chinese Communist Party— that, in spite of the fact that there has been no fundamental transformation in property relations in the Soviet Union, the class struggle has ended not simply in the generation of a new bourgeoisie and a new capitalist class but also in the restoration of capitalism itself. And this, from a "Chinese" standpoint, which Bettelheim is apparently struggling to respect, would mean precisely the abolition of "socialist production relations". Our disagreement with this kind of account will be obvious.

In fact, the subsistence of capitalist relations of production within socialism implies a *tendency* to the generation of a new bourgeoisie, but whether or not this tendency is *realized* depends on the outcome of the class struggle. Such a bourgeoisie *may* be generated, it *may* transform itself into a full-fledged capitalist class and it *may* succeed in restoring capitalism. But, as we shall see, a number of conditions, political as well as economic, must be fulfilled before such a thing can take place. And—to take a concrete example, *the* example—there is ample evidence, as far as the Soviet Union is concerned (especially of its remarkable stability), to refute the claim that it is rushing headlong towards such a restoration.

Be that as it may, it is no ground for complacency. On the contrary. Czechoslovakia in 1968, Poland in 1970 are the proof. If the principal contradiction dominating the complexity of the Czech events clearly lay in the relation to the USSR (as Althusser and the French Communist Party believe), it is just as clear that secondary contradictions operated which were internal to Czech society. But these internal contradictions were by no means specific to the Czech situation. They also touched the USSR. This is no secret. The Cambridge economist Michael Ellman, for example, has pointed out that "in Czechoslovakia in the early 1960s the distribution of incomes was exceptionally equal .... A major objective of the abortive Czech reform was to overcome this situation. Similarly one of the features of economic reform in the USSR has been to improve the position of the specialists relative to that of the workers".[29]

The Polish events demonstrate something important, too. The workers' protest itself was not—contrary to a common opinion—directed against "Stalinism": rather the opposite. It was the result of economic reforms, especially in pricing policy, which in effect constituted one step in the abandonment of the *relative* equality of the Stalin years. The fact that the protest had to take the *form* of riots was, on the other hand, in all probability a result of the legacy of the "administrative methods" preferred in those years. But that is a different question.

It is therefore impossible to paint the Stalin period in wholly black or white terms, and it is equally impossible to pretend that its faults can be eliminated simply by "democratizing" or "liberalizing" the political structures (for the sake of "liberty") and "reforming" the economy (for the sake of "productivity"). The effects of Stalin's *humanism* and *economism* cannot be rectified by a *more consistent humanism* and a *more consistent economism*.

Something ought perhaps to be said here—since the example will have occurred to the reader—about the policies of the Chinese Communist Party. It is true that these policies have been consciously anti-humanist and anti-economist. This is certainly true of the Cultural Revolution of 1966–69 (which was however widely misrepresented in the West as a utopian, humanist project; whatever it was, it was not *that*). But, as far as it is possible to determine, the Chinese critique of Stalin suffers from an inadequate supply of alternative theses. Thus two recently published texts of Mao (dating from 1958 and 1959) on Stalin's *Economic Problems of Socialism* make the following criticisms: Stalin failed to deal with the political and ideological conditions of the transition to communism; he put the accent on the "expert"

29. Michael Ellman, "What Kind of Economic Reform Does the Soviet Union Need?", in *Cambridge Review*, May, 1971, p. 210.

and not the "red" side of the specialist; and he relied on the cadres and not on the masses.

Mao also argues, correctly, that one must not confuse the demarcation line between socialism and communism with that which distinguishes collective-farm property from public property. But his reasoning actually relies on Stalin's thesis that commodity production under socialism is a consequence of the existence of a non-public, collective farm sector. Since the abolition of this sector is not equivalent to the transition to communism, the two lines of demarcation are not identical. Thus for Mao, as for Stalin, "labour [under socialism] is not a commodity". Finally, he sometimes tends to identify the principle of the *supremacy of politics* (anti-economism) with *planning*.[30]

None of these positions (to judge from the pages of *Peking Review*) appears to have been modified up to the present day.[31] Unless evidence to the contrary becomes available, it must be considered that the Chinese still share certain of Stalin's fundamental theses.[32] And they certainly appear

30. *Mao Tsé-Toung et la construction du socialisme*, ed. Hu Chi-hsi (Seuil, 1975), pp. 39, 41, 58.

31. See for example an article by Nan Ching, who argues that "commodity production and commodity exchange still exist in socialist society . . . because two kinds of socialist ownership, namely, ownership by the whole people and collective ownership, exist side by side . . . However, the socialist type of commodity production differs from the capitalist type. This is manifested chiefly by the fact that there no longer is the economic relation of exploitation of workers by the capitalists, anarchism in production has been eliminated and the scope of commodity production has been reduced" (*Peking Review*, May 30, 1975, p. 12).

32. What the Chinese *have* rejected—and this they did early on—is the thesis of the primacy of the productive forces. Thus they no longer define communism in terms of material superabundance. Interesting in this connexion is an episode which took place in China in 1958 concerning the translation of the so-called "fundamental principles" of socialism and communism. The communist principle: "From each according to his ability, to each according to his needs", had been mistranslated in Chinese, said Chang Chung-shih (Deputy Director of the CCP Central Committee's Translation Bureau), to imply that anyone could take for himself whatever he wanted, and as much of it as he liked. This was wrong, said Chang. The revised translation indicated that the members of a communist society would have to work as hard as they could, and would get what was distributed to them.

to accept the existence of a socialist mode of production.

So much for alternative interpretations of the Stalin period and of socialist construction in general. We have seen that they fail to grasp some of the essential characteristics of the construction process. Up to now we have looked mainly at the question of the socialist economy. But we ought also to glance quickly at the *political* sphere. As we have seen, the State must play a key role in the generation within a socialist system of any new bourgeoisie. It is not simply a site of struggle between the working class and its potential enemies; it is also itself an *obstacle* to the victory of the working class.

This question really must be clarified, since it is the source of much confusion. Communists believe, as everyone knows, in the "dictatorship of the proletariat". What everyone does not know is the meaning of this expression. One very common interpretation considers it to be a dictatorship indeed, but not of the kind suggested by the Communists. It involves, in this interpretation, the existence of an enormously powerful State machine capable of crushing all opposition to the rule, not of the workers, but of a handful of Party bosses. This is for example how not only openly bourgeois thinkers but also most Social Democrats understand the dictatorship of the proletariat.

They are wrong. The term *dictatorship*, in the Marxist sense, is not contrasted with (or identified with) democracy. It functions in a different (though connected) theoretical space. Marxists also talk about the dictatorship of the bourgeoisie, and this term they apply to the most "democratic" of bourgeois nations. They mean that the bourgeoisie rules; but not necessarily (or primarily) by *repression*. It rules through the State, that is true, but mainly (at least in the "free West") by the use of the *Ideological Apparatuses*—thus precisely *not* by the method of "dictatorship", in the *bourgeois* sense of the term. The term "dictatorship of the proletariat", similarly, implies that the proletariat rules. But not (necessarily) primarily by the use of the Repressive Apparatus. The bourgeoisie can in principle rule indefinitely in this way, but the proletariat, as we shall see, *cannot*.

Of course, everyone who has read Lenin's *State and*

Revolution knows that "the proletariat needs the State as a *special* form of organization of violence against the bourgeoisie". But it needs a State "which is withering away, *i.e.*, a State so constituted that it begins to wither away immediately". Why?

The withering away of the State means, here, the abolition of the State *Apparatus*. An uninterrupted struggle to abolish the State *Apparatus* is in fact a condition of the reinforcement of proletarian State *power*.[33] The reason is that to *strengthen* the "Proletarian State Apparatus"—even when it *must* be strengthened, in order to function as a means of repression against the bourgeoisie—is always at the same time, tendentially, to *weaken* the control of the proletariat over its political, *i.e.* (here) State representatives. This is because *every* State is more or less *bureaucratic*, and therefore distant from the masses (Lenin in *The State and Revolution*: bureaucrats are "privileged persons divorced from the people and standing *above* the people"). That is precisely why Marxists insist on the final abolition of the State.

In fact the (necessary) existence of a proletarian *State Apparatus* paradoxically constitutes one of the conditions of the emergence of a new bourgeoisie. But this condition, let it be noted, is only *one* condition, and certainly not a sufficient one. Indeed, the existence of a "bureaucracy" under socialism is not itself even evidence of the "degeneration" of the system, unless every form of socialism is degenerate. Because *some* bureaucratism under socialism is inevitable (that is one of the reasons why socialism is not communism). Lenin, by the way, seems to have admitted as much when arguing in 1921 that "it will take decades to overcome the evils of bureaucracy" (*Collected Works*, vol. 32, p. 56). But this is bureaucracy in the *narrow* sense. In a *wider and more fundamental* sense it is inevitable because, as Lenin also admitted a year earlier in an argument with Trotsky, "the dictatorship of the proletariat cannot be exercised by a mass proletarian organization. It cannot work without a number of 'transmission belts' running from the vanguard to the mass of the working people."

33. *Cf.* Balibar, *Cinq Etudes*, p. 95.

Or, in other words, the State (the dictatorship of the proletariat) subsists, as a necessary evil, under socialism— not only because of the need to repress the old exploiting classes, etc., but also because the working class emerges from capitalism and imperialism "divided" and even "corrupted" (*Collected Works*, vol. 32, p. 21).

We have already said that the subsistence of capitalist production relations under socialism implies a tendency to the generation of a new bourgeoisie. One of the conditions for the realization of this tendency is a progressive bureaucratization of the State Apparatus. That is why the struggle against bureaucratization is not simply a struggle for efficiency, or against abuses, but a class struggle for communism. Once again, therefore, the tendency—in this case to bureaucratism—cannot be avoided, but the extent to which this tendency is realized depends on the class struggle.

We ought to add, finally, that it is this same class struggle which will determine whether these two tendencies (to capitalism in the economy, to bureaucracy in politics) are allowed not only to develop but also to *converge* and to *unite* in a critical conjuncture.

The new proletarian State must therefore not only destroy the old bourgeois State; it must itself be of a new type, a "State which is no longer a State" (Lenin). How can this be? It can be because the proletarian State is *both* a State "of the old type" (this is especially true of its Repressive Apparatus) and *also* an "anti-State". It is an anti-State in so far as certain of its Ideological Apparatuses—especially the Party, the Trades Unions, and mass popular organizations of all kinds—are transformed into *non-State organizations* capable of "controlling" and eventually of replacing the State.[34]

It is, *very schematically*, with the State that the proletariat wages class struggle against the old bourgeoisie and against imperialism. It is with its non-State organizations that it

---

34. It would of course be absurd *simply* to contrast State and Party in this respect. The Party, like other mass organizations, is also a site of class struggle. The history of this struggle cannot be examined in the space available here.

wages class struggle against the emergence of a new bourgeoisie.

That is the proletarian "State which is no longer a State". Not only the formulation is contradictory, but also the reality. To put it another way: the two kinds of class struggle which the proletariat must wage can never be in perfect harmony with one another. The conditions for the success of one may be obstacles to the success of the other.

Stalin, in this connexion, found himself faced with a rather complex set of dilemmas. The threat posed by the old bourgeoisie (including the old intelligentsia) was countered by the use of the Repressive State Apparatus. (That was logical.) The threat posed by the new generation of specialists—though Stalin was not sure what kind of threat it was, or even, sometimes, whether it was a threat at all—was met by a combination of financial inducement and the use of the same Apparatus. The measures had two obvious effects. On the one hand they perpetuated the danger, by reproducing the specialists as a privileged social group; on the other hand they encouraged the growth and independence of the Repressive State Apparatus and its functionaries.

As we saw, Stalin all but ignored the problem of the generation of a new bourgeoisie. He considered the class struggle under socialism to be primarily a struggle against the old exploiting classes. When that difficulty was resolved, he therefore tended (only *tended*, however, because he was never *quite sure*) to consider that class struggle had ceased to exist in the USSR. Thus the dictatorship of the proletariat could be relaxed. That was a "right deviation". In fact, however, it could not be relaxed without putting socialism at risk. And a mechanism seems to have operated which substituted itself for this absent dictatorship, for the absent theoretical, political and ideological struggles of the *Party and masses*. Or, rather, the dictatorship of the proletariat was maintained, but by the use of the Repressive State Apparatus, by "administrative methods". This was a "left" deviation (rhetoric of the political police as a weapon of the proletarian masses, and so on). The cost was enormous, not only in terms of human suffering, but also in terms of the damage caused to the struggle for communism. Because in building such a State, which was, it is true, a "proletarian State", but a State very much *of the old type* (that is, without adequate corresponding non-State organizations), Stalin solved one set of problems at the cost of generating a whole new set.

The "Stalin deviation" was a deviation above all because it implied that the road to communism lay not so much through class struggle as through the development of the productive forces. That is why it can be characterized in terms of *humanism* and *economism*. But it is precisely Stalin's humanism and his economism which Khrushchev *did not touch*, which he *did not rectify*. Can we, in these circumstances, conclude that Stalin's ghost has been laid? Can the errors of so many years of Communist history be wiped out by injecting Marxism with a *bigger dose* of humanism? These are the political questions which lie behind Althusser's *Reply to John Lewis*.

1.
Reply to
John Lewis

Foreword

The reader will find an article and a note here, dating from June 1972.

The article, "Reply to John Lewis", appeared, translated by Grahame Lock, in two numbers of the theoretical and political journal of the Communist Party of Great Britain, *Marxism Today*, in October and November 1972.

"Reply": because, a few months earlier (in its January and February numbers of 1972), the same journal had published a long critical article by John Lewis (a British Communist philosopher known for his interventions in political-ideological questions) under the title: "The Althusser Case".

The present text of the *Reply to John Lewis* follows the English version of the article, except that I have made some corrections, added a few paragraphs for purposes of clarification, and also added a Remark.

To this text I have joined an unpublished *Note*, which was to have been part of my *Reply*, but which was cut to avoid extending the limits of an article which had already grown too long.

1 May 1973
L.A.

Reply to John Lewis
(Self-Criticism)

I.

I want to thank *Marxism Today* for having published John
Lewis's article about the books I have written on Marxist
philosophy: *For Marx* and *Reading Capital*, which appeared
in France in 1965. He took care to treat me in a special way,
in the way a medical specialist treats a patient. The whole
family, as it were, together with his silent colleagues, stood
motionless at the bedside, while Dr John Lewis leaned
over to examine "the Althusser case".[1] A long wait. Then
he made his diagnosis: the patient is suffering from an attack
of severe "dogmatism"—a "mediaeval" variety. The prog-
nosis is grave: the patient cannot last long.

It is an honour for this attention to be paid to me. But
it is also an opportunity for me to clear up certain matters,
twelve years after the event. For my first article [reprinted
in *For Marx*], which was concerned with the question of
the "young Marx", actually appeared in 1960, and I am
writing in 1972.

A good deal of water has flowed under the bridge of
history since 1960. The Workers' Movement has lived
through many important events: the heroic and victorious
resistance of the Vietnamese people against the most powerful imperialism in the world; the Proletarian Cultural Revolution in China (1966–69); the greatest workers' strike in
world history (ten million workers on strike for a month)
in May 1968 in France—a strike which was "preceded"

1. The title of John Lewis's article is *The Althusser Case*. Not surprisingly:
in his conclusion, John Lewis compares Marxism to . . . medicine.

and "accompanied" by a deep ideological revolt among
French students and petty-bourgeois intellectuals; the occupation of Czechoslovakia by the armies of the other countries
of the Warsaw Pact; the war in Ireland, etc. The Cultural
Revolution, May 1968 and the occupation of Czechoslovakia
have had political and ideological repercussions in the whole
of the capitalist world.

With hindsight one can judge things better. Lenin used
to say: the criterion of practice is only really valid if it bears
on a "process" which is of some length. With the help of
the "practical test" of the twelve, ten or even seven years
which have passed since the original articles were written,
one can look back and see more clearly whether one was
right or wrong. It is really an excellent opportunity.

Just one small point in this connexion. John Lewis, in
his article, never for one moment talks about this political
history of the Workers' Movement. In *For Marx*—that is,
in 1965—I was already writing about Stalin, about the
Twentieth Congress of the Soviet Communist Party, and
about the split in the International Communist Movement.
John Lewis, on the other hand, writes as if Stalin had never
existed, as if the Twentieth Congress and the split in the
International Communist Movement had never occurred,
as if May 1968 had never taken place, nor the occupation
of Czechoslovakia, nor the war in Ireland. John Lewis is
a pure spirit; he prefers not to talk about such concrete
things as politics.

When he talks about philosophy, he talks about philosophy.
Just that. Full stop. It has to be said that this is precisely
what the majority of so-called philosophy teachers do in
our bourgeois society. The last thing they want to talk
about is politics! They would rather talk about philosophy.
Full stop. That is just why Lenin, quoting Dietzgen, called
them "graduated flunkies" of the bourgeois state. What a
wretched sight they make! For *all* the great philosophers
in history, since the time of Plato, even the great bourgeois
philosophers—not only the materialists but even idealists
like Hegel—have talked about politics. They more or less
recognized that to do philosophy was to do politics in the
field of theory. And they had the courage to do their politics
openly, *to talk about politics*.

Heaven be thanked, John Lewis has changed all that. John Lewis is a Marxist and we are in 1972. He does not feel the need to talk about politics. Let someone work that one out.

But to *Marxism Today* I must express my thanks for giving an important place to a discussion about philosophy. It is quite correct to give it this important place. The point has been made not only by Engels and of course by Lenin, but by Stalin himself! And, as we know, it has also been made by Gramsci and by Mao: the working class *needs philosophy* in the class struggle. It needs not only the Marxist *science* of history (historical materialism), but also Marxist philosophy (dialectical materialism). Why?

I should like to reply by using a formula. I will take the (personal) risk of putting it this way: the reason is that *philosophy is, in the last instance,*[2] *class struggle in the field of theory.*[3]

All this is, as John Lewis would say, perfectly "orthodox".

---

2. *N.B.: in the last instance.* I do not want to be misunderstood. What I am saying is that philosophy is, in the last instance, class struggle in the field of theory. I am not saying that philosophy is *simply* class struggle in the field of theory.

3. This formula, which is extremely condensed, might mislead the reader. I would therefore like to add three points to help orient him. (1) Because of its abstraction, its rationality and its system, philosophy certainly figures "in" the field of theory, in the neighbourhood of the sciences, with which it stands in a specific set of relations. But philosophy is not (a) science. (2) Unlike the sciences, philosophy has an especially intimate relation with the class tendency of the *ideologies*; these, in the last instance, are *practical* and do not belong to theory ("theoretical ideologies" are in the last instance "detachments" of the practical ideologies in the theoretical field). (3) In all these formulations, the expression "in the last instance" designates "determination in the last instance", the principal aspect, the "weak link" of *determination*: it therefore implies the existence of one or more secondary, subordinate, overdetermined and overdetermining aspects—*other* aspects. Philosophy is therefore not simply class struggle in theory, and ideologies are not simply practical: but they are practical "in the last instance". Perhaps there has not always been a full understanding of the *theoretical* significance of Lenin's political thesis of the "weak link". It is not simply a question of choosing *the* "weak link" from a number of pre-existing and already identified links: the chain is so made that the process must be reversed. In order to recognize and identify the other links of the chain, in their turn, one must *first* seize the chain by the "weak link".

Engels, whom Lenin quotes on the point in *What is to be Done?*, wrote in 1874 in his Preface to *The Peasant War* that there are three forms of the class struggle. The class struggle has not only an economic form and a political form *but also* a theoretical form. Or, if you prefer: the same class struggle exists and must therefore be fought out by the proletariat in the economic field, in the political field *and in the theoretical field*, always under the leadership of its party. When it is fought out in the theoretical field, the concentrated class struggle is called philosophy.

Now some people will say that all this is nothing but words. But that is not true. These words are *weapons* in the class struggle in the field of theory, and since this is part of the class struggle as a whole, and since the highest form of the class struggle is the political class struggle, it follows that these words which are used in philosophy are weapons in the political struggle.

Lenin wrote that "politics is economics in a concentrated form". We can say: philosophy is, in the last instance,[4] the *theoretical* concentrate of politics. This is a "schematic" formula. No matter! It expresses its meaning quite well, and briefly.

Everything that happens in philosophy has, in the last instance, not only political consequences in theory, but also political consequences *in politics*: in the political class struggle.

We will show in a moment why that is so.

Of course, since I cite Engels and Lenin in support of my point, John Lewis will surely say, once again, that I am talking like "the last champion of an orthodoxy in grave difficulties".[5] O.K.! I am the defender of orthodoxy, of that "orthodoxy" which is called the theory of Marx and Lenin. Is this orthodoxy in "grave difficulties"? Yes, it is and has been since it came to birth. And these grave difficulties are the difficulties posed by the threat of bourgeois ideology. John Lewis will say that I am "crying in the wilderness". Is that so? No, it is not!

4. See note 2 above.
5. I cite the expressions of John Lewis himself.

For Communists, when they are Marxists, and Marxists when they are Communists, *never* cry in the wilderness. Even when they are practically alone.

Why? We shall see.

I therefore take my stand on this theoretical basis of Marxism—a basis which is "orthodox" precisely in so far as it is in conformity with the theory of Marx and Lenin. And it is on this basis that I want to take issue both with John Lewis and with *my own* past errors, on the basis of the need to carry on the class struggle in the field of theory, as Engels and Lenin argued, and on the basis of the definition of philosophy which I am now proposing (in June, 1972): *philosophy is, in the last instance, class struggle in the field of theory*.

I will therefore leave aside all the rather imprudent remarks, some of them "psychological", which John Lewis thought it worth making at the end of his article, about Althusser's "*whole style of life and writing*". John Lewis is for example very worried, very put out, quite upset—good "humanist" that he is—by the fact that Althusser "argues exhaustively and with an extreme dogmatism", in a way which makes him think not so much of the Scholastics, who were great philosophers of the Middle Ages, but of the *schoolmen*, commentators of commentators, erudite splitters of philosophical hairs, who could not rise above the level of quotation. Thank you! But really, this kind of argument has no place in a debate between Communists in the journal of a Communist Party. I will not follow John Lewis onto this ground.

I approach John Lewis as a comrade, as a militant of a fraternal party: the Communist Party of Great Britain.

I will try to speak plainly and clearly, in a way that can be understood by all our comrades.

So as not to make my reply too long, I will only take up those theoretical questions which are most important, politically speaking, for us today, in 1972.

II.

To understand my reply, the reader must obviously know what John Lewis, in his "radical" critique of my "philosophical writings", essentially holds against me.

In a few words, we can sum this up as follows.

John Lewis holds:

1. that I do not understand Marx's *philosophy*;
2. that I do not understand the history of the *formation* of Marx's thought.

In short, his reproach is that I do not understand *Marxist theory*.

That is his right.

I will consider these two points in succession.

III.

First Point: *Althusser does not understand Marx's philosophy.*

To demonstrate this point, John Lewis employs a very simple method. First he sets out Marx's *real* philosophy, which is Marx as he understands him. Then, beside this, he puts Althusser's interpretation. You just have to compare them, it seems, to see the difference!

Well, let us follow our guide to Marxist philosophy and see how John Lewis sums up his own view of Marx. He does it in three formulae, which I will call three *Theses*.[6]

1. *Thesis no. 1.* "It is man who makes history."

John Lewis's argument: no need of argument, since it is obvious, it is quite evident, everyone knows it.

John Lewis's example: revolution. It is man who makes revolution.

2. *Thesis no. 2.* "Man makes history by remaking existing history, by 'transcending', through the 'negation of the negation', already made history."

John Lewis's argument: since it is man who makes history,

6. In a *Philosophy Course for Scientists* (1967, to be published), I proposed the following definition: "Philosophy states propositions which are *Theses*". (It therefore differs from the sciences: "A science states propositions which are Demonstrations")

it follows that in order to make history man must transform the history which he has already made (since it is man who has made history). To transform what one has already made is to "transcend" it, to negate what exists. And since what exists is the history which man has already made, it is already negated history. To make history is therefore "to negate the negation", and so on without end.

John Lewis's example: revolution. To make revolution, man "transcends" ("negates") existing history, itself the "negation" of the history which preceded it, etc.

3. *Thesis no. 3.* "Man only knows what he himself does."

John Lewis's argument: no argument, probably because of lack of space. So let us work one out for him. He could have taken the case of science and said that the scientist "only knows what he himself does" because he is the one who has to work out his proof, either by experiment or by demonstration (mathematics).

John Lewis's example: no example. So let us provide one. John Lewis could have taken *history* as an example: man's knowledge of history comes from the fact that he is the one who makes it. This is like the Thesis of Giambattista Vico: *verum factum*.[7]

These then are the three Theses which sum up John Lewis's idea of Marx's philosophy:
Thesis no. 1: It is man who makes history.
Thesis no. 2: Man makes history by transcending history.
Thesis no. 3: Man only knows what he himself does.

This is all very simple. Everyone "understands" the words involved: *man, make, history, know*. There is only one word which is a bit complicated, a "philosopher's" word: "transcendence", or "negation of the negation". But if he wanted to, John Lewis could say the same thing more simply. Instead of saying: man makes history, in

7 "What is true is what has been done." Marx cites Vico in *Capital*, in connexion with the history of technology.

transcending it, by the "negation of the negation", he could say that man makes history by "transforming" it, etc. Wouldn't that be more simple?

But a little difficulty still remains. When John Lewis says that it is man who makes history, everyone understands. Or rather, everyone thinks he understands. But when it is a question of going a bit further in the explanation, when John Lewis honestly asks himself the question: "*what* is it that man *does* when he makes history?", then you realize that a nasty problem appears just when everything seemed simple, that there is a nasty obscurity just in the place where everything seemed clear.

What was obscure? The little word *make*, in the Thesis that "it is man who makes history". What can this little word *make* possibly mean, when we are talking about *history*? Because when you say: "I made a mistake" or "I made a trip around the world", or when a carpenter says: "I made a table", etc., everyone knows what the term "make" means. The sense of the word changes according to the expression, but in each case we can easily explain what it means.

For example, when a carpenter "makes" a table, that means he *constructs* it. But to *make* history? What can that mean? And the *man* who makes history, do you know that individual, that "species of individual", as Hegel used to say?

So John Lewis sets to work. He does not try to avoid the problem: he confronts it. And he explains the thing. He tells us: to "make", in the case of history, that means to "transcend" (negation of the negation), that means to transform the raw material of existing history by going beyond it. So far, so good.

But the carpenter who "makes" a table, he has a piece of "raw material" in front of him too: the wood. And he transforms the wood into a table. But John Lewis would never say that the carpenter "transcends" the wood in order to "make" a table out of it. And he is right. For if he said that, the first carpenter who came along, and all the other carpenters and all the other working people in the world would send him packing with his "transcendence". John Lewis uses the term "transcendence" (negation of the negation) *only* for history. Why? We have to work out the answer, for John Lewis himself does not provide any explanation.

In my opinion, John Lewis holds on to his "transcendence" for the following reason: because the raw material of history *is already history*. The carpenter's raw material is *wood*. But the carpenter who "makes" the table would never say that *he was the one who* "*made*" the wood, because he knows very well that it is nature which produces the wood. Before a tree can be cut up and sold as planks, it first has to have grown somewhere in the forest, whether in the same country or thousands of miles away on the other side of the equator.

Now, for John Lewis it is man who *has made* the history with which *he makes* history. In history man produces everything: the result, the product of his "labour", is history: but so is the *raw material* that he transforms. Aristotle said that man is a two-legged, reasoning, speaking, political animal. Franklin, quoted by Marx in *Capital*, said that man is a "tool-making" animal. John Lewis says that man is not only a tool-making animal, but an animal which makes history, in the strong sense, because he *makes everything*. He "makes" the raw material. He makes the instruments of production. (John Lewis says nothing about these—and for good reason! Because otherwise he would have to talk about the *class struggle*, and his "man who makes history" would disappear in one flash, together with his whole system.) And he makes the final product: history.

Do you know of any being under the sun endowed with such a power? Yes—there does exist such a being in the tradition of human culture: *God*. Only *God* "makes" the raw material with which he "makes" the world. But there is a very important difference. John Lewis's God is not outside of the world: the man-god who creates history is not outside of history—he is *inside*. This is something infinitely more complicated! And it is just because John Lewis's little human god—man—is *inside* history ("*en situation*", as Jean-Paul Sartre used to say) that Lewis does not endow him with a power of absolute creation (when one creates everything, it is relatively easy: there are no limitations!) but with something even more stupefying—the power of "transcendence", of being able to progress by indefinitely *negating-superseding* the constraints of the history *in which* he lives, the power to transcend history by *human liberty*.[8]

John Lewis's man is a little lay god. Like every living being he is "up to his neck" in reality, but endowed with the prodigious power of being able at any moment to step outside of that reality, of being able to change its character. A little Sartrian god, always *"en situation"* in history, endowed with the amazing power of "transcending" every situation, of resolving all the difficulties which history presents, and of going forward towards the golden future of the human, socialist revolution: man is an essentially revolutionary animal because he is a *free* animal.

Please excuse all this if you are not a philosopher. We philosophers are well acquainted with this kind of argument. And we Communist philosophers know that this old tune in philosophy has always had its political consequences.

The first people who talked about "transcendence" in philosophy were the idealist-religious philosophers of Plato's school: the Platonic and neo-Platonic philosophers. They had an urgent need of the category of "transcendence" in order to be able to construct their philosophical or religious theology, and this theology was then the official philosophy of the slave state. Later, in the Middle Ages, the Augustinian and Thomist theologians took up the same category again and used it in systems whose function was to serve the interests of the Church and feudal state. (The Church is a State Apparatus, and the number one Ideological State Apparatus of the feudal state.) Is there any need to say more?

Much later, with the rise of the bourgeoisie, the notion of "transcendence" received, in Hegelian philosophy, a new function: the same category, but "wrapped" in the veil of the "negation of the negation". This time it served the bourgeois state. It was quite simply the *philosophical name* for *bourgeois liberty*. It was then revolutionary in relation to the philosophical systems of feudal "transcen-

8. I do not know John Lewis's personal philosophical history. But I am not sticking my neck out much in betting that he has a weakness for Jean-Paul Sartre. Lewis's "Marxist Philosophy" in fact bears a remarkable resemblance to a copy of Sartrian existentialism, in a slightly Hegelianized form, no doubt designed to make it more acceptable to Communist readers.

dence". But it was *one hundred per cent bourgeois*, and it stays that way.

Since that time, Jean-Paul Sartre has taken up the same idea once more, in his theory of man *"en situation"*: the *petty-bourgeois* version of *bourgeois liberty*. And this is to cite only one example, for Sartre is not alone—"transcendence", in its authoritarian or eschatological form, is still flourishing today among large numbers of theologians, some reactionary, some very progressive, from Germany and Holland to Spain and Latin America. The bourgeois no longer has the same need to believe—and anyway has for the thirty years since 1940 no longer been able to believe— that his liberty is all-embracing. But the petty-bourgeois intellectual: he is quite a different kind of animal! The more *his* liberty is crushed and denied by the development of imperialist capitalism, the more he exalts the power of that liberty ("transcendence", "negation of the negation"). An *isolated* petty-bourgeois can protest: he does not get very far. When the petty-bourgeois *masses* revolt, however, they get much further. But their revolt is still limited by the objective conditions of the class struggle, whether it is helped or hindered by them. It is here that petty-bourgeois *liberty* meets *necessity*.

John Lewis now, in 1972, takes up the old arguments in his turn, in the theoretical journal of the British Communist Party. He can, if I may say so, rest assured: he is not "crying in the wilderness"! He is not the only person to take up this theme. He is in the company of many Communists. Everyone knows that. But why should it be that since the nineteen-sixties many Communists have been resurrecting this worn-out philosophy of petty-bourgeois liberty, while still claiming to be *Marxists*?

We shall see.

IV.

But first, I shall follow the procedure used by John Lewis. I shall compare his "Marxist" Theses with the Theses of Marxist-Leninist philosophy. And everyone will be able to compare and judge for himself.

I will go over the points in John Lewis's order. That way things will be clearer. I am making an enormous concession to him by taking his order, because his order is idealist. But we will do him the favour.

To understand what follows, note that in the case of each Thesis (1,2,3) I begin by repeating Lewis's Thesis and then state the Marxist-Leninist Thesis.

1. THESIS No. 1

John Lewis: "It is *man* who makes history".
Marxism-Leninism: "It is the *masses* which make history".
  What is this "man" who "makes" history? A mystery.[9]
  What are the "masses" which make history"? In a class society they are the *exploited* masses, that is, the exploited social classes, social strata and social categories, grouped around the exploited class *capable* of uniting them in a movement against the dominant classes which hold state power.
  The exploited class capable of doing this is not always *the most* exploited class, or *the most* wretched social "stratum".
  In Antiquity, for example, it was not the slaves (except in a few periods—Spartacus) who "made" history in the strong, political sense of the term, but the most exploited classes among the "free" men (at Rome, the urban or rural "plebs").[10]
  In the same way, under capitalism the "lumpenproletariat",

9. For us, struggling under the rule of the bourgeoisie. "man" who makes history is a mystery. But this "mystery" did have a sense when the revolutionary bourgeoisie was struggling against the feudal regime which was then dominant. To proclaim *at that time*, as the great bourgeois Humanists did, that it is *man* who makes history, was to struggle, *from the bourgeois point of view* (which was then revolutionary), against the religious Thesis of feudal ideology: it is *God* who makes history. But we are no longer in their situation. Moreover, the bourgeois point of view has always been idealist as far as history is concerned.

10. It is not certain—here I shall have to bow to the judgement of Marxist historians—that the slave class did not, in spite of everything, quietly but genuinely "make history". The transition from the small-property slave system to the large-scale system at Rome is perhaps significant here.

as Marx called it, groups together the most wretched of men, the "lazarus-layers of the working-class".[11] But it is around the proletariat (the class which is exploited in capitalist *production*) that you will find grouped the masses which "make history", which are going to "make history"— that is, who are going to make the revolution which will break out in the "weakest link" of the world imperialist chain.

Against John Lewis's Thesis—it is man who makes history—Marxism-Leninism has always opposed the Thesis: it is the masses which make history. The masses can be defined. In capitalism, *the masses* does not mean "*the mass*" of aristocrats of the "intelligentsia", or of the ideologists of fascism; it means the set of exploited *classes*, strata and categories grouped around *the class* which is exploited *in large-scale production*, the only class which is capable of uniting them and directing their action against the bourgeois state: the proletariat. Compare this with Lewis's Thesis.

2. THESIS No.2

John Lewis: "Man makes history by 'transcending' history". *Marxism-Leninism*: "The class struggle is the motor of history" (Thesis of the *Communist Manifesto*, 1847).

Here things become extremely interesting. Because Marxism-Leninism blows up John Lewis's whole philosophical system. How?

John Lewis said: it is man who makes history. To which Marxism-Leninism replied: it is *the masses*.

But if we said no more, if we went no further, we would give the impression that Marxism-Leninism gives a *different* reply to the *same* question. That question being: *who makes* history? This question therefore supposes that history is the result of the action of (what is done by) a *subject* (who)? For John Lewis, the subject is "man". Does Marxism-Leninism propose a *different subject*, the masses?

---

11. *Capital*, Part VII, Ch. XXV, sec. 4. Excluded from production, without fixed work or completely unemployed, (often) in the street, the sub-proletarians are part of the reserve army, the army of unemployed, which capitalism uses *against* the workers.

Yes and no. When we started to sketch out a definition of the masses, when we talked about this idea of the masses, we saw that the whole thing was rather complicated. The masses are actually *several* social classes, social strata and social categories, grouped *together* in a way which is both complex and *changing* (the positions of the different classes and strata, and of the fractions of classes within classes, *change* in the course of the revolutionary process itself). And we are dealing with huge numbers: in France or Britain, for example, with tens of millions of people, in China with hundreds of millions! Let us do no more here than ask the simple question: can we still talk about a "subject", identifiable by the *unity* of its "personality"? Compared with John Lewis's subject, "man", as simple and neat as you can imagine, the masses, considered as a subject, pose very exacting problems of identity and identification. You cannot hold such a "subject" in your hand, you cannot point to it. A subject is a being about which we can say: "that's it!". How do we do that when the masses are supposed to be the "subject"; how can we say: "that's it"?

It is precisely the Thesis of the *Communist Manifesto*— "the class struggle is the motor of history"—that *displaces the question*, that brings the problem into the open, that shows us how to pose it properly and therefore how to solve it. It is the masses which "make" history, but "it is the class struggle which is the motor of history". To John Lewis' question: "how does man make history?", Marxism-Leninism replies by replacing his idealist philosophical categories with categories of a quite different kind.

The question is no longer posed in terms of "man". That much we know. But in the proposition that "the class struggle is the motor of history", the question of "making" history is also eliminated. It is no longer a question of *who* makes history.

Marxism-Leninism tells us something quite different: that it is the *class struggle* (new concept) which is the *motor* (new concept) of history, it is the class struggle which moves history, which advances it: and brings about revolutions. This Thesis is of very great importance, because *it puts the class struggle in the front rank*.

In the preceding Thesis: "it is the masses which make history", the accent was put (1) on the exploited classes grouped around the class capable of uniting them, and (2) on their power to carry through a revolutionary transformation of history. It was therefore the masses which were put in the front rank.

In the Thesis taken from the *Communist Manifesto*, what is put in the front rank is no longer the exploited classes, etc., but the class struggle. This Thesis must be recognized as decisive for Marxism-Leninism. It draws a radical demarcation line between revolutionaries and reformists. Here I have to simplify things very much, but I do not think that I am betraying the essential point.

For *reformists* (even if they call themselves Marxists) it is not the class struggle which is in the front rank: it is simply the classes. Let us take a simple example, and suppose that we are dealing with just two classes. For reformists these classes exist *before* the class struggle, a bit like two football teams exist, separately, before the match. Each class exists in its own camp, lives according to its particular conditions of existence. One class may be exploiting another, but for reformism that is not the same thing as class struggle. One day the two classes come up against one another and come into conflict. It is only then that the class struggle begins. They begin a hand-to-hand battle, the battle becomes acute, and finally the exploited class defeats its enemy (that is revolution), or loses (that is counter-revolution). However you turn the thing around, you will always find the same idea here: the classes exist *before* the class struggle, *independently* of the class struggle. The class struggle only exists *afterwards*.[12]

12. To clarify this point, this reformist "position" must be related to its bourgeois origins. In his letter to Weydemeyer (5 March 1852), Marx wrote: "No credit is due to me for discovering the existence of classes in modern society, nor yet the struggle between them. Long before me bourgeois historians had described the historical development of this struggle of the classes, and bourgeois economists the economic anatomy of the classes". The thesis of the recognition of *the existence of social classes*, and of *the resulting class struggle* is not proper to Marxism-Leninism: for it puts the classes in the front rank, and the class struggle in the second. *In this form* it is a bourgeois thesis, which reformism naturally feeds on. The Marxist-

Revolutionaries, on the other hand, consider that it is impossible to separate the classes from class struggle. The class struggle and the existence of classes are one and the same thing. In order for there to be classes in a "society", the society has to be *divided* into classes: this division does not come *later in the story*; it is the exploitation of one class by another, it is therefore the class struggle, which constitutes the division into classes. For exploitation is already class struggle. You must therefore begin with the class struggle if you want to understand class division, the existence and nature of classes. *The class struggle must be put in the front rank*.

But that means that our Thesis 1 (*it is the masses which make history*) must be subordinated to Thesis 2 (*the class struggle is the motor of history*). That means that the revolutionary power of the masses comes precisely from the *class struggle*. And that means that it is not enough, if you want to understand what is happening in the world, just to look at the exploited classes. You also have to look at the exploiting classes. Better, you have to go beyond the football match idea, the idea of two antagonistic groups of classes, to examine the basis of the existence *not only* of classes but also of the antagonism between classes: that is, the *class struggle*. Absolute primacy of the class struggle (Marx, Lenin). Never forget the class struggle (Mao).

But beware of idealism! The class struggle does not go on in the air, or on something like a football pitch. It is rooted in the mode of production and exploitation in a given class society. You therefore have to consider the *material basis* of the class struggle, that is, the material *existence* of the class struggle. This, in the last instance, is the unity of the relations of production and the productive forces *under* the relations of production of a given mode of production, in a concrete historical social formation. This

---

Leninist thesis, on the other hand, puts the *class struggle* in the front rank. Philosophically, that means: it affirms the *primacy of contradiction* over the *terms* of the contradiction. The class struggle is not a product of the existence of classes which exist *previous* (in law and in fact) to the struggle: the class struggle is the historical form of the *contradiction* (internal to a mode of production) which *divides* the classes into classes.

materiality, in the last instance, is at the same time the "base" (*Basis*: Marx) of the class struggle, and its material existence; because exploitation takes place in production, and it is exploitation which is at the root of the antagonism between the classes and of the class struggle. It is this profound truth which Marxism-Leninism expresses in the well-known Thesis of class struggle in the infrastructure, in the "economy", in class exploitation—and in the Thesis that *all the forms of the class struggle are rooted in economic class struggle*. It is on this condition that the revolutionary thesis of the primacy of the class struggle is a materialist one.

When that is clear, the question of the "subject" of history disappears. History is an immense *natural-human* system in movement, and the motor of history is class struggle. History is a process, and a *process without a subject*.[13] The question about how "*man* makes history" disappears altogether. Marxist theory rejects it once and for all; it sends it back to its birthplace: bourgeois ideology.

And with it disappears the "necessity" of the concept of "transcendence" and of its subject, man.

That does not mean that Marxism-Leninism *loses sight* for one moment of real men. Quite the contrary! It is precisely in order to *see* them as they are and to free them from class exploitation that Marxism-Leninism brings about this revolution, getting rid of the bourgeois ideology of "man" as the subject of history, *getting rid of the fetishism of "man"*.

Some people will be annoyed that I dare to speak about the fetishism of "man". I mean those people who interpret Marx's chapter in *Capital* on "The Fetishism of Commodities" in a particular way, drawing two necessarily complementary idealist conclusions: the condemnation of "reification"[14] and the exaltation of the *person*. (But the pair of notions *person/thing* is at the root of every bourgeois ideology!

13. I put this idea forward in a study called "Marx and Lenin before Hegel" (February 1968), published with *Lenin and Philosophy*, Maspero, Paris, 1972 [English translation in Louis Althusser, *Politics and History*, NLB, 1972]. For more details, see below the *Remark on the Category: "Process without a Subject or Goal(s)"*.

14. Transformation into a *thing (res)* of everything which is *human*, that is, a *non-thing* (man = non-thing = Person).

Social relations are however not, except for the law and for bourgeois legal ideology, "relations between persons"!). Yet it is the same mechanism of social illusion which is at work—when you start to think that a social relation is the natural quality, the natural attribute of a *substance* or a *subject*. Value is one example: this social relation "appears" in bourgeois ideology as the natural quality, the natural attribute of the commodity or of money. The class struggle is another example: this social relation "appears" in bourgeois ideology as the natural quality, the natural attribute of "man" (liberty, transcendence). In both cases, the social relation is "conjured away": the commodity or gold have *natural* value; "man" is *by nature* free, *by nature* he makes history.

If John Lewis's "man" disappears, that does not mean that real men disappear. It simply means that, for Marxism-Leninism, they are something quite different from copies (multiplied at will) of the original bourgeois image of "man", a free subject by nature. Have the warnings of Marx been heeded? "My analytical method *does not start from man*, but from the economically given social period" (*Notes on Adolph Wagner's "Textbook"*). "Society *is not composed of individuals*" (*Grundrisse*).

One thing is certain: one cannot *begin* with man, because that would be to begin with a bourgeois idea of "man", and because the idea of *beginning with* man, in other words the idea of an absolute point of departure (= of an "essence") belongs to bourgeois philosophy. This idea of "man" as a starting-point, an absolute point of departure, is the basis of all bourgeois ideology; it is the soul of the great Classical Political Economy itself. "Man" is a myth[15] of bourgeois ideology: Marxism-Leninism cannot *start* from "man". It starts "from the economically given social period"; and, at the end of its analysis, when it "arrives", *it may find real men*. These men are thus the *point of arrival* of an analysis which starts from the social relations of the existing mode

15. The word "man" is not simply a word. It is the place which it occupies and the function which it performs in bourgeois ideology and philosophy that give it its *sense*.

of production, from class relations, and from the class struggle. These men are quite different men from the "man" of bourgeois ideology.

"Society is not *composed of individuals*", says Marx. He is right: society is not a "combination", an "addition" of individuals. What constitutes society is the system of its social relations in which *its* individuals live, work and struggle. He is right: society is not made up of individuals in general, in the abstract, just so many copies of "man". Because each society has *its own* individuals, historically and socially determined. The slave-individual is not the serf-individual nor the proletarian-individual, and the same goes for the individual of each corresponding ruling class. In the same way, we must say that even a class is not "composed" of individuals in general: each class has *its own* individuals, fashioned in their individuality by their conditions of life, of work, of exploitation and of struggle—by the relations of the class struggle. In their mass, real men are what class conditions make of them. These conditions do not depend on bourgeois "human nature": liberty. On the contrary: the liberties of men, including the forms and limits of these liberties, and including their will to struggle, depend on these conditions.

If the question of "man" as "subject of history" disappears, that does not mean that the question of *political action* disappears. Quite the contrary! This political action is actually given its strength by the critique of the bourgeois fetishism of "man": it is forced to follow the conditions of the class struggle. For class struggle is not an individual struggle, but an *organized* mass struggle for the conquest and revolutionary transformation of state power and social relations. Nor does it mean that the question of the revolutionary *party* disappears—because without it the conquest of state power by the exploited masses, led by the proletariat, is impossible. But it does mean that the "role of the individual in history", the existence, the nature, the practice and the objectives of the revolutionary party are not determined by the omnipotence of "transcendence", that is, the liberty of "man", but by quite different conditions: by the state of the class struggle, by the state of the labour movement, by the ideology of the labour movement (petty-bourgeois or proletarian), and by its relation to Marxist theory, by its mass line and by its mass work.

3. THESIS No. 3

John Lewis: "Man only knows what he himself *does*". *Marxism-Leninism*: "One can only know what *exists*" (ce qui *est*).

I am deliberately putting these propositions into such direct opposition: so that everyone can see the difference.

For John Lewis, "man" only knows what he "does". For dialectical materialism, the philosophy of Marxism-Leninism, one can only know what *exists*. This is the fundamental Thesis of materialism: "the primacy of being over thought".

This Thesis is at one and the same time a Thesis about existence, about materiality and about objectivity. It says that one can only know what *exists*; that the principle of all existence is *materiality*; and that all existence is *objective*, that is, "prior" to the "subjectivity" which knows it, and independent of that subjectivity.

One can only know what *exists*. This Thesis, difficult to understand, and easy to misrepresent, *is the basis* of all Marxist Theses about knowledge. Marx and Lenin never denied the "activity" of thought, the work of scientific experiment, from the natural sciences to the science of history, whose "laboratory" is the class struggle. Indeed, they insisted on this activity. They even, now and again, said and repeated that certain idealist philosophers (Hegel, for example) had understood this "activity" better, though in "mystified" forms, than certain non-dialectical materialist philosophers. This is where we get to the dialectical Theses of Marxist philosophy, But—and this is where it differs fundamentally from John Lewis—*Marxism-Leninism has always subordinated the dialectical Theses to the materialist Theses*. Take the famous Thesis of the primacy of practice over theory: it has no sense unless it is subordinated to the Thesis of the primacy of being over thought. Otherwise it falls into subjectivism, pragmatism and historicism. It is certainly thanks to practice (of which scientific practice is the most developed form) that one can know what exists: primacy of practice over theory. But in practice one only ever knows what exists: primacy of being over thought.

"One can only know what exists." As far as nature is concerned, there ought not to be much problem: who could claim that "man" had "made" the natural world which he knows? Only idealists, or rather only that crazy species of idealists who attribute God's omnipotence to man. Even idealists are not normally so stupid.

But what about history? We know that the Thesis: "it is man who makes history" has, literally, no sense. Yet a trace of. the illusion still remains in the idea that history is *easier* to understand than nature because it is completely "human". That is Giambattista Vico's idea.

Well, Marxism-Leninism is categorical on this point: history is as difficult to understand as nature. Or, rather, it is even more difficult to understand. Why? Because "the masses" do not have the same *direct practical* relation with history as they have with nature (in productive work), because they are always *separated* from history by *the illusion that they understand it*. Each ruling exploiting class offers them "its own" explanation of history, in the form of its ideology, which is dominant, which serves its class interests, cements its unity, and maintains the masses under its exploitation.

Look at the Middle Ages: the Church and its ideologists offered all its flock—that is to say, primarily the exploited masses, but also the feudal class and itself—a very simple and clear explanation of history. History is made by God, and obeys the laws, that is, the ends, of Providence. An explanation for the "masses".

Look at the eighteenth century in France. The situation is different: the bourgeoisie is not yet in power, it is critical and revolutionary. And it offers everyone (without distinction of class! not only to the bourgeoisie and its allies, but also to the masses it exploits) a "clear" explanation of history: history is moved by Reason, and it obeys the laws or follows the ends of Truth, Reason and Liberty. An explanation for the "masses".

If history is difficult to explain scientifically, it is because *between* real history and men there is always a screen, a separation: *a class ideology of history* in which the human masses "spontaneously" believe: because this ideology is pumped into them by the ruling or ascending class, and serves it in its exploitation. In the eighteenth century the bourgeoisie is already an exploiting class.

To succeed in piercing this ideological and idealist "smoke-screen" of the ruling classes, the special circumstances of the first half of the nineteenth century were required: the experience of the class struggles following the French Revolution (1789, 1830) and the first proletarian class struggles, *plus* English political economy, *plus* French socialism. The result of the conjuncture of all these circumstances was Marx's discovery. He was the first to open up the "Continent of History" to scientific knowledge.

But in history, as in nature, one can only know what *exists*. The fact that, in order to get to know what really does *exist*, an enormous amount of scientific work and gigantic practical struggles were necessary, does not disprove the point. One can only know what *exists*, even if this is *changing*, under the effect of the material dialectic of the class struggle, even if what *exists* is only known on condition that it is *transformed*.

But we must go further. You will notice that I said that the Marxist-Leninist Thesis is not "man can only know what exists", but: "*one* can only know what exists".[16] Here too the term "man" has disappeared. We are forced to say in this connexion that scientific history, like all history, is a *process without a subject*, and that scientific knowledge (even when it is the work of a particular individual scientist, etc.) is actually the historical result of a process which has no real subject or goal(s). That is how it is with Marxist science. It was Marx who "discovered" it, but as the result of a dialectical process, combining German philosophy, English political economy and French socialism, the whole thing based on the struggles between the bourgeoisie and the working class. All Communists know that.

16. I wrote "one can only know what exists", in order not to complicate things. But it might be objected that this impersonal "one" bears the traces of "man". Strictly speaking, we should write: "only what exists *can be known*".

Scientists, in general, do not know it. But if they are prepared to, and if they have enough knowledge of the history of the sciences, Communists can help scientists (including natural scientists and mathematicians) to understand its truth. Because all scientific knowledge, in every field, really is the result of a process without any subject or goal(s). A startling Thesis, one which is doubtless difficult to understand. But it can give us "insights" of a certain importance, not only into scientific work, but also into the political struggle.

V.

For all these philosophical Theses, these philosophical positions (Thesis = position) produce *effects* in the social practices. Among them, effects in political practice and scientific practice.

But we have to generalize: it is not only the philosophical Theses which we have already discussed that produce these effects, but *all* philosophical Theses. Because if there is one idea which is popular today—even among some Marxists— it is the idea of philosophy as pure contemplation, pure *disinterested* speculation. Now this dominant idea is actually the very self-interested representation of idealism created by idealism itself. It is a mystification of idealism, necessary to idealism, to represent philosophy as purely speculative, as a pure revelation of Being, Origin and Meaning. Even speculative ideologies, even philosophies which content themselves with "*interpreting the world*", are in fact active and practical: their (hidden) goal is to act on the world, on all the social practices, on their domains and their "hierarchy"—even if only in order to "place them under a spell", to sanctify or modify them, in order to preserve or reform "the existing state of things" against social, political and ideological revolutions or the ideological repercussions of the great scientific discoveries. "Speculative" philosophies have a political *interest* in making believe that they are *disinterested* or that they are only "moral", and not really practical and political: this in order to gain their practical ends, in the shadow of the ruling power which they support with their arguments. Whether this strategy is "conscious" and deliberate or "unconscious" means little: we know that it is not consciousness which is the motor of history, even in philosophy.

You will remember the definition of philosophy which I proposed above. We can apply this definition to every philosophy: philosophy is, in the last instance, class struggle in the field of theory.

If philosophy is *class struggle* in theory, if it depends in the last instance on politics, then—as philosophy—it has political effects: in political practice, in the *way* in which "the concrete analysis of the concrete situation" is made, in which the mass line is defined, and in which mass work is carried out. But if it is class struggle in the field of *theory*, then it has theoretical effects: in the sciences, and also within the field of the ideologies. If it is *class struggle in the field of theory*, it has effects on the union of theory and practice: on the *way* in which that union is conceived and realized. It therefore has effects, of course, not only in political practice and scientific practice, but also in *every* social practice,[17] from the "struggle for production" (Mao) to art, etc.[18]

But I cannot deal with everything here. I will just say that philosophy, as class struggle in the field of theory, has two main effects: in politics and in the sciences, in

17. John Lewis is right to criticize me on this point: philosophy is not only "concerned" with politics and the sciences, but with *all* social practices.

18. How are these effects produced? This question is very important. Let us limit ourselves to the following comment: (1) Philosophy is not Absolute Knowledge; it is neither the Science of Sciences, nor the Science of Practices. Which means: it does not possess the Absolute Truth, either about any science or about any practice. In particular, it does not possess the Absolute Truth about, nor power over, political practice. On the contrary, Marxism affirms the primacy of politics over philosophy. (2) But philosophy is nevertheless not "the servant of politics", as philosophy was once "the servant of theology": because of its position *in theory*, and of its *"relative autonomy"*. (3) What is *at stake* in philosophy is the real problems of the social practices. As philosophy is not (a) science, its relation to these problems is not a *technical relation of application*. Philosophy does not provide formulae to be "applied" to problems: philosophy cannot be applied. Philosophy works in a quite different way: by modifying the *position* of the problems, by modifying the *relation* between the practices and their object. I limit myself to stating the principle, which would require a long explanation.

political practice and in scientific practice. Every Communist knows that, or ought to know it, because Marxism-Leninism has never ceased to repeat it and argue for it.

So let us now set out our schematic "proof", by comparing John Lewis's Theses with the Theses of Marxism-Leninism. That will allow us to show a little more clearly how philosophy "functions".

John Lewis's Thesis: "It is man who makes history".
Thesis of Marxism-Leninism: "It is the masses which make history; the class struggle is the motor of history".
Let us look at the *effects* of these Theses.

1. *Effects in the Field of Science*

When someone, in 1972, defends the idealist Thesis that "it is man who makes history", what effect does that have as far as the *science* of history is concerned? More precisely: can one make use of it to produce scientific discoveries?

It is a very regrettable fact, no doubt, but it is in fact no use at all from this point of view. John Lewis himself does not get anything out of it which might help us to see how the class struggle works. You might say that he didn't have the space in a single article. That is perhaps true. So let us turn to his (unavowed) Master, Jean-Paul Sartre, to the philosopher of "human liberty", of man-projecting-himself-into-the-future (John Lewis's transcendence), of man "*en situation*" who "transcends" his place in the world by the liberty of the "project". This philosopher (who deserves the praise given by Marx to Rousseau: that he never compromised with the powers-that-be) has written two enormous books— *Being and Nothingness* (1939), and the *Critique of Dialectical Reason* (1960), the latter devoted to proposing a philosophy for Marxism. More than two thousand pages. Now, what did Sartre get out of the Thesis: "it is man who makes history"?[19] What did it contribute to the science of history? Did the ingenious developments of the Sartrian positions finally permit the production of a few pieces of scientific

19. Sartre's Theses are obviously more subtle. But John Lewis's version of them, schematic and poor as it is, is not basically unfaithful to them.

knowledge about the economy, the class struggle, the state, the proletariat, ideologies, etc.—knowledge which might help us to understand history, to act in history? We have, unfortunately, reason to doubt it.

But then someone is going to say: here is an example which proves just the opposite of your Thesis about the effects of philosophy, because, as you recognize, this "humanist" philosophy has *no effect at all* on scientific knowledge. Sorry! I claim that Theses like those defended by John Lewis and Jean-Paul Sartre really do have such an effect, even though it is a *negative* one: because they "prevent" the development of existing scientific knowledge. Lenin said the same of the idealist philosophies of his own time. These Theses are an obstacle to the development of knowledge. Instead of helping it to progress, they hold it back. More precisely, they drag knowledge back to the state it was in *before* the scientific discoveries made by Marx and Lenin. They take us back to a pre-scientific "philosophy of history".

It is not the first time that this has happened in the history of humanity. For example, half a century after Galileo—that is, half a century after physics had been founded as a *science*—there were still philosophers who defended Aristotelian "physics"! They attacked Galileo's discoveries and wanted to drag knowledge of the natural world back to its pre-scientific Aristotelian state. There are no longer any Aristotelian "physicists"; but the same process can be observed in other fields. For example: there are anti-Freudian "psychologists". And there are anti-Marxist philosophers of history, who carry on as if Marx had never existed, or had never founded a science. They may be personally honest. They may even, like Sartre, want to "help" Marxism and psychoanalysis. But it is not their intentions that count. What count are the real *effects* of their philosophies in these sciences. The fact is that although he comes *after* Marx and Freud, Sartre is, paradoxically, in many respects a pre-Marxist and pre-Freudian ideologian from the philosophical point of view. Instead of helping to build on the scientific discoveries of Marx and Freud, he makes a spectacular appearance in the ranks of those whose work does more to hinder Marxist research than to help it.

That is how, in the end, philosophy "works" in the sciences. *Either* it helps them to produce new scientific knowledge, *or* it tries to wipe out these advances and drag humanity back to a time when the sciences did not exist. Philosophy therefore works in the sciences in a progressive or retrogressive way. Strictly speaking, we should say that it *tends* to act in one way or another—for every philosophy is always contradictory.[20]

You can see what is at stake. It is not enough to say that what John Lewis or Sartre says does not help us to produce any scientific knowledge of history. It is not even enough to argue that what they say represents an "epistemological obstacle" (to use Bachelard's term). We are forced to say that their Thesis produces or can produce effects which are extremely harmful to scientific knowledge, retrogressive effects, because instead of helping us, in 1972, to understand the great scientific treasure that we possess in the knowledge given us by Marx, and to develop it,[21] it goes back to zero. It takes us back to the good old days of Descartes, or Kant and Fichte, of Hegel and Feuerbach, to the time *before* Marx's discovery, before his "epistemological break". This idealist Thesis mixes everything up, and thus it paralyses revolutionary philosophers, theoreticians and militants. It disarms them, because in effect it deprives them of an irreplaceable weapon: the objective knowledge of the conditions, mechanisms and forms of the class struggle.

If you now look at the Marxist-Leninist Theses—"it is the masses which make history", "the class struggle is the motor of history"—the contrast is striking. These Theses do not paralyse research: they are *on the side of* a scientific understanding of history. They do not wipe out the science of history founded by Marx—for these two philosophical

20. There is no absolutely *pure* idealist or materialist philosophy, even if only because every philosophy must, in order to take up its own theoretical class positions, *surround* those of its principal adversary. But one must learn to recognize the *dominant tendency* which results from its contradictions, and masks them.

21. Lenin said: Marx has given us the "corner-stones" of a theory which we must "develop in every direction".

Theses are at the same time proven propositions of the science of history, of historical materialism.[22]

These Theses, then, take account of the *existence* of the science of history. But at the same time they help the working out of *new* concepts, of new scientific discoveries. For example, they lead us to define the masses which make history—in class terms. For example, they lead us to define the form of union between the classes which make up the masses. As far as the class struggle under capitalism is concerned, they put the question of taking state power, the long transition (to communism) and the proletariat in the forefront. For example, they cause us to conceive the unity of the class struggle and of class division, and all their consequences, *in the material forms* of exploitation and of the division and organization of labour, and therefore to study and come to understand these forms. For example, they lead us to define the proletariat as a class whose conditions of exploitation render it capable of directing the struggle of all the oppressed and exploited classes, and to understand the proletarian class struggle as a form of class struggle without precedent in history, inaugurating a "new practice of politics",[23] which is the secret of many still enigmatic or evaded questions.

The theoretical consequences of these questions are obvious. They force us above all to break with the bourgeois—that is, the *economist* conception—of political economy ("criticized" as such by Marx in *Capital*), with the bourgeois conception of the state, of politics, of ideology, of culture, etc. They prepare the ground for new research and new discoveries, some of which might cause a few surprises.

On the one side, then, we have idealist philosophical Theses which have theoretically retrograde effects on the science of history. On the other side we have materialist philosophical Theses which have theoretically progressive effects in the existing fields of the Marxist science of history, and which can have revolutionary effects in those fields

22. The fact that scientific propositions may *also*, in the context of a philosophical debate, "function philosophically" is worthy of thought.

23. Cf. Etienne Balibar, "La Rectification du *Manifeste communiste*", *La Pensée*, August 1972.

which have not yet been really grappled with by the science of history (for example in the history of the sciences, of art, of philosophy, etc.).

This is what is at stake as far as the class struggle in the theoretical field is concerned.

2. *Political effects*

I think that, as far as political effects are concerned, things are rather clear.

How could one carry on the class struggle on the basis of the philosophical Thesis: "it is man who makes history"? It might be said that this Thesis is useful in fighting against a certain conception of "History": history in submission to the decisions of a Deity or to the Ends of Providence. But, speaking seriously, that is no longer the problem!

It might be said that this Thesis serves *everyone*, without distinction, whether he be a capitalist, a petty-bourgeois or a worker, because these are all "men". But that is not true. It serves *those* whose interest it is to talk about "man" *and not* about the masses, about "man" *and not* about classes and the class struggle. It serves the bourgeoisie, above all; and it also serves the petty-bourgeoisie. In his *Critique of the Gotha Programme*, Marx wrote: "The bourgeois have very good grounds for falsely ascribing *supernatural creative power* to [human] labour".[24] Why? Because by making "men" think that "labour is the source of all wealth and all culture", the bourgeoisie can keep quiet about the power of "*nature*", about the decisive importance of the *natural*, *material conditions* of human labour. And why does the bourgeoisie want to keep quiet about the natural-material conditions of labour? Because *it controls them*. The bourgeoisie knows what it is doing.

If the workers are told that "it is men who make history", you do not have to be a great thinker to see that, sooner or later, that helps to disorient or disarm them. It tends

24. Marx's emphasis. Marx was therefore criticizing the formula of the socialist John Lewises of his time, inscribed in the Unity Programme of the German Social-Democratic Party and Lassalle's Party: "*Labour is the source of all wealth and all culture*".

to make them think that they are all-powerful as men, whereas in fact they are disarmed as workers in the face of the power which is really in command: that of the bourgeoisie, which controls the material conditions (the means of production) and the political conditions (the state) determining history. The humanist line turns the workers away from the class struggle, prevents them from making use of the only power they possess: that of their *organization as a class* and their *class organizations* (the trade unions, the party), by which they wage *their* class struggle.

On the one hand, therefore, we have a philosophical Thesis which, directly or indirectly, serves the political interests of the bourgeoisie, even inside the labour movement (that is called reformism), and even within "Marxist" theory (that is called revisionism), with all the consequent political effects.

On the other hand we have Theses which directly help the working class to understand its role, its conditions of existence, of exploitation and of struggle, which help it to create organizations which will lead the struggle of all exploited people to seize state power from the bourgeoisie.

Need I say more?

None of this is affected by the fact that these bourgeois or petty-bourgeois Theses are defended, in 1972, by a militant of a Communist Party. Read chapter 3 of the *Communist Manifesto*. You will see that in 1847 Marx distinguished three kinds of socialism: reactionary (feudal, petty-bourgeois, *humanist*[25]) socialism, conservative or bourgeois socialism, and critical-utopian socialism and communism. You have the choice! Read the great polemical writings of Engels and Lenin about the influence of bourgeois ideology in the workers' parties (reformism, revisionism). You have the choice!

What we want to know now is how, after so many solemn warnings and so many testing experiences, it is possible for a Communist—John Lewis—to present his "Theses" as Marxist.

We shall see.

25. Then called "True" or "German" socialism.

VI.

So as not to hold things up, I will be brief in dealing with John Lewis's second reproach: *that "Althusser" does not understand anything of the history of the formation of Marx's thought.*

Here I must make my self-criticism, and give way to John Lewis on one precise point.

In my first essays, I suggested that after the "epistemological break" of 1845 (after the discovery by which Marx founded the science of history) the philosophical categories of *alienation* and *the negation of the negation* (among others) disappear. John Lewis replies that this is not true. And he is right. You certainly do find these concepts (directly or indirectly) in the *German Ideology*, in the *Grundrisse* (two texts which Marx never published) and also, though more rarely (alienation) or much more rarely (negation of the negation: only one explicit appearance) in *Capital*.

On the other hand John Lewis would have a hard job finding these concepts in the *Communist Manifesto*, in the *Poverty of Philosophy*, in *Wage Labour and Capital*, in his *Contribution to the Critique of Political Economy*, in the *Critique of the Gotha Programme* or in the *Notes on Wagner's Textbook*. And this is to cite only some of Marx's texts. As far as the political texts are concerned—and this of course is equally true of the texts of Lenin,[26] Gramsci or Mao—well, he can always try!

But in any case, formally speaking John Lewis is right. And so, even if his argument in fact depends on leaving aside all the texts which could bother him, I must reply.

Here, in a few words, is my reply.

1. If you look at the whole of Marx's work, there is no doubt that there does exist a "break" of some kind in 1845. Marx *says so* himself. But of course no one should be believed simply on his word, not even Marx. You have to judge on the evidence. Nevertheless, the whole work of Marx

---

26. He can certainly cite Engels's use of the negation of the negation in *Anti-Dühring*—which can be found in Lenin's *What the "Friends of the People" Are*. But it is a rather "peculiar" defence: an anti-Hegelian one.

shows him to be right on this point. In 1845 Marx *began* to lay down the foundations of a science which did not exist before he came along: the science of history. And in order to do that he set out a number of new concepts which cannot be found anywhere in his humanist works of youth: *mode of production, productive forces, relations of production, infrastructure-superstructure, ideologies*, etc. No one can deny that.

If John Lewis still doubts the reality of this "break", or rather—since the "break" is only the effect—of this *irruption* of a new science in a still "ideological" or pre-scientific universe, he should compare two judgements made by Marx on Feuerbach and Proudhon.

Feuerbach is described in the *1844 Manuscripts* as a philosopher who has made extraordinary discoveries, who has discovered both the basis and the principle of the critique of political economy! But a year later, in the *Theses on Feuerbach*, and in the *German Ideology*, he is object of an all-out attack. After that he simply disappears.

Proudhon is described in the *Holy Family* (end of 1844) as someone who "does not simply *write* in the interest of the proletariat, but is himself a proletarian, a worker. His work is *a scientific manifesto of the French proletariat*."[27] But in 1847, in the *Poverty of Philosophy*, he gets a hiding from which he will never recover. After that he simply disappears.

If, as John Lewis says, *nothing* really happened in 1845, and if everything that I have said about the "epistemological break" is "a complete myth", then I'll be hung for it.

2. So something *irreversible* really does start in 1845: the "epistemological break" is a point of *no return*. Something begins which will have no end.[28] A "continuing break", I wrote, the beginning of a long period of work, as in every other science. And although the way ahead is open, it is difficult and sometimes even dramatic, marked by events— theoretical events (additions, rectifications, corrections)—

27. *The Holy Family*, English translation, Moscow 1956.
28. Lenin speaking of the study of imperialism: "This study is only beginning, and *it is without an end*, by its very nature, like science in general". (*The Collapse of the Second International*.)

which concern the scientific knowledge of a particular object: the conditions, the mechanisms and the forms of the class struggle. In simpler terms, the science of history.

We can say, then, that this science does not emerge, ready-made, from Marx's head. It merely *has its beginning* in 1845, and has not yet got rid of all its past—of all the ideological and philosophical prehistory out of which it has emerged. There is nothing astonishing in the fact that for some time it continues to contain ideological notions or philosophical categories which it will later get rid of.

We can also say: look at Marx's texts, look at the birth and development of his scientific concepts, and—since John Lewis insists on talking about them—you will at the same time see the gradual disappearance of these two philosophical categories inherited from the past and still subsisting as remnants, known as *alienation* and the *negation of the negation*. Now in fact, the more we advance in time, the more these categories disappear. *Capital* speaks only once of the negation of the negation in explicit terms. It is true that Marx several times uses the *term* "alienation". But all that disappears in Marx's later texts and in Lenin. Completely.[29] We could therefore simply say: what is important is the *tendency*: and Marx's scientific work does *tend* to get rid of these philosophical categories.

3. But this is not sufficient. And here is my self-criticism.

I was not attentive enough to the *fact* which John Lewis points out, that is, to the fact of the continuing presence of the said philosophical categories *after* the "epistemological break". And that was because I identified the "epistemological (= *scientific*) break" with Marx's philosophical revolution. More precisely, I did not separate Marx's philosophical revolution from the "epistemological break", and I therefore talked about philosophy as if it were science, and quite logically wrote that in 1845 Marx made a *double* break, scientific *and* philosophical.

29. One really must be short of arguments to have to use, as a proof of Lenin's "humanist philosophy", a few lines from *The German Ideology* (1844) which Lenin copied into his notebook! John Lewis is obviously not worried about gaining the reputation of "schoolman" himself.

That was a mistake. It is an example of the *theoreticist* (=rationalist-speculative) deviation which I denounced in the brief self-criticism contained in the Preface to the Italian edition of *Reading Capital* (1967), reproduced in the English edition.[30] Very schematically, this mistake consists in thinking that philosophy is a *science*, and that, like every science, it has: (1) an *object*; (2) a *beginning* (the "epistemological break" occurs at the moment when it *looms up* in the pre-scientific, ideological cultural universe); and (3) a *history* (comparable to the history of a science). This theoreticist error found its clearest and purest expression in my formula: Philosophy is "Theory of theoretical practice".[31]

Since that time, I have begun to "put things right". In a philosophy course for scientists, dating from 1967, and then in *Lenin and Philosophy* (February 1968), I put forward other propositions:

1. Philosophy is not (a) science.
2. Philosophy has no object, in the sense in which a science has an object.
3. Philosophy has no history, in the sense in which a science has a history.
4. Philosophy is politics in the field of theory.
   What are the consequences?

1. It is impossible to reduce philosophy to science, and it is impossible to reduce Marx's philosophical revolution to the "epistemological break".
2. Marx's philosophical revolution preceded Marx's "epistemological break". It *made the break possible*.

One can of course put forward serious arguments to the effect that there is a sense in which philosophy, as Hegel said, and as I repeated in *Lenin and Philosophy*, always

---

30. And in the edition of *Reading Capital* published in the Petite Collection Maspero, 1968, vol. 1.
31. The corrections which I later made to this formula (for example: Philosophy is "Theory of theoretical practice in its distinction from the *other* practices", or "Theory of the processes of the production of knowledge", or " ... of the material and social conditions of the processes of production of knowledge", etc., in *For Marx* and *Reading Capital*) do not touch the root of this error.

"lags behind" science or the sciences. But from another point of view, which is important here, one has to say the opposite, and argue that in the history of Marx's thought the scientific breakthrough is based on the philosophical revolution, which gives the breakthrough its form: that of a *revolutionary science*.

In the case of other sciences, we often lack evidence and proof of what happened. But in the case of Marx, we are able to say that while both the philosophical revolution and the epistemological break take place "at the same time", the scientific break is based on the philosophical revolution.

In practical terms, that means the following. The young Marx, born of a good bourgeois family in the Rhineland, entered public life as editor of a liberal newspaper of the same land. That was in 1841. A young and brilliant intellectual, he was, within three or four years, to undergo an astonishing evolution *in politics*. He was to pass from radical bourgeois liberalism (1841–42) to petty-bourgeois communism (1843–44), then to proletarian communism (1844–45). These are incontestable facts. But parallel to this political evolution you can observe an evolution in philosophy. *In philosophy*, over the same period, the young Marx was to pass from a position of subjective neo-Hegelianism (of a Kant-Fichte type) to theoretical humanism (Feuerbach), before rejecting this to pass over to a philosophy which would no longer merely "interpret" the world: a completely new, materialist-revolutionary philosophy.

If you now compare Marx's political evolution with his philosophical evolution, you will see:

1. that his philosophical evolution is based on his political evolution; and
2. that his scientific discovery (the "break") is based on his philosophical evolution.

That means, in practice, that it is because the young Marx had "settled accounts" with his previous philosophical consciousness (1845), because he had finally abandoned his bourgeois liberal and petty-bourgeois revolutionary positions to adopt (even if only in principle, at a moment when he was letting go the ropes) new revolutionary-proletarian class positions in theory, it was because of all this that he was able to lay down the foundations of the scientific theory of history as history of the class struggle. *In principle*: because the process of recognizing and occupying these new positions in theory needed time. Time, in a ceaseless struggle to contain the pressure of bourgeois philosophy.

4. On the basis of these points it should be possible to account for the intermittent survival of categories like those of *alienation* and of the *negation of the negation*. Note that I talk about intermittent survival. For alongside their *tendency* to disappear in Marx's work, considered as a whole, there is a strange phenomenon which must be accounted for: their total disappearance in certain works, then their *subsequent* reappearance. For example, the two categories in question are absent from the *Communist Manifesto* as well as from the *Poverty of Philosophy* (published by Marx in 1847). They seem to be hidden in his *Contribution to the Critique of Political Economy* (which he published in 1859). But there are many references to alienation in the *Grundrisse* (preparatory notes made by Marx in the years 1857–58, and which he *did not publish*). We know, because of a letter sent to Engels, that Marx had "by chance" re-read Hegel's *Logic* in 1858 and had been fascinated by it. In *Capital* (1867) alienation comes up again, but much more rarely, and the negation of the negation appears just once. And so on.[32]

32. One must be careful with philosophical categories taken *one by one*: for it is less their name than their function in the theoretical apparatus in which they operate that decides their "nature". Is *a particular* category idealist or materialist? In many cases we have to reply with Marx's answer: "That depends". But there are limit-cases. For example, I do not really see that one can expect anything positive from the category of the *negation of the negation*, which contains within it an irreparable idealist charge. On the other hand it seems to me that the category of alienation can render *provisional* services, given a double and absolute condition: (1) that it be "cut" from every philosophy of "reification" (or of fetishism, or of self-objectivization) which is only an anthropological variant of idealism; and (2) that alienation is understood as *secondary* to the concept of exploitation. On this double condition, the category of alienation can, *in the first instance* (since it disappears in the final result) help to avoid a purely *economic*, that is, economist conception *of surplus-value*: it can help to introduce the idea that, in exploitation, *surplus-value is inseparable from the concrete and material forms in which it is extorted*.

However that might be, and without anticipating other studies which must be made if the *contradictory* dialectic of Marx's development and the elaboration of his work is to be understood, one fact is clear. The Marxist science of history did not progress in a simple straight line, according to the classic *rationalist* scheme, without problems or internal conflicts, and under its own power, from the moment of the "point of no return"—the "epistemological break". There certainly is a "point of no return", *but* in order not to be forced to retreat, it is necessary to advance—and to advance, how many difficulties and struggles there are! For if it is true that Marx had to pass over to proletarian class positions in theory in order to found the science of history, he did not make that leap all at once, once and for all, for ever. It was necessary to *work out* these positions, to take them up over and against the enemy. The philosophical battle continued within Marx himself, in his work: around the principles and concepts of the new revolutionary science, which was one of the stakes of the battle. Marxist science only gained its ground little by little, in theoretical struggle (class struggle in theory), in close and constant relation to the class struggle in the wider sense. This struggle lasted all of Marx's life. It continued after his death, in the labour movement, and it is still going on today. A struggle without an end.

It is therefore possible to understand, at least in principle, the partial disappearance and reappearance of certain categories in Marx's work as indicative of survivals of old ideas or attempts to work out new ones, of advances and retreats in the long dual struggle to take up class positions in theoretical work and to found the science of history.

When I said that it was the "epistemological break" which was primary, and when I said that it was at the same time a *philosophical* "break", I therefore made two mistakes. In the case of Marx it is the philosophical revolution which is *primary*—and this revolution is not a "break". The theoretical terminology itself is important here: if one can legitimately

A number of texts from the *Grundrisse* and from *Capital* go, in my opinion, in this sense. But I know that others go in a different and much more ambiguous sense.

keep the term "break" to denote the beginning of the science of history, the clear effect of its irruption in the cultural universe, the point of no return, one cannot employ the same term in talking about philosophy. In the history of philosophy, as in very long periods of the class struggle, one cannot really talk about a point of no return. So I shall use the term: philosophical "revolution" (in the strong sense in Marx's case). This expression is more correct: for—to evoke once again the experiences and terms of the class struggle—we all know that a revolution is always open to attacks, to retreats and reverses, and even to the risk of counter-revolution.

Nothing in philosophy is *radically* new, for the old Theses, taken up again in new form, survive and return in a new philosophy. Nor is anything ever settled *definitively*: there is always the struggle of antagonistic tendencies, there are always "come-backs", and the oldest philosophies are always ready to mount an offensive disguised in modern— even the most revolutionary—trappings. Why?

Because philosophy is, in the last instance, class struggle in the field of theory. Because the revolutionary classes are always opposed by the old conservative and reactionary ruling classes, who will never give up their ambition for revenge, even when they no longer hold state power. According to the state of affairs, these classes will either defend their power or, if they have lost power, they will try to regain it, using among other things the arguments of such-and-such a philosophy: that which serves them best politically and ideologically, even if it comes out of the depths of history. It only has to be done up a bit and given a modern coat of paint. Philosophical Theses, in the end, have "no age". That is the sense in which I took up Marx's comment in the *German Ideology* that "philosophy has no history".

In practice, when the state of the class struggle enables it to put on enough pressure, bourgeois ideology can penetrate Marxism itself. The class struggle in the field of theory is not just a phrase: it is a reality, a terrible reality. Without understanding that, it is impossible to understand either the dramatic history of the formation of Marx's thought or the "grave difficulties" which even today, in 1972, weigh on the "orthodoxy" defended by a certain number of Communists.

The dramatic history of Marx and of his thought can be reduced, if we follow John Lewis, to a peaceful and problem-free university career! A certain Marx appears on the literary and philosophical scene. Quite naturally, he begins to talk about politics in the *Communist Manifesto*, then about economics in *Capital*. He founds and directs the First International, opposes the insurrection in Paris, then in the space of two months, takes a firm stand on the side of the Paris Commune. He wages a battle to the death against the anarchists and followers of Proudhon, etc., etc. All this without the hint of a problem, of a drama, aside from all the assaults of the struggle, with no regard to the difficulties, the questions, all the torments of the search for "truth" in that struggle itself. Like a good bourgeois intellectual, as well installed in his thought as he is in the comfort of his existence, Marx, in this view, *always thought the same thing*, without any revolution or "break" in his thinking: he always taught that "man makes history", by the "negation of the negation", etc. I think I am justified in saying here that only someone who has no experience of the class struggle, including class struggle in the field of theory—or even simply of the way in which scientific research is done—could argue such nonsense, and thus insult the life and sufferings not only of Marx himself but of all Communists (and also of all those scientists who succeed in *finding something out*). Now, not only did Marx "find something out" (and at what risk, and of what importance!), but he was also a *leader* of the labour movement for thirty-five years. He always did his thinking and his "investigating" *in and through the struggle*.

The whole history of the labour movement is marked by endless crises, dramas and struggles. There is no need for me to go over them here. But as far as philosophy is concerned, we ought at least to mention the great struggles of Engels and Lenin against the intervention of the idealism of Dühring and of Bernstein, both of them declared neo-Kantians and humanists, whose theoretical revisionism covered their political reformism and political revisionism.

John Lewis would do well to re-read the first pages of *What is to be Done?* In this text a petty-bourgeois intellectual named Lenin is defending Marx's "orthodoxy", which is "in grave difficulties". With "extreme dogmatism" (I use Lewis's terms). Yes, Lenin declared himself proud to be attacked as a "dogmatist" by the international coalition of "critical" revisionists, with the "English Fabians" and "French Ministerialists" at their head! (I am quoting Lenin.) Yes, Lenin declared himself proud to defend this old problem-ridden "orthodoxy", the orthodoxy of Marx's teaching. Yes, he thought it was "in grave difficulties". The cause: reformism and revisionism!

Some Communists, today, are thinking and doing the same. There certainly are not too many of them.

That is how things are. Why? We shall see.

VII.
We have to answer two questions.

1. Why are there Communists like John Lewis (and there are quite a lot of them) who, in 1972, can openly argue in Communist journals for a philosophy which they call Marxist, but which is in fact simply a variant of bourgeois idealism?

2. Why are the Communist philosophers who defend Marx's philosophy so few in number?

To answer these two questions, which are really one and the same, we must—all apologies to John Lewis—briefly enter the field of political history.

I have made the basic points in *For Marx*. But John Lewis does not seem to have read the political pages of *For Marx*. John Lewis is a pure spirit.

And yet I was rather clear in explaining that the articles collected in *For Marx* had to be considered as a philosophical intervention in a political and ideological conjuncture dominated by the Twentieth Congress and the "split" in the International Communist Movement.[33] The fact that

33. Cf. the Introduction to *For Marx*.

I was able to make such an intervention is a consequence of the Twentieth Congress.

Before the Twentieth Congress it was actually not possible for a Communist philosopher, certainly in France, to publish texts which would be (at least to some extent) relevant to politics, which would be something other than a pragmatist commentary on consecrated formulae. That is the good side of the Twentieth Congress, for which we must be grateful. From that time on it was possible to publish such texts. The French Party, to take only one example, explicitly recognized (at the Argenteuil Central Committee meeting in 1966) the right of party members to carry out and publish their philosophical research.

But the "criticism of Stalin's errors" was formulated at the Twentieth Congress in terms such that there inevitably followed what we must call an unleashing of *bourgeois* ideological and philosophical themes within the Communist Parties themselves. This was the case above all among Communist intellectuals, but it also touched certain leaders and even certain leaderships. Why?

Because the "criticism of Stalin's errors" (some of which—and rather a lot—turned out to be crimes) was made in a non-Marxist way.

The Twentieth Congress criticized and denounced the "cult of personality" (the cult in general, personality in general ...) and summed up Stalin's "errors" in the concept of "violation of Socialist *legality*". The Twentieth Congress therefore limited itself to denouncing certain *facts* about what went on in the *legal superstructure*, without relating them—as every Marxist analysis must do—firstly, to the rest of the Soviet superstructure (above all, the state and party), and secondly, to the infrastructure, namely the relations of production, class relations and the forms of the class struggle in the USSR.[34]

34. Lenin: "In theory there is undoubtedly a certain period of transition between capitalism and communism. It must necessarily combine the traits or particularities of these two economic structures of society. This transitory period can only be a period of struggle between the death agony of capitalism and the birth of communism, or, in other terms: between vanquished, but not yet eliminated capitalism, and already born, but still weak communism.

76

Instead of relating the "violations of socialist legality" to: 1. the state, *plus* the party, and: 2. the class struggle, the Twentieth Congress instead related them to ... the "cult of personality". That is, it related them to a concept which, as I pointed out in *For Marx*, cannot be "found" in Marxist theory. I now venture to say that it can perfectly well be "found" elsewhere: in *bourgeois* philosophy and psycho-sociological ideology.

If you take Communist philosophers and other Communist "intellectuals" and set them officially on a bourgeois ideological and philosophical line, in order to "criticize" a regime under which they (among others) have suffered deeply, you must not be surprised when the same Communist philosophers and intellectuals quite naturally take the road of bourgeois philosophy. It has been opened up right in front of them! You must not be surprised when they make up their own little bourgeois Marxist philosophy of the Rights of Man, exalting Man and his Rights, the first of which is *liberty*, whose reverse is *alienation*. It is quite natural for them to lean on Marx's early works—that is what they are there for—and then on humanism in all its forms! Shall it be Garaudy's socialist humanism, the pure humanism of John Lewis, the "true" or "real" socialism of others, or even (why not?) "scientific" humanism itself? Between these different varieties of the philosophy of human *liberty*, each philosopher can of course *freely* take his choice! All that is perfectly normal.

Having said that, we must add that it is important not to mix things up which, politically speaking, ought not to be confused, things which are quite different from one another. The humanist reactions of western Communist theoreticians, and even of some from eastern Europe, are one thing. It would however be an extremely serious political mistake, for example, to claim to judge and condemn—on account of an adjective ("human")—something like the

---

[...] Classes remain and will remain in the era of the dictatorship of the proletariat. [...] Classes remain, but each class has undergone a change in the era of the dictatorship of the proletariat; the relations between the classes have also changed. The class struggle does not disappear under the dictatorship of the proletariat, it simply takes other forms" *(Economics and Politics in the Era of the Dictatorship of the Proletariat).*

slogan "*socialism with a human face*", a slogan under which the Czech masses let everyone know—even if the form was sometimes confused—about their class and national grievances and aspirations. It would be an extremely serious political mistake to confuse this national mass movement, this important historical fact, with the humanist pedantry of our western, sometimes Communist philosophers (or of such-and-such a philosopher of eastern Europe). There were intellectuals in the Czech national mass movement, but it was not a "movement of intellectuals". What the Czech people wanted was *socialism*, and not humanism. It wanted a socialism whose *face* (not the *body*: the body does not figure in the formula) would not be disfigured by practices unworthy both of itself (the Czech people: a people of a high political culture) and of socialism. A socialism with a human face. The adjective is in the right place. The national mass movement of the Czech people, even if it is no longer to be heard of (and the struggle is nevertheless still going on) merits the respect and support of all Communists. Exactly as the "humanist" philosophies of western intellectuals (at ease in their academic chairs or wherever), the philosophies of "Marxist humanism", whether they are called "true" or "scientific," merit the criticism of all Communists.

It is for all the reasons outlined above, then, that there are cases like John Lewis in the western Communist Parties— and that there are rather a lot of them.

It is for the same reasons that, in these parties, there exists a certain number of Communist philosophers who are fighting against a certain current—and that there are rather few of them.

And it is for these reasons—directly political reasons— that I want to repeat my thanks to *Marxism Today*, journal of the Communist Party of Great Britain, for accepting to publish my reply.

Paris, July 4 1972

Note on "The Critique of the Personality Cult"

Not for one moment does the idea strike John Lewis that "philosophy is as close to politics as the lips are to the teeth", that, "in the last instance", what is at stake—indirectly, but also very directly—where *philosophical Theses* are concerned is always a number of *political* problems or arguments of real history, and that every philosophical text (including his own) is "in the last instance" *also* a political intervention in the theoretical conjuncture *as well as*, through onc of its effects, today the main effect, a theoretical intervention in the political conjuncture. Not for a moment does the idea strike him of wondering about the political conjuncture in which my texts (and his own) were written, about what theoretical-political "effects" I had in mind when thinking them out and publishing them, about the framework of theoretical argument and political conflicts in which the enterprise was undertaken, or about the reactions it caused.

I am not expecting John Lewis to have a detailed knowledge of French political and philosophical history, of the struggle of ideas (even unimportant or erroneous ideas) within the French Communist Party since the war, and especially between 1960 and 1965. But all the same! Communists have a history in common: a long, difficult, happy and unhappy history, one which to a large extent is linked to the Third International, itself dominated since the thirties by Stalin's political "line" and leadership. We have a common past, as Communists, in the Popular Fronts, the Spanish War, the Second War and the anti-fascist resistance, and the Chinese Revolution. But we also have Lysenko's "science", which was no more than ideology, and a few formulae and slogans which were claimed to be "scientific" but were no more than "ideological", and which concealed very strange practices.[1] We all share, as Communists, a past which includes Khrushchev's "criticism of the personality cult" at the Twentieth Congress of the Soviet Party, and the ordeal of the split in the International Communist Movement. We have the Chinese Cultural Revolution in common, whatever we think of it, and May '68 in France. A few ups and downs, in short, from which one ought to be able to abstract so as to "talk philosophy" between Communists in 1972...

It is not too serious a matter. Because one day we really shall have to try and call things by their *name*, and to do that, as Marxists, we have to look for that *name*; I mean the right *concept* (even if we have to do it while we advance), so that we can come to understand our own history. Our history is not like a peaceful stream flowing between secure banks, its course marked out in advance, any more than Marx's own history was, or the tragic and glorious history of the first two decades of the century. Even if we do not go back so far, even if we only speak of the recent past— whose memory, whose shadow even, still reaches over us today—no one can deny that for thirty years we lived through a period of ordeals, heroism and dramas under the domination of a political line and political practices which, for lack of a concept, we have to call by a proper name: that of Stalin. Do we quite simply leave all this behind as a consequence of Stalin's death and on the strength (and through the effects) of a little phrase: "the personality cult," pronounced at the Twentieth Congress of the Communist Party of the Soviet Union as the "last word" (in every possible sense) in the affair? I wrote, during the 1960s, in a

---

1. A few examples, remaining at the *theoretical* level: the economist evolutionism of Stalin's *Dialectical Materialism and Historical Materialism;* the conjuring away of the historical role of Trotsky and others in the Bolshevik Revolution *(Short History of the CPSU [B])*; the thesis of the sharpening of the class struggle under socialism; the formula: "everything depends on the cadres", etc. Among ourselves: the thesis of "bourgeois science/proletarian science", the thesis of "absolute pauperization", etc.

philosophical text which John Lewis has right in front of him, that the concept of the "personality cult" was a concept which *"cannot be found* in *Marxist theory"*, that it had no value in terms of knowledge, that it explained nothing and left us in the dark. This was quite clear: it still is.

"A concept which cannot be found in Marxist *theory."* This must be recognized. In the form in which it was put forward and used, both theoretically and politically, the concept of the "personality cult" was not simply the name of something: it did not satisfy itself with simply pointing out the *facts* (the "abuses", the "violations of Soviet legality"). It claimed at the same time—this was openly stated—*theoretical* pretensions: it was supposed to give an account of the "essence" of the facts which it revealed. And this is how it was used politically.

Now this pseudo-concept, the circumstances of whose solemn and dramatic pronouncement are well known, did indeed expose certain practices: "abuses", "errors", and in certain cases "crimes". But it explained nothing of their conditions, of their causes, in short of their *internal* determination, and therefore of their forms.[2] Yet since it *claimed* to explain what in fact it did not explain, this pseudo-concept could only mislead those whom it was supposed to instruct. Must we be even more explicit? To reduce the grave events of thirty years of Soviet and Communist history to this pseudo-explanation by the "cult" was not and could not have been a simple mistake, an oversight of an intellectual hostile to the practice of divine worship: it was, as we all know, a political act of responsible leaders, a certain *one-sided* way of putting forward the problems, not of what is vulgarly called "Stalinism", but of what must, I think, be

2. For Marxism the explanation of any phenomenon is in the last instance *internal:* it is the *internal* "contradiction" which is the "motor". The external circumstances are active: but "through" the internal contradiction which they overdetermine. Why the need to be precise on this question? Because certain Communists, finding the "explanation" in terms of the "cult" inadequate, thought of the idea of adding a *supplement*, which could only be *external:* for example, the explanation by capitalist encirclement, whose reality no one can deny. Marxism, however, does not like supplements: when you need a supplement too much, you have probably missed the *internal* cause.

called (unless one objects to *thinking* about it) by the name of a concept: provisionally, *the "Stalinian" deviation*.[3] And, at the same time, it was a certain way of *not posing* the problems. More precisely, it was (and still is) a way of seeking the causes of grave events and of their forms in certain defects of the functioning of the *legal* superstructure ("violations of socialist legality"), without (even in the form of a hypothesis!) looking into the whole of the State Apparatuses constituting the Superstructure (the Repressive Apparatus, the Ideological Apparatuses, including the Party), and above all without getting to the root of the problem (one which was so serious and lasted so long): the *contradictions* of the construction of socialism and of its line, that is, without dealing with the existing forms of production relations, class relations and the class struggle, the last of which is then said—in a formula which has not yet been withdrawn—to have been "transcended" in the U.S.S.R. Yet this is where the *internal* causes of the facts of the "cult" must be sought— at the risk of finding other facts.

Of course, it is not true that everything is always connected with everything else—this is not a Marxist thesis—and one does not need to invoke the whole infrastructure and superstructure to sort out a simple legal detail, if it is only a *detail*,

3. The term "Stalinism", which the Soviet leaders have avoided using, but which was widely used by bourgeois ideologians and the Trotskyists, before penetrating into Communist circles, offers in general the same "disadvantages" as the term "personality cult". It designates a *reality* which innumerable Communists, above all, have experienced, either in direct and tragic form, or less directly and with more or less serious consequences. Now this terminology also has theoretical pretensions: among bourgeois ideologists and many Trotskyists. It *explains* nothing. To set out on the road of a Marxist explanation, to be able to pose the problem of the explanation of these facts, the least that is required is to put forward *Marxist concepts*, and to see whether they are suitable. That is why I am proposing the concept of "*deviation*", which is a concept that can certainly be "found" in Marxist-Leninist theory. Thus one might, first of all, talk of a "*Stalinian*" *deviation*: first of all, because to talk of a deviation necessarily requires that it should next be *qualified*, that one should explain *in what* it consisted, and always in Marxist terms. One thing, at the present stage, must be made clear: to speak of a "Stalinian" deviation is not to explain it by an individual, who would be its "cause". The adjective certainly refers to a man in history, but above all to a certain *period* in the history of the International Labour Movement.

and only *legal*. But is the "Stalin" deviation a detail? A simple legal detail?! Of course, one cannot, at any and every moment, in a moment, remake what many years have unmade—this is not a Marxist thesis. There are of course historical constructions which are so interconnected with neighbouring buildings, which are so much propped up by these latter that one cannot simply and brutally chop down their surroundings to give them some air: one must sometimes proceed "cautiously". But the precautions of the Twentieth Congress ...!

The "Stalinian" deviation, in the form revealed to us by the terms of the official declarations, pointed out certain facts, without—for lack of Marxist explanations—avoiding the trap of repeating much earlier denunciations: those of the most anti-Communist bourgeois ideology, and those of the "anti-Stalinist" theory of Trotskyism. *As it was revealed to us*, limited in its scope to "violations of socialist *legality*" alone—while the Communists of the U.S.S.R. and of the world had an infinitely more "extensive" experience of it—this deviation could, finally, only provoke two possible reactions (leaving aside its "classical" exploitation by anti-Communist and anti-Soviet elements). *Either a left-wing critique*, which accepts the term "deviation", even if in a very contradictory sense, and which, in order to *account for it*, undertakes serious research into its basic historical causes: that is, if John Lewis will excuse me, not into Man (or Personality), but into the Superstructure, relations of production, and therefore the state of class relations and the class struggle in the U.S.S.R. Such a critique may then, but only then, be justified in talking not only about a violation of the law but also about the reasons for this violation. *Or a right-wing critique*, which attacks only certain aspects of the *legal* superstructure, and of course can then invoke Man and his Rights, and oppose Man to the violation of his Rights (or simple "workers' councils" to the "bureaucracy").

The fact is: one practically *never* hears anything but the second critique. And the official formulation of the critique of the "cult", of the "violations of socialist legality", far from keeping the most violent bourgeois anti-Communism and Trotskyist anti-Stalinism at arm's length, actually provides them with a historical argument *they could hardly have hoped for*: it gives them a justification, a second wind, a second life. Which explains, let it be said in passing, a good number of apparently paradoxical phenomena: for example, the resurgence fifty years after the October Revolution and twenty years after the Chinese Revolution of Organizations which have lasted forty years *without winning a single historical victory* (because, unlike some of the present-day "ultra-left", they are organizations, and they also have a theory): the Trotskyist Organizations. And that is not to speak of the "effectiveness" of bourgeois anti-Sovietism, thirty years after Stalingrad!

However that may be, we did not need to wait long before seeing the official critique of the "Stalinian" deviation, that of the "personality cult", produce—in the special circumstances—its inevitable ideological effects. After the Twentieth Congress an openly rightist wave carried off (to speak only of them) many Marxist and Communist "intellectuals", not only in the capitalist countries, but also in the socialist countries. It is not of course a question of putting the intellectuals of the socialist countries and Western Marxists into the same bag—and especially not of confusing the mass political protest of our comrades in Prague, known as "socialism with a human face", with Garaudy's "integral humanism", etc. In Prague they did not have the same choice of words (the words did not have the same sense) nor the same choice of roads. But here ...! Here we see Communists following the Social-Democrats and even religious thinkers (who used to have an almost guaranteed monopoly in these things) in the practice of *exploiting* the works of Marx's youth in order to draw out of them an ideology of Man, Liberty, Alienation, Transcendence, etc.—without asking whether the *system* of these notions was idealist or materialist, whether this ideology was petty-bourgeois or proletarian. "Orthodoxy", as John Lewis says, was almost submerged: not Stalin's "thought", which continued and continues to hold itself comfortably above the uproar, in its bases, its "line" and certain of its practices—but quite simply the theory of Marx and Lenin.

It was in these conditions that I came to intervene, let us say "accidentally", in the form of a critical review I wrote of a number of Soviet and East German articles which had been translated into French. This review, "On the Young Marx", appeared in the magazine *La Pensée* in 1960.* I was trying, to the best of my ability and with the makeshift tools at my disposal, by criticizing a few received ideas and asking a few questions, to combat the contagion which was "menacing" us. That is how it was. At the beginning there were not very many of us, and John Lewis is right: "we" were crying "in the wilderness", or in what certain people might call "the wilderness". But one must be very wary of this kind of "wilderness"; or rather, know how not to be frightened by it. In reality "we" have never been alone. Communists are never alone.

So, against the rightist-idealist interpretations of Marxist theory as a "philosophy of man", of Marxism as a theoretical humanism; against the tendentious confusion—whether positivist or subjectivist—of science and Marxist "philosophy"; against the evolutionist reduction of the materialist dialectic to the "Hegelian" dialectic; and in general against bourgeois and petty-bourgeois positions, I have tried to defend, we have tried to defend, come what may, at the cost of rash actions and errors, a few vital ideas which can be summed up in a single idea: that which is special and specific to Marx, which is revolutionary in both the theoretical and political senses, and this in the face of bourgeois and petty-bourgeois ideology, with which he had to *break* in order to become a Communist and found the science of history, the same ideology with which even today we must still and always will have to *break*, to become, remain or become again Marxists.

The forms may have changed: but the root of the question has remained, for 150 years or so, substantially the same. This bourgeois ideology, which is the *dominant* ideology, and which weighs so heavily on the labour movement and threatens its most vital functions—unless the movement fights resolutely back on the basis of its *own positions*, quite exterior to bourgeois ideology because *proletarian*—this

*Reprinted in *For Marx* [Translator's note].

bourgeois ideology is actually, in its deepest essence, constituted by the ideological pair *economism/humanism*. Behind the abstract categories of the philosophy which provides it with titles and airs, it was this pair of notions which I was aiming at when I made a joint attack, *both* on theoretical humanism (I repeat: theoretical; not on a word, or a few phrases, or even an inspired idea of the future, but on a *philosophical* language in which "man" is a category with a *theoretical function*) *and*, passing by the vulgar forms of Hegelianism or evolutionism which join with it, on *economism*.

For no one (at least, no revolutionary Marxist) can fail to see that when, in the midst of the class struggle, the litanies of humanism hold the theoretical and ideological stage, it is economism which is quietly winning. Even under feudalism, when humanist ideology was revolutionary, it was still profoundly bourgeois. In a bourgeois class society it always has played and still does play the role of hiding the class-determined economic and economistic practices governed by the relations of production, exploitation and exchange, and by bourgeois law. In a bourgeois class society there is always the risk that humanist ideology—when it is not just a slip of the pen or an image of political rhetoric, when it is of a lasting and organic character—serves as a cover for an *economistic* deviation in the workers' organizations, which are not immune to the contagion of the dominant ideology. This deviation is in principled contradiction to proletarian class positions. The whole history of the Rights of Man proves it: behind Man, it is Bentham who comes out the victor.[4] Much of the history of the Second International, whose dominant tendency Lenin denounced, also goes to prove it: behind Bernstein's neo-Kantian idealism, it is the economist current which comes out on top. Who can seriously claim that the whole of this long history, with all its conflicts and dangers, is behind us, and that it will never again menace us, that we shall never again be at risk?

I am talking about the ideological *pair* economism/humanism. It is a pair in which the two terms are complementary. It is not an accidental link, but an organic and

4. Karl Marx, *Capital*, vol. 1, Part I, section 2.

consubstantial one. It is born spontaneously, that is to say necessarily, of the bourgeois practices of production and exploitation, *and at the same time* of the legal practices of bourgeois law and its ideology, which provide a sanction for the capitalist relations of production and exploitation and their reproduction.

And it is quite true that bourgeois ideology is fundamentally *economist*, that the capitalist sees everything from the point of view of commodity relations and from the point of view of the material conditions (means of production are also commodities) which allow him to exploit that very special "commodity", the labour power of the workers. Thus, he sees things from the point of view of the *techniques* of the extortion of surplus-value (which are linked together with capitalist organization and division of labour), from the point of view of the technology of exploitation, of economic "performance" and development: from the point of view of capitalist accumulation. And what does the Bourgeois Economist do? Marx showed that, even when he raised himself to the point of thinking in terms of capitalism, he did no more than theorize the economistic viewpoint of the capitalist. Marx criticized the very project of "Political Economy", *as such, because it was economistic*.

But at the same time it is true that the reverse side of the same coin, the necessary "cover", the alibi, the "point of honour" of this economism is humanism or bourgeois liberalism. This is because ideas find their foundations in the categories of Bourgeois *Law* and the legal ideology materially indispensable to the functioning of Bourgeois Law: liberty of the Person, that is, in principle, his right freely to dispose of himself, his right to his property, his free will and his body (the proletarian: a Person "free" to sell himself!), and his other goods (private property: real property—which abolishes others—that of the means of production).

This is the breeding ground of economism/humanism: the capitalist mode of production and exploitation. And this is the precise link by which, the precise place in which these two ideologies join together as a *pair*: *Bourgeois Law*, which at the same time both provides a real support for capitalist relations of production, and lends its categories to liberal and humanist ideology, including bourgeois philosophy.

The question then arises: when this bourgeois ideological pair penetrates into Marxism, "when it pursues the struggle, not on its own terrain but on the general terrain of Marxism, as revisionism" (Lenin), what does it become? It remains what it was before: a *bourgeois* point of view, but this time "functioning" within Marxism. As astonishing as this may seem, the whole history of the Labour Movement and Lenin's theses are witness to it:[5] Marxism itself can, in certain circumstances, be considered and treated as, *even practised as a bourgeois point of view*. Not only by "armchair Marxists", who reduce it to academic bourgeois sociology, and who are never anything but "functionaries of the dominant ideology"—but also by sections of the Labour Movement, and their leaders.

This is something which depends on the relations of power in the class struggle, and, at the same time, on *class position* in the class struggle, in the "line", the organization and the functioning of the class struggle fought by the Labour Movement. That is to say that it is a historical form in which the *fusion* between the Labour Movement and Marxist theory—which alone can assure the *objectively* "revolutionary" character of the "movement" (Lenin)—is held up or reversed, in the face of what must perhaps, for purposes of understanding, also be called a "fusion": but quite another kind of "fusion", that between the Labour Movement and bourgeois ideology.

The economism/humanism pair, when it is introduced into Marxism, does not really change in form, even if it is forced to make some changes (only some) in its vocabulary. Humanism remains humanism: it takes on a Social-Democratic accent, one which raises not the question of the *class struggle* and its abolition, through the emancipation of the *working class*, but that of the defence of Human Rights, of liberty and justice, even of the liberation and free develop-

5. Cf. *Marxism and Revisionism, The Collapse of the Second International, The Renegade Kautsky*, etc.

ment of the "personality" or the "integral personality". Economism remains economism: for example, in the exaltation of the development of the Productive Forces, of their "socialization" (what kind of socialization?), of the "scientific and technical revolution", of "productivity", etc.

Can we make a comparison? Yes, we can. And we discover the factor which permits us to identify the ideological pair *economism/humanism* and its practices as bourgeois: it is the elimination of something which never figures in economism or humanism, *the elimination of the relations of production and of the class struggle*.

The fact that the bourgeoisie, in its own ideology, keeps *silent* about the relations of production and the class struggle, in order to exalt not only "expansion" and "productivity" but also Man and his liberty—that is its own affair, and it is quite in order, in *bourgeois order*: because it needs this silence, which allows economism/humanism, expressing *the bourgeois point of view*, to work at the concealment of the relations of production while helping to guarantee and reproduce them. But when the Workers' Parties, before the revolution, or even after, themselves keep *silent* (or semi-silent) about the relations of production, the class struggle, and their concrete forms,[6] while exalting *both* the Productive Forces *and* Man—this is quite a different matter! Because, unless it is only a question of words or of a few speeches, if it is really a question of a consistent political line and practice, then you can bet—as Lenin did, when he spoke about the pre-1914 Second International—that this bourgeois point of view is a contaminating agent which can threaten or even overcome the *proletarian point of view* within *Marxism itself*.

And since we have been talking about the Second International, let us say a brief word about the Third, about the last ten years of its existence. After all, why be silent about a question which is burning to be expressed? Why meet the official silence with nothing but another silence, and thus give it sanction? For an official silence does still reign—

6. Lenin: in the "transition" between capitalism and communism, classes remain, the class struggle remains, but *takes on new forms*.

beneath a facade of feigned or embarrassed "explanations"—over this period, one whose heroism, whose greatness, whose dramas we have lived through or known. Why should we not try to *understand*, whatever the risks of what we say, not only the merits of the International but also the inevitable *contradictions* of its positions and its line (and how could it have avoided them, especially given the tragic times with which it had to deal)? I am rather afraid that we may one day have to recognize the existence within it of a certain *tendency* which, held in bounds by Lenin's efforts, could not finally be mastered, and ended up by quietly taking over the leading role. I am rather afraid that a long time might be allowed to go by—for apparently pragmatic reasons, which doubtless have deeper roots—before a "hypothesis" such as that which I want to put forward today could hope to be stated in black and white, and *put to the test of a genuine Marxist analysis*. I shall take the personal risk of advancing this hypothesis now, in the form of necessarily schematic propositions:

1. The International Communist Movement has been affected since the 1930s, to different degrees and in very different ways in different countries and organizations, by the effects of a *single* deviation, which can provisionally be called the "Stalinian deviation".

2. Keeping things *well in proportion*, that is to say, respecting essential distinctions, but nevertheless going beyond the most obvious phenomena—which are, in spite of their extremely serious character, historically secondary: I mean those which are generally grouped together in Communist Parties under the heading "personality cult" and "dogmatism"—the Stalinian deviation can be considered as *a form* (a *special form*, converted by the state of the world class struggle, the existence of a single socialist State, and the State power held by the Bolshevik Party) of the *posthumous revenge of the Second International*: as a revival of its main tendency.

3. This main tendency was, as we know, basically an economistic one.

This is only a hypothesis, and I am simply laying down its reference points. It naturally poses very great problems. The most obvious of these problems can be stated in the following way: *how* could a basically economistic tendency have combined with the superstructural effects we know so well, effects which it produced as the transformation of its own forms? *What* were the material forms of existence of this tendency, which enabled it to produce these effects in the existing conjuncture? *How* did this tendency, centred from a certain time onwards on the USSR, spread through the whole International Communist Movement, and what special—and sometimes differing—forms did it take?

If some readers are disconcerted by the comparison between the economism of the Second International and that of the "Stalinian deviation", I will first of all reply: you must look and see what is the *first* principle of analysis recommended and used by Lenin at the beginning of Chapter 7 of *The Collapse of the Second International* to help understand a *deviation* in the history of the Labour Movement. The first thing you have to do is to see if this deviation is not "linked *with some former current of socialism*". Not because of some vulgar "historicism", but because there exists a continuity, in the history of the Labour Movement, of its difficulties, its problems, its *contradictions*, of correct solutions and therefore *also of its deviations*, because of the continuity of a single class struggle against the bourgeoisie, and of a single class struggle (economic, political *and ideological-theoretical*) of the bourgeoisie against the Labour Movement. The possibility of cases of "posthumous revenge", of "revivals", is based on this continuity.

But I would like to add something else. There are of course serious political questions at stake in the summary and schematic hypotheses which I am proposing—but, above all, there exists the possibility of serious ambiguities which must at all costs be guarded against. Look how Lenin—who was uncompromising in his denunciation of the idealist-economist tendency of the Second International—treated this very organization: he never *reduced* the Second International to its deviation. He recognized the different periods in its history, he distinguished the main question from the secondary one—and, for example, he always gave the International credit for having developed the organizations of the proletarian class struggle, the trade unions and workers' parties; nor did he ever refuse to cite Kautsky, or to defend Plekhanov's philosophical work. In the same way, and for infinitely more obvious and powerful reasons, Stalin cannot be *reduced* to the deviation which we have linked to his name; even less can this be done with the Third International which he came in the thirties to dominate. He had other historical merits. He understood that it was *necessary* to abandon the miraculous idea of an imminent "world revolution" and to undertake instead the "construction of socialism" in one country. And he drew the consequences: it must be defended at any cost as the foundation and last line of defence of socialism throughout the world, it must be made into an impregnable fortress capable of withstanding the imperialist siege; and, to that end, it must be provided with a heavy industry. It was this very industry that turned out the Stalingrad tanks which served the heroic struggle of the Soviet people in their fight to the death to liberate the world from Nazism. Our history *also* passed in that direction. And in spite of the deformations, caricatures and tragedies for which this period is responsible, it must be recalled that millions of Communists also learned, even if Stalin "taught" them in dogmatic form, that there existed *Principles of Leninism*.

Thus, if it seems possible, keeping everything *in proportion*, to talk about the posthumous revenge of the Second International, it must be added that it is a revenge which took place in other times, in other circumstances, and of course in other *forms*, which cannot be the subject of a literal comparison. But in spite of these considerable differences one can talk about the revenge, or the revival, or the resurgence of a tendency which is *basically* the same: of an economistic conception and "line", even when these were hidden by declarations which were, in their own way, cruelly "humanist" (the slogan "Man, the most precious capital", the measures and dispositions, which remained a dead letter, of the Soviet Constitution of 1936).

If this is true, if the "Stalinian" deviation cannot be

reduced to "violations of Soviet legality" alone; if it is related to more profound causes in history and in the *conception* of the class struggle and of class *position*; and even supposing that the Soviet people are now protected from all violations of *legality*—it does not follow that either they or we have completely overcome the "Stalinian" deviation (neither the causes, nor the mechanisms, nor the effects of which have been the object of a "concrete analysis" in the Leninist sense, that is to say, of a scientific Marxist analysis) *simply on account of the denunciation of the "personality cult"*, or by a patient work of rectification unenlightened by any analysis. In these conditions, with all the information, past and present, available to us (including the official silence, which refuses to pronounce against these facts), we can bet that the Stalinian "line", purged of "violations of legality" and therefore "liberalized"—with economism and humanism working together—has, for better or worse, survived Stalin and—it should not be astonishing!—the Twentieth Congress. One is even justified in supposing that, behind the talk about the different varieties of "humanism", whether restrained or not, this "line" continues to pursue an honourable career, in a peculiar kind of silence, a sometimes talkative and sometimes mute silence, which is now and again broken by the noise of an explosion or a split.

So that I do not have to leave anything out of consideration, I will advance one more risky hypothesis which will certainly "say something" to John Lewis, specialist of Chinese politics. If we look back over our whole history of the last forty years or more, it seems to me that, in reckoning up the account (which is not an easy thing to do), the only *historically existing* (left) "critique" of the fundamentals of the "Stalinian deviation" to be found—and which, moreover, is *contemporary* with this very deviation, and thus for the most part precedes the Twentieth Congress—is a concrete critique, one which exists in the facts, in the struggle, in the line, in the practices, their principles and their forms, of the Chinese Revolution. A silent critique, which speaks through its actions, the result of the political and ideological struggles of the Revolution, from the Long March to the Cultural Revolution and its results. A critique *from afar*. A critique "from behind the scenes". To be looked at more closely, to be interpreted. A *contradictory* critique, moreover— if only because of the disproportion between acts and texts. Whatever you like: but a critique from which one can learn, which can help us to test our hypotheses, that is, help us to see our own history more clearly. But here too, of course, we have to speak in terms of a tendency and of specific forms—without letting the forms mask the tendency and its contradictions.

If I have been able—with the means at my disposal, and from afar—èven very feebly to echo these historic struggles and to indicate, behind their ideological effects, the existence of some real problems: this, for a Communist philosopher, is no more than his duty.

These, to go no further, are some of the very concrete "questions"—where politics stares you in the face—which haunt the margins of the simple philosophical work undertaken by me, for better or worse, more than ten years ago.

As far as John Lewis is concerned, it seems that it never occurred to him to ask such questions! From our point of view I hope that it is so. Because the matter would be that much more serious if, having understood what was at stake, he had kept silent about it: so as not to get his fingers burned.

June 1972

Remark on the Category: "Process without a Subject or Goal(s)"

This formula ["process without a Subject", "process without a Subject or Goal(s)"] has everything required to offend against the "evidence" of common sense, that is (Gramsci) of the dominant ideology, and thus without any trouble at all to make some determined enemies.

For example, the objection will be raised that "the masses" and "classes" are, when all is said and done, "made up of" *men*! And that, if Man (a category which is then simply declared to be ... an "abstraction", or, to add weight, a "speculative abstraction") cannot be said to make history, at least *men* do so—concrete, living men, human subjects. In support of this idea Marx himself will be cited as witness, his testimony being the *beginning* of a little remark in the *Eighteenth Brumaire*: "Men make their own history ..." With the backing of evidence and quote, the conclusion is quickly drawn: history has "subjects"; these subjects are obviously "men"; "men" are therefore, if not the Subject of history, at least *the subjects* of history ...

This kind of reasoning unfortunately only stands up at the cost of confusions, sliding meanings and ideological word-games: on Man-men, Subject-subjects, etc.

Let us be careful, therefore, not to play with words, and let us look at the thing a bit closer.

In my opinion: men (plural), in the concrete sense, are necessarily subjects (plural) *in* history, because they act *in* history as subjects (plural). But there is no Subject (singular) *of* history. And I will go even further: "men" are not "the subjects" *of* history. Let me explain.

To understand these distinctions one must define the *nature* of the questions at issue. The question of the constitution of individuals as historical *subjects*, active *in* history, has nothing in principle to do with the question of *the "Subject* of history", or even with that of *the "subjects* of history". The first question is of a *scientific* kind: it concerns historical materialism. The second question is of a *philosophical* kind: it concerns dialectical materialism.

First question: *scientific*.

That human, i.e. social individuals are *active* in history—as *agents* of the different social practices of the historical process of production and reproduction—that is a fact. But, considered as *agents*, human individuals are not "free" and "constitutive" subjects in the philosophical sense of these terms. They work in and through the determinations of the *forms of historical existence* of the social relations of production and reproduction (labour process, division and organization of labour, process of production and reproduction, class struggle, etc.). But that is not all. These agents can only be agents *if they are subjects*. This I think I showed in my article on "Ideology and Ideological State Apparatuses". [See *Lenin and Philosophy and other Essays*, London NLB, 1971] No human, i.e. social individual can be the agent of a practice if he does not have the *form of a subject*. The "subject-form" is actually the form of historical existence of every individual, of every agent of social practices: because the social relations of production and reproduction necessarily comprise, as an *integral part*, what Lenin calls "(juridico-) *ideological social relations*", which, in order to function, impose the subject-form on each agent-individual. The agent-individuals thus always act in the subject-form, as subjects. But the fact that they are necessarily subjects does not make the agents of social-historical practices into the *subject* or *subjects* of history (in the philosophical sense of the term: *subject of*). The subject-agents are only active *in* history through the determination of the relations of production and reproduction, and in their forms.

Second question: *philosophical*.

It is for precise ideological ends that bourgeois philosophy has taken the legal-ideological notion of the *subject*, made it into a philosophical category, its number one philosophical category, and posed the question of *the* Subject of knowledge (the *ego* of the cogito, the Kantian or Husserlian transcendental subject, etc.), of morality, etc., and of *the Subject of* history. This illusory question does of course have a purpose, but in its position and form it has *no sense* as far as dialectical materialism is concerned, which purely and simply rejects it, as it rejects (for example) the question of God's existence. In advancing the Thesis of a "process without a Subject or Goal(s)", I want simply but clearly to say this. To be dialectical-materialist, Marxist philosophy must break with the idealist category of the "Subject" as Origin, Essence and Cause, *responsible* in its internality for all the determinations of the external "Object",[1] of which it is said to be the internal "Subject". For Marxist philosophy there can be no Subject as an Absolute Centre, as a Radical Origin, as a Unique Cause. Nor can one, in order to get out of the problem, rely on a category like that of the "ex-Centration of the Essence" (Lucien Sève), since it is an illusory compromise which—using a fraudulently "radical" term, one whose root is perfectly conformist (ex-*centration*)—safeguards the umbilical cord between Essence and Centre and therefore remains a prisoner of idealist philosophy: since there is no Centre, every *ex*-centration is superfluous or a sham. In reality Marxist philosophy thinks in and according to quite different categories: determination in the last instance— which is quite different from the Origin, Essence or Cause *unes*—determination by Relations (*idem*), contradiction, process, "nodal points" (Lenin), etc.: in short, in quite a different configuration and according to quite different categories from classical idealist philosophy.

Naturally, these philosophical categories do not only concern history.

But if we *restrict* ourselves to history (which is what concerns us here), the philosophical question presents itself in the following terms. There is no question of contesting the

---

1. The category of "process without a Subject or Goal(s)" can therefore take the form: "*process without a Subject or Object*".

gains of historical materialism, which says that individuals are agent-subjects *in* history under the determination of the forms of existence of the relations of production and reproduction. It is a question of something quite different: of knowing whether history can be thought philosophically, in its modes of determination, according to the idealist category of the *Subject*. The position of dialectical materialism on this question seems quite clear to me. One cannot seize (*begreifen*: conceive), that is to say, *think* real history (the process of the reproduction of social formations and their revolutionary transformation) as if it could be reduced to *an* Origin, *an* Essence, or *a* Cause (even Man), which would be its Subject—a Subject, a "being" or "essence", held to be *identifiable*, that is to say existing in the form of the *unity* of an *internality*, and (theoretically and practically *responsible* identity, internality and responsibility are constitutive, among other things, of every subject), thus accountable, thus capable of *accounting for* the whole of the "phenomena" of history.

The matter is quite clear when we are confronted with classical idealism, which, within the openly stated category of liberty, takes Man (= the Human Race = Humanity) to be the Subject and the Goal of history; cf the *Enlightenment*, and Kant, the "purest" philosopher of bourgeois ideology. The matter is also clear when we are confronted with the *philosophical* petty-bourgeois communitarian *anthropology* of Feuerbach (still respected by Marx in the 1844 Manuscripts), in which the Essence of Man is the Origin, Cause and Goal of history.

But the same position evidently takes on a more deceptive air in the post-Husserlian and pre-Kantian (Cartesian) phenomenological interpretations, like those of Sartre, where the Kantian Theses of the Transcendental *Subject*, unique because one, and of the Liberty of *Humanity*, are mixed up and "squashed together", and where the Subject is multiplied within a theory of the *originating* Liberty of an infinity of "concrete" transcendental subjects (Tran Duc Thao said, explaining Husserl: "We are all, you and I, each one of us, 'transcendental egos' and 'transcendental equals' ['*egos*' and '*egaux*']", which brings us back to the

Thesis that "men" (the concrete individuals) are *the* subjects (transcendental, constitutive) of history). This is the basis of Sartre's special interest in a "little phrase" from the *Eighteenth Brumaire*, and a similar phrase from Engels, which fit him like a glove. Now this position—which brings the Kantian categories *down* to the level, no longer of an anthropological philosophy (Feuerbach), but of a vulgar philosophical psycho-sociology—not only has nothing to do with Marxism, but actually constitutes a quite dubious theoretical position which it is practically impossible to *conceive* and to defend. You just have to read the *Critique of Dialectical Reason*, which announces an Ethics that never appeared, to be convinced of this point.

In proposing the category of the "process without a Subject or Goal(s)", we thus draw a "demarcation line" (Lenin) between dialectical-materialist positions and bourgeois or petty-bourgeois idealist positions. Naturally, one cannot expect *everything* from a first intervention. This "demarcation line" must be "worked on". But, as Lenin said for his part, a demarcation line—if it is correct—is in principle sufficient, just as it is, to defend us from idealism and to mark out the way forward.

These philosophical positions are of course not without their consequences. Not only, for example, do they imply that Marxism has nothing to do with the "anthropological question" ("What is man?"), or with a theory of the realization-objectification-alienation-disalienation of the *Human Essence* (as in Feuerbach and his heirs: theoreticians of *philosophical* reification and fetishism), or even with the theory of the "excentration of the Human Essence", which only criticizes the idealism of the Subject from within the limits of the idealism of the Subject, dressed up with the attributes of the "ensemble of social relations" of the sixth *Thesis on Feuerbach*—but they also allow us to understand the sense of Marx's famous "little phrase" in the *Eighteenth Brumaire*.

This comment, in its *complete* form, reads as follows: "Men make their own history, but they do not make it out of freely chosen elements (*aus freien Stücken*), under circumstances chosen by themselves, but under circumstances (*Umstände*) directly encountered (*vorgefundene*), given by and transmitted from the past." And—as if he had foreseen the exploitation of these first five words, and even these "circumstances" from which Sartre draws out such dazzling effects of the "practico-inert", that is, of liberty— Marx, in the Preface to the *Eighteenth Brumaire*, written seventeen years later (in 1869, two years after *Capital*), set down the following lines: "I show something quite different (*different* from the ideology of Hugo and of Proudhon, who both hold the individual Napoleon III to be the [detestable or glorious] *cause* "*responsible*" for the *coup d'état*), namely how the *class struggle* (Marx's emphasis) in France created the circumstances (*Umstände*) and the relations (*Verhältnisse*) which allowed (*ermöglicht*) a person (a subject) so mediocre and grotesque to play the role of a hero".

One must read one's authors closely. History really is a "process without a Subject or Goal(s)", where the given *circumstances* in which "men" act as subjects under the determination of social *relations* are the product of the *class struggle*. History therefore does not have a Subject, in the philosophical sense of the term, but a *motor*: that very class struggle.

1 May 1973

2.
Elements of
Self-Criticism

Foreword

The reader will find two previously unpublished essays here.

The first dates from June 1972. It was to be included in the *Reply to John Lewis*, thus adding to the elements of self-criticism to be found there, which in fact, it may be remembered, were limited to a rectification of the definition of philosophy. But in the end it could not be included in that text, which had to be kept to the length of what was actually only a magazine article, and also because I wanted to preserve the unity of the same text when it was published in French.

In this essay there can be found, for the first time, a critical examination of the positions I took in *For Marx* and *Reading Capital*—positions which, two years after the publication of these works, in the Preface to the Italian edition of *Reading Capital*, I characterized as affected by a "theoreticist tendency".

I have taken the opportunity of adding to these *Elements of Self-Criticism*, as a supplement, an earlier essay (from July 1970), which deals with the development of the young Marx, and indicates in what direction I was then working.

This self-criticism, whose "*logic*" and *internal* arguments I present here, in the form in which they came to disturb our course of thought on the subject, is naturally not a purely internal phenomenon. It can only be understood as the effect of *a quite different, external* "*logic*", that of the political events which I referred to in the *Reply to John Lewis*.

The reader will work out for himself the necessary relation between these two "*logics*", without forgetting the primacy of practice over theory—that is, the primacy of the class struggle in economics and politics over the class struggle in theory.

May 20, 1974

To Waldeck Rochet
who admired Spinoza
and spent a long day with me
talking about him, in June 1966.

Elements of
Self-Criticism

I really think that, after John Lewis has given *his* point of view on my essays (which are now between seven and twelve years old, since the first article collected in *For Marx* dates from 1960), after so many critics, indeed, have given *their* points of view, that I should now present *my own*.

I have never disowned my essays: there was no good reason to do so. But, in 1967, two years after their publication, I admitted (in an Italian edition of *Reading Capital*, as well as in other foreign editions) that they were marked by an erroneous tendency. I pointed out the existence of this error, and I gave it a name: *theoreticism*. Today, I think I can go further, and define the special "object" of the error, its essential forms and its reverberations.

I should add that instead of talking about an error it would be better to talk about a deviation. A theoreticist deviation. You will see why I am suggesting a change of terminology—that is, in this case, a change of category— and what is at stake philosophically and politically when I stress this *nuance*.

The whole thing can be summed up in a few words.

I wanted to defend Marxism against the real dangers of *bourgeois* ideology: it was necessary to stress its revolutionary new character; it was therefore necessary to "prove" that there is an antagonism between Marxism and bourgeois ideology, that Marxism could not have developed in Marx or in the labour movement except given a radical and un- remitting *break* with bourgeois ideology, an unceasing struggle against the assaults of this ideology. This thesis was correct. It still is correct.

But instead of explaining this *historical* fact in all its dimensions—social, political, ideological and theoretical— I reduced it to a simple *theoretical* fact: to the epistemological *"break"* which can be observed in Marx's works from 1845 onwards. As a consequence I was led to give a *rationalist* explanation of the "break", contrasting *truth* and *error* in the form of the speculative distinction between *science* and *ideology*, in the singular and in general. The contrast between Marxism and bourgeois ideology thus became simply a special case of this distinction. Reduction + interpretation: from this rationalist-speculative drama, the class struggle was practically absent.

All the effects of my theoreticism derive from this rationalist-speculative interpretation.

Thus, to straighten things out, I must re-examine the situation from a critical perspective: not in order to introduce new subjects of discussion (which would create a diversion), but in order to come back to that departure point, to that special "object", on which my theoreticist tendency took the opportunity to fix itself—in short, to the question of the "break", to that extraordinary political-theoretical adventure which took form and developed, from 1845 onwards, in Marx's work—so that I can show how I interpreted it when I carried out this reduction.

1. The "Break"

The "break" is not an illusion, nor a "complete myth", as John Lewis claims. I am sorry: I will not give way on this point. That one must explain the "break" without reducing it, I have just admitted. But look at the situation: I reduced the "break" to a simple rationalist-speculative antithesis; but most of my critics *reduced it to nothing*! They rubbed it out, obliterated it, erased it, denied it. And how passionately they carried out this work of proscription and destruction! Let us be explicit: there really does exist, in the history of Marx's theoretical reflection, something like a "break", which is not a nullity, but of vital importance for the history of the whole labour movement. And between those who recognize the fact of the "break" and those who want to reduce it to nothing, there exists an opposition which, it must be acknowledged, is ultimately *political*.

Let us look at this question a little more closely.

It is clear to every reader who knows the theoretical works which preceded those of Marx—and which one can list (following Lenin) as: German Philosophy, including the Philosophy of Law and of History; English Political Economy; and French Socialism (utopian or proletarian)—it is clear and undeniable, because empirically verifiable by a process of comparison (as long as what is analysed is not this or that isolated formula, but the structure and mode of functioning of the texts) that, with *The German Ideology*, something new and unprecedented appears in Marx's work, something which will never disappear. An historical event in the strong sense, but one which concerns the field of theory, and within theory what I called, using a metaphor, "the opening of the Continent of History". Thus, using metaphors which we shall retain (and we must retain both, and play on the distinction between them),[1] we may speak of this

---

1. And later create more "correct" ones, and play again on the distinction between them and make it function. Because in philosophy you can only think—*i.e.*, adjust existing, borrowed categories and produce new ones within the terms required by the theoretical *position* taken up—*by the use of* metaphors.

event as the "opening of the Continent of History", or (and) of the irruption, of the sudden appearance of the Continent of History *within* scientific theory.

In fact, something radically new—though in an often very unstable form, clumsy in working out its new object and terminology,[2] or even still trapped in the old philosophical category,[3] and yet terribly anxious to make its appearance in the world—really did arrive on the theoretical scene: it had never been seen before, it was in fact unprecedented, and, as we now know, with the benefit of hindsight, it was destined to remain there.

This thesis, which my critics have not spared, I maintain. It is of course very schematic, both in the form in which I originally had to present it and in the form in which I now take it up again. It would need to be backed up by lengthy research and analysis, for which it is only the hypothesis. But none of the objections which have been raised to the thesis, even among the more or less serious ones, seems to me to have weakened it in principle. Because, bare and schematic as it was, it did in the last resort simply register a fact.

What I said was that it is possible to locate, even among the ambiguities and hesitations of *The German Ideology*, a set of fundamental theoretical concepts, which cannot be found in Marx's earlier texts, and which present the special characteristic of being able to function in quite another manner than in their prehistory. I will not enter here into a study of these new concepts, whose novel organization gave them a quite new meaning and function: mode of production, relations of production, productive forces, social classes rooted in the unity of the productive forces and relations of production, ruling class/oppressed class, ruling

2. *Cf.* the term "*Verkehrsverhältnisse*", which, in *The German Ideology*, is the theoretical centre around which all the new concepts gravitate: yet which itself "turns" around a so far absent concept, which has not yet been produced in its definitive form: the concept of *relations of production*.

3. *Cf.* the "division of labour", which, in *The German Ideology*, in fact functions as a substitute for the concept of *alienation*. Thus the theory of the individual, of the human "personality" and of communism which is found in this text.

ideology/oppressed ideology, class struggle, etc. To take only one example, which can be proved beyond doubt by a process of comparison, I repeat that the theoretical system of the *1844 Manuscripts* rested, in contrast, on three basic concepts: Human Essence/Alienation/Alienated Labour.[4] And it should be noted that the "mode of functioning" of this new system or

---

4. John Lewis, like so many other critics, may well object that one can find in the *1844 Manuscripts* most of the concepts of Classical Political Economy—for example: capital, accumulation, competition, division of labour, wages, profit, etc. Exactly. These are concepts of Classical Political Economy, which Marx borrows *just as* he finds them there, without changing them one iota, without adding to them any new concept, and without modifying anything at all of their theoretical organization. In the *1844 Manuscripts*, Marx actually speaks of the Economists as having said *the last word* on Economics. He does not modify their concepts, and when he criticizes them, he does so "philosophically", therefore from outside, and in the name of a philosophy which admits its inspiration: "*Positive criticism [of political economy] owes its true foundation to the discoveries of Feuerbach*", author of a "*real theoretical revolution*", which Marx then considered decisive (*Cf.* the *1844 Manuscripts*, Moscow 1967, pp. 19–20).

To measure what we might call the difference, we need only to consider the break with Feuerbach which took place a few months later (see the *Theses on Feuerbach*), and to note this fact: nowhere in the *Manuscripts* does the entirely new triadic conception appear, which forms the basis of the hitherto unknown theoretical system that begins to come into view in *The German Ideology*—Mode of Production, Relations of Production, Productive Forces. The appearance of this new system produces, from the moment of *The German Ideology*, a new arrangement of the concepts of Classical Political Economy. They change their place, and also their meaning and function. Soon, the "discovery" (Engels) of surplus-value, placed in the centre of the theory of the capitalist mode of production (surplus-value = capitalist exploitation = class struggle) produces a complete upheaval among these concepts. A quite different form of the *critique* of Political Economy then appears, which bears no relation to the (Feuerbachian) "philosophical critique" of the *Manuscripts*, a critique based not on "Feuerbach's great discoveries", but on the reality of the contradictory process of the capitalist mode of production and of the antagonistic class struggle of which it is the site, that is, both cause and effect. The Critique of Political Economy (sub-title of *Capital*) now becomes a denunciation of the economism of Classical Political Economy, of political economy as such (which does not take account of relations of exploitation and class struggle)—and at the same time it becomes an *internal* account of the contradictions of the capitalist mode of production, a critique of the capitalist mode of production from the standpoint of its own tendential laws, which announce its future disappearance under the blows of the proletarian class struggle. All this can be proved, textually.

conceptual apparatus proved to be quite simply *different* (without any relation in its "nature", without either a continuity or an "inversion") from the "mode of functioning" of the earlier systems. Because what we are seeing here is a "change of terrain" (I proposed, early on, the use of this important metaphor), therefore a "new terrain" on which the new concepts, after much elaboration, can lay down the foundations of a *scientific* theory, or (another metaphor) "open the road" to the development of what will, irresistibly, become a science, an unusual science, a *revolutionary science*, but a theory which contains what we recognize in the sciences, because it provides *objective knowledge* [*connaissances objectives*]. As a matter of fact, it is possible on this new terrain to pose, little by little and for the first time, by using the new concepts, the real problems of concrete history, in the form of scientific problems. It is possible to produce (as Marx does in *Capital*) proven theoretical results, that is, results which can be verified by scientific *and* political practice,[5] and are open to methodical rectification.

Now, the historical appearance[6] of this new Scientific Continent, of this new apparatus of fundamental theoretical concepts, went together—as you can see empirically in Marx, even if the process is clearly contradictory—with the theoretical *rejection* of the old basic notions and (or) of

---

5. This little "and" (scientific *and* political practice) naturally poses important problems which cannot be dealt with here. The problems and their solution can be ascribed to what is called the "union" or "fusion" of the Labour Movement with Marxist theory: Lenin, Gramsci and Mao have written crucial texts on these questions.

6. A moment ago I drew a contrast—in order to bring home the "reduction" which I had made—between the simple "theoretical fact" of the "break" [*coupure*], and the "historical fact" of the break [*rupture*] between Marxism and bourgeois ideology. But, considered in itself, the break is also an historical fact. Historical: because we have the right to speak of *theoretical* events in history. Historical: because it is a case of an event *of historical importance*, of such great importance that we could, supposing that such a comparison makes any sense, talk of Marx's discovery as the greatest event in the history of knowledge since the "appearance" of mathematics, somewhere in Greece, associated with the name of Thales. And we are as yet far from having appreciated the full importance of this theoretical event and of its political consequences.

their organization, which were recognized and rejected as *erroneous*.

Caution: we have reached a very sensitive theoretical and political point.

This process of explicit *rejection* begins in 1845 in *The German Ideology*, but it is disguised by its very general and abstract form, which contrasts "positive *science*", dealing in empirical realities, with the mistakes, the illusions and dreams of *ideology*, and very precisely of philosophy, which is at this time conceived of simply as ideology: better, as ideology *par excellence*. But in 1847, in *The Poverty of Philosophy*, the "settling of accounts" takes place directly on the new scientific terrain, and it is the pseudo-scientific concepts of Proudhon—who three years earlier, in *The Holy Family*, had been celebrated as the scientific theoretician of the proletariat—which now have to pay the price.

What is decisive in all this is the manner in which the accounts are settled. We no longer have a philosophical "critique", which works in part, or *can* in case of need work by "inversion";[7] we have instead the scientific denunciation of errors as errors, and their elimination, their removal pure and simple: Marx *puts an end* to the reign of conceptual errors, which he can call errors because he is advancing "truths", scientific concepts. This very special way of "settling accounts" is repeated again and again. It reappears throughout Marx's work, in *Capital* and later (*cf.* the showers of

---

7. Self-criticism on the question of the "inversion". In my first essays I tended to reduce philosophy to science, and, in consequence, I refused to recognize that the figure of the "inversion" had its place in the history of philosophical relations. I began to rectify my position in an article of February 1968, "Marx's Relation to Hegel" [contained in the collection *Politics and History*, NLB, 1972; Translator's note]. It must be said, however, that philosophy is not (a) science, and that the relation between philosophical *positions* in the "history" of philosophy does not reproduce the relation between a body of scientific *propositions* and their (pre-scientific) prehistory. The "inversion" is *one* of the necessary forms of the internal dialectic between philosophical positions: but only in certain well defined conditions. For there exist many other forms of the same relation, given other conditions. To recognize only one form ("inversion") is to be caught in speculative idealism. Materialism takes very seriously the plurality of forms of relation, and their determinate conditions.

criticism directed at the Social-Democratic leaders for their
theoretical *errors*, contained in the Gotha Programme, and
at Wagner for the Hegelian theoretical nonsense which he
talked about the concept of value and its "division" into
exchange-value and use-value). It is repeated in Lenin
(polemic with the Narodniks, the "romantics", with Rosa
Luxemburg over *Capital*, with Kautsky on the State and
Imperialism, etc.), in Gramsci (polemic with Bukharin
over historical materialism, etc.), and in Mao. It never
comes to an end. A science (Lenin repeats it again and again
when he talks about historical materialism) never comes to
an end.

But every science[8] begins. Of course, it always has a
prehistory, out of which it emerges. But it does emerge, in
two senses: in the ordinary sense, and in another sense, its
own special sense, which distinguishes it above all from the
philosophy with which it coexists within theory, but also
from other realities, like the practical and theoretical
ideologies.

It emerges in the ordinary sense: this means that it is not
born out of nothing, but out of a process of labour by which
it is hatched, a complex and multiple process, sometimes
brightened by a flash of lightning, but which normally
operates blindly, in the dark, because "it" never knows where
it is headed, nor, if ever it arrives, where it is going to surface.
It is born out of the unpredictable, incredibly complex and
paradoxical—but, in its contingency, necessary—*conjunction*
of ideological, political, scientific (related to other sciences),
philosophical and other "*elements*", which at some moment[9]
"*discover*", *but after the event, that they needed each other,*

8. What follows should not be understood as a relapse into a theory of
science (in the singular), which would be quite speculative, but as the *minimum
of generality* necessary to be able to grasp a concrete object. *Science* (in the
singular) does not exist. But nor does "production in general": and yet
Marx talks about "production in general", and deliberately, consciously,
in order to be able to analyse concrete modes of production.

9. Not necessarily at any precise moment (though, in exceptional circumstances this just could be: certain scientists, following Pascal, talk about
their "night", that is, about the sudden proof which comes at "daybreak",
when they are suddenly blessed with "sight"), but at a moment which can
still be roughly fixed in historical time and its periods.

since they come together, without however recognizing one another, in the theoretical shape of a new-born science. This is the first sense in which a science emerges from its prehistory, like everything that comes into the world, from atoms to living things and to men, including the code for their genetic reproduction.

But a science also emerges from its prehistory in its own special way: in quite another manner which, at least in theory, is proper to itself, since it distinguishes it, among other things, from the way in which a philosophy "emerges" from *its* history. In this second sense, you can almost say that a science emerges from its prehistory in the same way as Marx emerged from the room of the Communist Weitling, with the famous remark: "Ignorance will never be an argument!", taking hold of the door and slamming it. Rejecting all or part of its prehistory, calling it erroneous: an *error*. And, at least in the very beginning, it is not too bothered with the "detail". It hardly matters that its judgement is, strictly speaking, "unjust"—it is not a question of morality. And it hardly matters—on the contrary!—that ideologists arrive on the scene much later, when it is clear that this fatherless infant can no longer be got rid of, and provide it with an official genealogy which, in order to conjure the child away,[10] looks into its prehistory, chooses for it and imposes on it *The* father who *had to* have this child (to keep it a bit quiet). It hardly matters—or, on the contrary, it matters very much!—that genuine scholars, rather heretically of course, come on the scene very much later to re-establish the existence of lines of descent so complex and so contingent in their necessity that they force the conclusion that the child *was born without a* (single-identifiable) *father*: but one must

10. Thus the bourgeois ideologists: they have discovered that Marx is nothing else *than* Ricardo, that *Capital* is nothing else *than* the chapter of Hegel's *Philosophy of Right* on *Sittlichkeit* (family apart): Civil Society + State, inverted (of course). "Find the lady", says the conventional Wisdom of detective novels. When the slogan is "find the father", it is obviously out of interest in the child: in order to make it disappear. Lenin, at all events, without going into detail, said, as if in passing, that Marxism had *three* "sources", no less!—a way, which has hardly been understood, of rejecting the question of THE father.

nevertheless accept the evidence and try to take account of this fact. Every recognized science not only has emerged from its own prehistory, but continues endlessly to do so (its prehistory remains always contemporary: something like its *Alter Ego*) by *rejecting* what it considers to be *error*, according to the process which Bachelard called "the epistemological *break* [*rupture*]".

I owe this idea to him, but to give it (to use a metaphor) the sharpest possible cutting-edge, I called it the "epistemological break [*coupure*]". And I made it the central category of my first essays.

What a fuss I raised! The use of this expression caused a real Holy Alliance to be formed against me; it united first those—bourgeois—who will defend to the death the Continuity of History, of which they are the masters, and of Culture, which provides them with the façade that they need in order to believe in their empire and its uninterrupted future; it also included those Communists who know that, according to Lenin, all the resources of human knowledge are required in order to construct socialism once the revolution is made, but who think—like the Marxists of the Gotha Programme—that it is not worth risking the loss of their political allies for a few "displaced" scientific concepts in the unity platform; and it included too those more or less anarchist elements which, using different political arguments, accused me of having introduced "bourgeois" concepts into Marxism, because I talked about it in terms of a "break".

But I shall continue to defend my theses, while of course rectifying them, at least until others—better suited and thus more correct—are proposed. I repeat: I shall continue to defend them, both for clear political reasons and for compelling theoretical reasons.

Let us not try to fool ourselves: this debate and argument are, in the last resort, political. This is not only the case with my openly bourgeois critics, but also with the others. Who, really, is naïve enough to think that the expressions: Marxist *theory*, Marxist *science*—sanctioned, moreover, time and time again by the history of the Labour Movement, by the writings of Marx, Engels, Lenin and Mao—would have produced the storms, the denunciations, the passions which we have witnessed,[11] if nothing had been at stake except a simple quarrel over words? This is not a debate about philology! To hang on to or to reject these *words*, to defend them or to destroy them—something real is at stake in these struggles, whose ideological and political character is obvious. It is not too much to say that what is at stake today, behind the argument about words, is *Leninism*. Not only the recognition of the existence and role of Marxist theory and science, but also the concrete forms of the fusion between the Labour Movement and Marxist theory, and the conception of materialism and the dialectic.

I know that it is not always easy to be fair. I agree that the ideological struggle is often confused, that the camps in this struggle are partly mixed up, and that arguments some-times go on above the heads of the combatants. I recognize that not everyone who declares himself for one side really takes up all its positions, and that he may while trying for one result produce another. The attacks against the idea of a Marxist *science* may even, as a result of certain of the argu-ments used, knock down by *ricochet* certain definite errors. Let us say that public positions must always be judged against the system of positions actually held *and* against the effects they produce. For example, to look at only one side of the question, you may declare yourself for Marxist theory and yet defend this theory on the basis of *positivist*, therefore non-Marxist positions—with all the consequences. Because you cannot really defend Marxist theory and science except on the basis of dialectical-materialist (therefore non-specu-lative and non-positivist) positions, trying to appreciate that quite *extraordinary*, because unprecedented, reality: Marxist theory as a *revolutionary* theory, Marxist science as a *revolutionary* science.

What is really unprecedented in these expressions is the combination of the terms "revolutionary" and "theory" ("Without an objectively/revolutionary/theory there can

11. Need it be recalled that these are not recent ... That long before the arrival of Raymond Aron, Benedetto Croce (and he was not the first) denied all *scientific* value to *Capital?* That (without going back to Stirner's "anti-theoretical" reactions) the "left" critique of the idea of a *Marxist* science can already be found in the young Lukács, in Korsch, in Pannekoek, etc.?

be no objectively/revolutionary/movement": Lenin), and, since science is the index of objectivity of theory, the combination of the terms "revolutionary" and "science". But in these combinations, which, if taken seriously, upset the received idea of theory and of science, the terms "theory" and "science" nevertheless remain. This is neither "fetishism" nor bourgeois "reification", nor is it a slip of the pen. Politically and theoretically, we cannot do without these words: because until it is proved otherwise, within the bounds of existing practices *we have no others, and we have no better.* And if Marx, Engels and Lenin, throughout their political battles and theoretical work, never abandoned them as guides and as weapons, that is because they considered them indispensable to their political and theoretical struggle: to the revolutionary liberation of the proletariat.

We therefore have the right, and the duty, to speak (as all the classics have done) of Marxist *theory*, and, within Marxist theory, of a *science* and a philosophy: provided that we do not thereby fall into theoreticism, speculation or positivism. And, to touch immediately on the most delicate point: yes, we have the right, as far as theory is concerned, and the duty, politically, to use and defend—by fighting for the *word*—the philosophical category of "science", with reference to Marxism-Leninism, and to talk about the foundation by Marx of a *revolutionary science*. But we must then explain the reason for, the conditions and sense of this unprecedented combination, which brings about a decisive "shift" in our conception of science. To use and defend the word "science" in the context of this programme is a necessity, in order to resist the bourgeois subjective idealists and the petty-bourgeois Marxists who, all of them, shout "positivism" as soon as they hear the term, no doubt because the only picture they can conjure up of the practice and history of a science, and *a fortiori* of Marxist science, is the classical positivist or vulgar, bourgeois picture. It is a necessity if we want to resist the petty-bourgeois ideologists, Marxists or not, who like to weep over the "reification" and "alienation" of objectivity (as Stirner used to weep over "the Holy"), no doubt because they attach themselves without any embarrassment to the very antithesis which constitutes the basis of bourgeois legal and philosophical ideology, the antithesis between *Person* (Liberty = Free Will = Law) and *Thing*.[12] Yes, it is quite correct for us to speak of an unimpeachable and undeniable *scientific* core in Marxism, that of Historical Materialism, in order to draw a vital, clear and unequivocal line (even if you must— and you must indeed—continue forever to "work" on this line, to avoid falling into positivism and speculation) between: *on the one hand* the workers, who need objective, verifiable and verified—in short scientific—knowledge, in order to win victory, not in words, but in facts, over their class opponents; and, *on the other hand*, not only the bourgeoisie, which of course refuses Marxism any claim to be scientific, but also those who are willing to content themselves with a personal or fake theory, put together in their imagination or according to their petty-bourgeois "desire", or who refuse the very idea of a scientific theory, even the *word* "science", even the word "theory", on the pretext that

12. One only has to open a textbook of law or jurisprudence, to see clearly that Law [*Droit*]—which, uniquely, works as one with its ideology, because it needs it to be able to "function"—and therefore legal ideology, is, in the last instance, and usually surprisingly transparently, the basis of all bourgeois ideology. One needs a Marxist lawyer to demonstrate it, and a Marxist philosopher to understand it. As far as philosophers in general are concerned, they have not yet cut through the fog that surrounds them, and they hardly suspect the presence of Law and of legal ideology in their ruminations: in philosophy itself. However, the evidence is there: the dominant classical bourgeois philosophy (and its by-products, even the modern ones) is built on legal ideology, and its "philosophical objects" (philosophy has no object, it has *its* objects) are legal categories or entities: the Subject, the Object, Liberty, Free Will, Property (Properties), Representation, Person, Thing, etc. But those thinkers, those Marxists, who have recognized the bourgeois legal character of these categories and who criticize them, must still find their way out of the trap of traps: the idea and programme of a "*theory* of *knowledge*". This is the keystone of classical bourgeois philosophy, which is still dominant. Now unless (like Lenin and Mao) we use this expression in a context which indicates *where to get out of* the circle, in the philosophical rather than the scientific sense, then the idea may be taken as constitutive of philosophy, and even of "Marxist philosophy", and you remain caught in bourgeois ideology's trap of traps. For the simple *question* to which the "theory of knowledge" replies is still a *question of Law*, posed in terms of the validity of knowledge.

every science or even every theory is essentially "reifying", alienating and therefore bourgeois.[13]

And I should add: we also have the right to speak about an "epistemological break" and to use this philosophical category to mark the historical-theoretical *fact* of the birth of a science, including, in spite of its unique character, Marxist revolutionary science, by the visible symptom of its emergence from its prehistory, its *rejection of the errors* of that prehistory. On condition, of course, that what are only effects are not taken for the cause—but instead that the signs and effects of the "break" are considered as the theoretical phenomenon of the appearance of a science in the history of theory, which brings up the question of the social, political, ideological and philosophical conditions of this irruption.

13. One day it will be necessary to clear up the problem of the theory which serves as a philosophical *alibi* for all this "reification" literature: the theory of commodity fetishism in Book I, Part I of *Capital*. Meanwhile it may be hoped that all those who, in spite of their aversion to the idea of Marxist *science* and even Marxist *theory*, nevertheless go out of their way to call themselves Marxists, will not satisfy themselves with the bad passages from Reich (who also wrote some good ones) and Marcuse (who did not) and others, but will take the trouble to read Stirner, a real man of the (Parisian) moment, and Marx's reply to him in *The German Ideology*. These are texts which, on the question of "theory", do not lack a certain bite.

2. "Science and Ideology"

Now this is the very point at which I must—since no-one else has really rendered me the service—[14] declare my *theoreticist* error: on the question of the "break".

In the end, and in spite of all my precautions, I conceived and defined this "break" in the rationalist terms of science and non-science. Not openly in the "classical" terms of the opposition between *truth and error* (of a Cartesian type, reproducing an antithesis "fixed" from its origins, from Platonism onwards). Not in terms of an opposition between *knowledge and ignorance* (that of Enlightenment philosophy). But, if I may say so, worse: in terms of an opposition between *science* (in the singular) and *ideology* (in the singular).

Why was this worse?

Because in this way a very important but very equivocal—and thus misleading—notion was brought into play, based on its contrast with that of science, a notion which appears in *The German Ideology*, where one and the same term plays two different roles, designating a philosophical category on the one hand (illusion, error), and a scientific concept on the other (formation of the superstructure): the notion of *ideology*. And although *The German Ideology* encourages this confusion, Marx did after all overcome it, and so made it easier for us to avoid the trap. But this equivocal notion of ideology was brought into play *within the rationalist context* of the antithesis between truth and error. And so ideology was reduced to error, and error called ideology, and this whole rationalist game was given a fraudulent Marxist appearance.

I do not need to say what this led to, ideologically and

14. It may be that someone has done it, and that I simply have not heard. My excuses. In what I have been able to read, I have often come across absolute condemnations, very strong reservations and also some severe but correct remarks: and yet no coherent criticism which goes to the root of the matter, nothing really enlightening and convincing. But perhaps I have simply been deaf and blind ...

practically.[15] And in fact this disguise, which disguised *nothing*, did have its consequences. But Marxism, although it is rational, is not Rationalism, not even "modern" Rationalism (of which some of our predecessors, before the war, dreamed, in the heat of the struggle against Nazi irrationalism). And, in spite of everything which I said in another connexion about the basically *practical*, social and political function of ideology, because (encouraged by *The German Ideology*) I used one and the same term in two senses, the importance which I placed in its first use, a philosophical and definitely rationalist one (= the exposure of illusions, of errors) caused my interpretation, objectively, to fall into theoreticism on this point.

Nevertheless, and even in the equivocal terms of *The German Ideology*, this disguise of error as ideology could take on and in fact did take on another meaning. Ideology was only the Marxist "name" for error. But even in *The German Ideology*, which itself carried out this reduction, you could feel that behind the contrast between "positive truth" and ideological illusion, a quite different break with the past—not simply theoretical, but political and ideological, and on a quite different scale—was making its appearance and working itself out. This break was the one which Marx made not with ideology in general, not only with the existing ideological conceptions of history, but with *bourgeois* ideology, with the dominant, reigning *bourgeois* conception of the world, which held sway not only over social practices but also within the practical and theoretical ideologies, in philosophy, and even in the products of Political Economy and utopian socialism. The fact that this domination was

15. I will mention only one name as an example and as an exemplary case: that of Lysenko. And with it, his deceptive contrast: "bourgeois science/proletarian science". In short, two memories of a certain period (to say no more). A number of my critics, Communists and others, understood very well *at the time* (1960–65) when I published my first essays, that even at the very modest level at which they intervened political questions were *also* at stake. Certain were quite correct, at least at the time. For what is often forgotten is that the "conjuncture" has changed in the last ten years, in some of its least apparent aspects, and, in its contingent respects, the front of the theoretical struggle has moved, just like the front of the political struggle. But the basis has remained largely unchanged.

not absolute, but the result of a struggle against survivals of the feudal conception of the world and against the fragile foundations of a new, proletarian conception of the world—this too is a fact of vital importance for understanding Marx's position. *For he was only able to break with bourgeois ideology in its totality because he took inspiration from the basic ideas of proletarian ideology, and from the first class struggles of the proletariat, in which this ideology became flesh and blood.* This is the "event" which, behind the rationalist façade of the contrast between "positive truth" and ideological illusion, gave this contrast its real historical dimension. I certainly "sensed" that what was at stake in this debate was the break with *bourgeois* ideology, since I set to work to identify and characterize this ideology (in terms of humanism, historicism, evolutionism, economism, idealism, etc.). But for want of understanding at that time the mechanisms of ideology, its forms, its functions, its *class tendencies*, and its necessary relations with philosophy and the sciences, I was not really able to clarify the link existing between, on the one hand, Marx's break with bourgeois ideology, and on the other hand, the "epistemological break".

This latter "break" is not an illusion.

Behind this disguise of error as ideology, there stood a fact: the declaration of opposition between truth and error which is objectively one of the symptoms of the birth, of the appearance of a science (when this really is what has taken place). Whatever has been claimed, there is no doubt that I did not hold to a "non-dialectical" opposition between science and ideology: for I showed that this opposition was recurrent, therefore historical and dialectical, since it is only if the truth has been "discovered" and "acquired", and then alone, that the scientist can look back from this established position towards the prehistory of his science, and declare that it consists in part or whole of error, of a "tissue of errors" (Bachelard), even if he recognizes within it partial truths which he exempts or anticipations which he retains (for example: Classical Political Economy, utopian socialism). But this very exemption is only possible because the partial truths and anticipations of its prehistory are now recognized and identified as such, on the basis of the finally discovered and established truth. "*Habemus* enim *ideam veram* . . ." (Spinoza). It is just because (*enim*) we possess (*habemus*) a true idea that . . . that we can also say: "*Verum index sui* et *falsi*"; what is true is the sign both of itself and of what is false, and the recognition of error (and of partial truths) depends on starting from what is true.

It is still the case, however, that in reducing and extending the "break" to this simple opposition between science and ideology—even if I did call it recurrent, even "perpetual" and "endless"—I uncritically adopted the point of view which "science" (in the singular) holds about itself (and, all too clearly, not only about itself!); or rather—since this formula is still idealist—I adopted the point of view which the "agents" of scientific practice hold about their own practice and the history of its results; or rather—since this formula is even now still idealist—[16] the point of view of the "spontaneous philosophy of scientists" (Lenin) who see, in the beginnings of a science, only the finished contrast between before and after, between the truth (or truths) discovered and the errors rejected. Now I have since (in a Philosophy Course for Scientists, 1967) tried to show precisely that this "spontaneous philosophy of scientists" is not spontaneous, and does not at all derive from the philosophical imagination of the scientists as such: for it is quite simply the repetition, by these scholars and scientists, of Theses of contradictory tendencies developed publicly by philosophy itself—that is, ultimately, by the "philosophy of philosophers".

I did, then, note the existence of the "break", but since I treated it in terms of the Marxist disguise of error as ideology, and—in spite of all the history and dialectics which I tried

16. *Cf.* on this subject all the ambiguities which arise—like a bird at the footsteps of the huntsman—from the simple use of Bachelard's formula: "*les travailleurs de la preuve*", especially when they are gathered into the "*cité des savants*". But the "*cité des savants*" only exists in the bourgeois division between manual and intellectual labour, and in the bourgeois ideology of "science and technique" which helps this division to function by approving it and justifying it from a simply bourgeois point of view. The proletarian point of view on the question is quite different: the suppression of the "*cité des savants*", the "union" of the scientists with the workers and militants, and onwards to communist forms of the division of labour totally unknown and unimaginable from the bourgeois viewpoint.

to "inject"[17] into it—in categories which in the last resort were rationalist, I could not explain what was the basis of this break; and if, deep down, I sensed it, I was incapable of grasping it[18] and expressing it.

Thus in fact I reduced the break between Marxism and bourgeois ideology to the "epistemological break", and the antagonism between Marxism and bourgeois ideology to the antagonism between science and ideology.

This false position, like any correct one, had its consequences. It might not have done so if I had been satisfied with limiting its expression to a few phrases. But I was naïve enough (or logical enough) to make a theoretical argument out of it, and to insert it into a line of argument rigorous enough for me to have to pay the price.

I *theorized* this "error" of the rationalist opposition between science (truths) and ideology (errors), in spite of all kinds of necessarily inoperative reserves, in terms of three figures which embodied and summed up my theoreticist (*i.e.* rationalist-speculative) tendency:

1. A (speculative) sketch of the theory of the difference between science (in the singular) and ideology (in the singular) in general.

2. The category of "theoretical practice" (*in so far as*, in

17. For the inevitable—and inevitably negative—results of the attempt to "inject" dialectics into all kinds of theses and theories, compare Marx's experience with Proudhon: "I tried to inject him with the Hegelian dialectic . . ." Without success. Indeed, if we take the word of *The Poverty of Philosophy*, criticizing *The Philosophy of Poverty*, we should perhaps even speak of a catastrophe! The dialectic cannot be "injected", nor, following the technical metaphor strictly, can it be "*applied*". Hegel pointed this out forcefully. On this point at least we must follow Hegel. On this point—which still leaves others to be debated—Marx and Lenin are Hegelians. One cannot talk of the injection or application of the dialectic. Here we touch on a very sensitive philosophical point (indicated by two simple words). In philosophy "*lines* of demarcation" meet and intersect at *points*, which thus become sensitive points: an encounter at the crossroads.

18. I say: incapable of *grasping* it. Because it is not possible, if you want to do serious work, to remain satisfied with general and established formulae, which, parasitic on others, give you the impression and conviction of being on the right road and of having found just the right word for the thing.

the existing context, it tended to reduce philosophical practice to scientific practice).

3. The (speculative) thesis of philosophy as "Theory of theoretical practice"—which represented the highest point in the development of this theoreticist tendency.[19]

Of course, this last thesis on philosophy was not without its secondary effects on the Marxist conception of *science*,

19. You only need to bring these three theses together to understand the term by which I have named my deviation: theoreticism. Theoreticism here means: primacy of theory over practice; one-sided insistence on theory; but more precisely: *speculative-rationalism*. To explain only the pure form: to conceive matters in terms of the contrast between truth and error was in fact *rationalism*. But it was *speculation* to want to conceive the contrast between established truths and acknowledged errors within a General Theory of Science and Ideology and of the distinction between them. Of course I am simplifying and forcing things to the extreme, reasoning them out to their ultimate conclusions—for our analyses never actually went so far, certainly not reaching these conclusions. But the tendency is undeniable.

It was organized, as is often the case, around the manifest form of a word, whose credentials seemed beyond doubt: *Epistemology*. Thus we went back to Bachelard, who makes constant use of the term, and also to Canguilhem, who, though we did not notice it, uses it very little. We (especially I) used it and abused it, and did not know how to control that use. I point this out because a whole number of our readers jumped on to this, reinforcing by their own philosophical inclinations the theoreticist tendency of our essays.

What did we understand by *Epistemology*? Literally: the theory of the conditions and forms of scientific practice and of its history in the different concrete sciences. But this definition could be understood in two ways. In a *materialist* way, which could lead us to study the material, social, political, ideological and philosophical conditions of the theoretical "modes of production" and "production processes" of already existing knowledge: but this would properly fall within the domain of Historical Materialism! Or in a *speculative* way, according to which Epistemology could lead us to form and develop the theory of scientific practice (in the singular) in distinction to other practices: but how did it now differ from philosophy, also defined as "Theory of theoretical practice"? We were now within the domain of "Dialectical Materialism", since philosophy was and is nothing but Epistemology. This was the crossroads. If Epistemology is philosophy itself, their speculative unity can only reinforce theoreticism. But if Epistemology is based on Historical Materialism (though naturally possessing a minimum of concepts which are its own and specify its object), then it must be placed within it; and, at the same time, the illusion and deception involved in the very project must be recognized. It follows (as we have since pointed out) that one must give up this project, and criticize the idealism or idealist connotations of all Epistemology.

of historical materialism, not so much because of the use to which I put the distinction (correct in principle) between science and Marxist "philosophy" as because of the way in which I treated this relation (philosophy being, ultimately, treated as theory like science, made of the same stuff, with the added capital letter: Theory). Very unfortunate consequences resulted as far as the presentation of the *modality* of Marxist science, of Historical Materialism, was concerned—especially in *Reading Capital*.

It was no doubt on this occasion that the accidental by-product of my theoreticist tendency, the young pup called structuralism, slipped between my legs . . .

3. Structuralism?

It must be admitted that it thus became tempting to flirt (*kokettieren*), not with the structure and its elements, etc. (because all these concepts are in Marx), but for example with the notion of the "effectivity of an absent cause"—which is, it must be said, much more Spinozist than structuralist!—in order to account at one and the same time for Classical Political Economy's "mistakes", for the Relations of Production, and even for fetishism (but I did not do so: the theory of fetishism always seemed to me ideological)—and to herald, by the term *structural causality* (*cf.* Spinoza), something which is in fact an "immense theoretical discovery" of Marx but which can also, in the Marxist tradition, be termed dialectical *materialist* causality. Provided that their critical effects are kept under control, these notions are not entirely useless—an example is the notion of the "absent cause".[20] But we were not always able to restrain ourselves,

---

20. In three senses:
  1. *Political*. For example, it is difficult to "put your finger" on "the" cause of what some have called "Stalinism" and others "the personality cult". The effects were certainly present, but the cause was absent;
  2. *Scientific*. Supposing that, by scientific analysis, "the" cause was found, and that we call it (in order to call it something) the "Stalinian deviation", even so this cause is itself only one link in the dialectic of the class struggle of the Labour Movement in a situation dominated by the construction of socialism in one country, itself a moment of the history of the International Labour Movement, in the world-wide class struggles of the imperialist stage of capitalism, the whole thing being determined "in the last instance" by the "contradiction" between the Relations of Production and Productive Forces.
  But it is also not possible to "put your finger" on this contradiction, determinant "in the last instance", as *the* cause. One can only grasp it and understand it within the forms of the class struggle which constitutes, in the strict sense, its *historical* existence. To say that "the cause is absent" thus means, in Historical Materialism, that the "contradiction determinant in the last instance" is *never present in person* on the scene of history ("the hour of the determination in the last instance never strikes") and that one can never grasp it directly, as one can a "person who is present". It is a "cause", but in the dialectical sense, in the sense that it determines *what*, on the stage of the class struggle, is the "decisive link" which must be grasped;

in certain pages of *Reading Capital*, in that Spring of 1965, and our "flirt" with structuralist terminology obviously went beyond acceptable limits, because our critics, with a few exceptions, did not see the irony or parody intended. For we had in mind quite another Personage than the anonymous author of structuralist themes and their vogue! We shall soon see who.

There were however certain indications in our essays which might have given cause for reflexion. I have for example always wondered how structuralism could swallow and digest categories like "determination in the last instance", "domination/subordination", to mention only these. But what did it matter? For flagrant reasons of convenience, we were called "structuralists", and it was in a coffin marked "structuralism" that the great family of Social-Democrats from all parties and lands solemnly bore us to our grave and buried us, in the name of Marxism—that is, of *their* Marxism. The spadefuls of earth—of "history", of "practice", of the "dialectic", of the "concrete", of "life", and of course of "Man" and "Humanism"—fell thick and fast. For a funeral, it was a nice one. With this rather special characteristic: that the years have passed, but the ceremony is still going on.

I will say no more about these episodes, for while they are not lacking in interest (it still remains to show why), they can distract us from the essential point, and for a very simple reason. This is that the criticisms which were then addressed to us put things in the wrong order: they called us structuralists, but they said little about our theoreticism. In a sense, they certainly did bury something: the main deviation, theoreticism, was buried beneath a secondary deviation (and problematic), structuralism. And it is easy

---

3. *Philosophical*. It is true that the dialectic is a thesis of *the* "absent" *cause*, but in a sense which must be understood as quite distinct from the supposed structuralist connotation of the term. The dialectic makes the reigning cause disappear, because it destroys, surpasses and "transcends" *the* mechanistic, pre-Hegelian category of cause, conceived as *the* billiard ball in person, something which can be grasped, cause identified with substance, with *the* subject, etc. The dialectic makes mechanical causality disappear, by *putting forward* the thesis of a quite different "causality".

to understand why: the point is that the Marxist thesis of theoretical anti-humanism, the formulation of which may have "overlapped" with *certain* good "structuralist" (anti-psychologistic, anti-historicist) reflexes of some important thinkers (Saussure and his school), who of course were no Marxists, came directly into conflict with their humanist ideology. What our critics, fascinated by the pseudo-antago-nism between structuralism and humanism, and fixed within an antithesis which suited them, could neither see nor understand, was that certain demarcation lines can overlap in this way, can meet at certain sensitive points; that in the philosophical battle you sometimes have to take over a certain key point occupied by others (who may be enemies) in order to make it part of your own defensive positions (it may then change its significance, because it will then be part of a quite different system); that this in-tegration procedure is not guaranteed by anyone in advance, and that it involves risks, precisely those risks to which Marx draws attention when, in Book I of *Capital*, he "flirts" with Hegel and his terminology. That is why things must be put back in their proper order. With hindsight, and benefiting from the criticisms which were made of me (I did not ignore them: some were very much to the point) and from further thought, I believe that six years later I can stand by the terms of my brief but precise self-criticism of 1967 and identify a fundamental *theoreticist* (= rationalist-speculative) deviation in my first essays (*For Marx*, *Reading Capital*) and also, in *Reading Capital*, its circumstantial by-product, a very ambiguous "flirtation" with structuralist terminology.

But since the question of structuralism has arisen, I should like to say a few words about it.

This very French speciality is not a "philosophers' philoso-phy": no philosopher gave it its name, nor its seal, and no philosopher has taken up its vague and changing themes in order to create the unity of a systematic *conception* out of them. This is not an accident. Structuralism, born of theoreti-cal problems encountered by scientists in their practical work (in linguistics from the time of Saussure, in social anthropology from the time of Boas and Lévi-Strauss, in psychoanalysis, etc.), is no "philosophers' philosophy", but a "philosophy" or "philosophical ideology of scientists". That its themes are vague and changing, that their boundary is very ill-defined, does not mean that its *general tendency* cannot be characterized: as rationalist, mechanistic, and above all *formalist*. Ultimately (and this can be seen in certain of the texts of Lévi-Strauss, and among linguists or other philosophizing logicians) structuralism (or rather: certain structuralists) tends towards the ideal of *the production of the real as an effect of a combinatory of elements*. But of course since "it" uses a whole lot of concepts drawn from existing disciplines, we could not honestly accuse structuralism of being the first to use the concept of structure!

At this point it is important to remember that structuralism is not a completely worked-out philosophy, but a jumble of vague themes which only *realizes* its ultimate tendency under certain definite conditions. According to what you "understand" by structuralism (*e.g.*, anti-psychologism), according to what you see in it when you come up against concepts which it has in fact borrowed, and according to whether you follow the extreme logic which inspires it, either you are not a structuralist or you are one more or less, or you really are one. Now no-one can claim that we ever gave way to the crazy formalist idealism of the idea of producing the real by a combinatory of elements. Marx does speak of the "combination" of elements in the structure of a mode of production. But this combination (*Verbindung*) is not a formal "combinatory": we expressly pointed that out. Purposely. In fact this is where the most important demarcation line is drawn.

For example, there is no question of deducing (therefore of predicting) the different "possible" modes of production by the formal play of the different possible combination of elements; and in particular, it is not possible to construct in this way, a priori ... the communist mode of production! Marx constantly uses the concepts of position and function, and the concept of *Träger* ("*supports*"), meaning a support of *relations*: but this is not in order to make concrete realities disappear, to reduce real men to pure functions of supports— it is in order to make mechanisms intelligible by grasping them through their concept, and *beginning with these* (since this is the only possible way) to make intelligible the concrete realities which can only be grasped by making a *detour* through abstraction. But just because Marx uses the concepts of structure, elements, point, function, *Träger*, relations, determination by relations, forms and transformed forms, displacement, etc., that does not make him a structuralist, since he is not a *formalist*. Here the second demarcation line is drawn.

Marx's concepts are actually used and confined within precise limits; and they are subjected to other concepts which define their *limits of validity*: the concepts of process, contradiction, tendency, limit, domination, subordination, etc. Here a third demarcation line is drawn.

For there are those who have said, or will one day say, that Marxism is distinguished from structuralism by *the primacy of the process over the structure*. Formally, this is not false; but it is also true of Hegel! If you want to go to the heart of the matter, you must go much deeper. For it is possible to conceive of a *formalism of the process* (of which the bourgeois economists offer us daily a caricature), therefore a structuralism ... of the process! In truth what we need to look at is the strange status of a decisive concept in Marxist theory, the concept of *tendency* (tendential law, law of a tendential process, etc.). In the concept of tendency there appears not only the *contradiction* internal to the process (Marxism is not a structuralism, not because it affirms the primacy of the process over the structure, but because it affirms the primacy of contradiction over the process: yet even this is not enough) but something else, which politically and philosophically is much more important—the special, unique status which makes Marxist science a *revolutionary* science. Not simply a science which revolutionaries can use in order to make revolution, but a science which they can use because it rests on *revolutionary class theoretical positions*.

Of course we did not see this last point clearly in 1965. Which means that we had not yet appreciated the exceptional importance of the role of the class struggle in Marx's philosophy and in the theoretical apparatus of *Capital* itself. It is a fact: although we suspected that Marxist science was not "a science like the others", we did finally treat it as "a science like the others", thus falling into the dangers of theoreticism. But we were never structuralists.

4. On Spinoza

If we never were structuralists, we can now explain why: why we seemed to be, even though we were not, why there came about this strange misunderstanding on the basis of which books were written. We were guilty of an equally powerful and compromising passion: *we were Spinozists*. In our own way, of course, which was not Brunschvicg's! And by attributing to the author of the *Tractatus Theologico-Politicus* and the *Ethics* a number of theses which he would surely never have acknowledged, though they did not actually contradict him. But to be a heretical Spinozist is almost orthodox Spinozism, if Spinozism can be said to be one of the greatest lessons in heresy that the world has seen! In any case, with very few exceptions our blessed critics, imbued with conviction and swayed by fashion, never suspected any of this. They took the easy road: it was so simple to join the crowd and shout "structuralism"! Structuralism was all the rage, and you did not have to read about it in books to be able to talk about it. But you have to read Spinoza and know that he exists: that he still exists today. To recognize him, you must at least have heard of him.

Let us clarify this business in a few words. After all, to lump structuralism and theoreticism together is hardly satisfactory or illuminating, because something in this combination is always "hidden": *formalism*, which happens to be essential to structuralism! On the other hand, to bring structuralism and Spinozism together may clarify certain points, and certain limits, as far as the theoreticist deviation is concerned.

But then comes the important objection: why did we make reference to Spinoza, when all that was required was for us simply to be Marxists? Why this detour? Was it necessary, and what price did we have to pay for it? The fact is: we did make the detour, and we paid dearly. But that is not the question. The question is: what is the meaning of the question? What can it mean to say that we should *simply* be Marxists (in philosophy)? In fact I had found out (and I was not the only one, but the reasons which I gave at the time are still almost all relevant) just how hard it was in practice to be a Marxist in philosophy. Having for years banged our heads against a wall of enigmatic texts and wretched commentaries on them, we had to decide to step back and make a detour.

In itself, nothing scandalous. It is not simply accidental, personal factors which are relevant here: we all begin from a given point of view, which we do not choose; and to recognize it and understand it we need to have moved on from this point, at the cost of so much effort. It is the work of philosophy itself which is at stake here: *for it requires steps back and detours.* What else did Marx do, throughout his endless research, but go back to Hegel in order to rid himself of Hegel and to find his own way, what else but rediscover Hegel in order to distinguish himself from Hegel and to define himself? Could this really have been a purely personal affair—fascination, rejection, then a return to a youthful passion? Something was working in Marx which went beyond the individual level: the need for every philosophy to make a detour *via* other philosophies in order to define itself and grasp itself in terms of its difference: its *division.* In reality (and whatever its pretensions) no philosophy is given in the *simple,* absolute fact of its presence—least of all Marxist philosophy (which in fact never made the claim). It only exists in so far as it "works out" its difference from other philosophies, from those which, by similarity or contrast, help it sense, perceive and grasp itself, so that it can take up its own *positions.* Lenin's attitude to Hegel is an example: working to separate out from the "debris" and useless "rubbish" those "elements" which might help in the effort to work out a differential definition. We are only now beginning to see a little more clearly into this necessary procedure.[21] How can it be denied that this procedure is indispensable to every philosophy, including Marxist philosophy itself? Marx, it has often been pointed out, was not content with making a single detour, *via* Hegel; he also constantly and explicitly, in his insistent use of

21. *Cf.* D. Lecourt, *Une Crise et son enjeu*, Maspero, 1973.

certain categories, measured himself against Aristotle, "that great thinker of the Forms". And how can it be denied that these detours, indispensable as they were, nevertheless had to be paid for, that we do not yet know (though we have our suspicions) what the theoretical cost really is, and that we can only find out *by ourselves working on these detours*?

This—keeping the matter (of course) in proportion— is how we approached Spinoza, courageously or imprudently (as you prefer). In our subjective history, and in the existing ideological and theoretical conjuncture, this detour became a necessity.

Why?

If a reason, one single and therefore fundamental reason must be given, here it is: we made a detour *via* Spinoza in order to improve our understanding of Marx's philosophy. To be precise: since Marx's materialism forced us to *think out* the meaning of the necessary detour *via* Hegel, *we made the detour via Spinoza in order to clarify our understanding of Marx's detour via Hegel.* A detour, therefore; but with regard to another detour. At stake was something enormously important: the better understanding of how and under what conditions a dialectic borrowed from the "most speculative" chapters of the *Great Logic* of Absolute Idealism (borrowed conditionally on an "inversion" and a "demystification", which also have to be understood) can be materialist and critical. Now this astonishing and enigmatic game of manoeuvres between idealism and materialism had already taken place once in history, in other forms (with which Hegel typically identified) two centuries earlier, under astonishing conditions: how could this philosophy of Spinoza have been materialist and critical—a philosophy terrifying to its own time, which began "not with the spirit, not with the world, but with God", and never deviated from its path, whatever form or appearance of idealism and "dogmatism" it might take on? In Spinoza's anticipation of Hegel we tried to see, and thought that we had succeeded in finding out, under what conditions a philosophy might, in what it said or did not say, and in spite of its form—or on the contrary, just because of its form, that is, because of the theoretical apparatus of its theses, in short because of its *positions*—produce effects useful to materialism. Thus, some light would be thrown on what philosophy really is, therefore on what a philosophy is, and on materialism. And then other things would begin to become clear.

I mentioned Hegel and the *Great Logic*, and not without reason. Hegel *begins* with Logic, "God before the creation of the world". But as Logic is alienated in Nature, which is alienated in the Spirit, which reaches its end in Logic, there is a circle which turns within itself, without end and without beginning. The first words of the beginning of the *Logic* tell us: Being is Nothingness. The posited beginning is negated: there is no beginning, therefore no origin. Spinoza for his part begins with God, but in order to deny Him as a Being (Subject) in the universality of His *only* infinite power (*Deus = Natura*). Thus Spinoza, like Hegel, rejects every thesis of Origin, Transcendence or an Unknowable World, even disguised within the absolute interiority of the Essence. But with this difference (for the Spinozist negation is not the Hegelian negation), that within the void of the Hegelian Being there exists, through the negation of the negation, the contemplation of the dialectic of a *Telos* (Telos = Goal), a dialectic which reaches its Goals in history: those of the Spirit, subjective, objective and absolute, Absolute Presence in transparency. But Spinoza, because he "begins with God", never gets involved with any Goal, which, even when it "makes its way forward" in immanence, is still figure and thesis of transcendence. The detour *via* Spinoza thus allowed us to make out, by contrast, a radical quality lacking in Hegel. In the negation of the negation, in the *Aufhebung* (= transcendence which conserves what it transcends), it allowed us to discover the Goal: the special form and site of the "mystification" of the Hegelian dialectic.

Is it necessary to add that Spinoza refused to use the notion of the Goal, but explained it as a necessary and there-fore well-founded illusion? In the Appendix to Book I of the *Ethics*, and in the *Tractatus Theologico-Politicus*, we find in fact what is undoubtedly the first theory of *ideology* ever thought out, with its three characteristics: (1) its *imaginary* "reality"; (2) its internal *inversion*; (3) its "centre": the illusion of the *subject*. An abstract theory

of ideology, it will be said. I agree: but try to find something
better before Marx, who himself said little on the subject—
except in *The German Ideology*, where he said too much.
And above all: it is not sufficient to spell out the letter of a
theory, one must also see how it operates, that is, since it is
always an apparatus of theses, what it refuses and what it
accepts. Spinoza's "theory" rejected every illusion about
ideology, and especially about the number one ideology
of that time, religion, by identifying it as imaginary. But
at the same time it refused to treat ideology as a simple
error, or as naked ignorance, because it based the system
of this imaginary phenomenon on the relation of men to
the world "expressed" by the state of their bodies. This
materialism of the imaginary opened the way to a surprising
conception of the First Level of Knowledge: not at all,
in fact, as a "piece of knowledge", but as the material world
of men *as they live it*, that of their concrete and historical
existence. Is this a false interpretation? In certain respects,
perhaps, but it is possible to read Spinoza in such a way.
In fact his categories do function, daringly, in this way in
the *history* of the Jewish people, of its prophets, of its religion,
and of its politics, where the primacy of politics over religion
stands out clearly, in the first work which, after Machiavelli,
offered a theory of history.

But this theory of the imaginary went still further. By
its radical criticism of the central category of imaginary
illusion, *the Subject*, it reached into the very heart of bourgeois
philosophy, which since the fourteenth century had been
built on the foundation of the legal ideology of the Subject.
Spinoza's resolute anti-Cartesianism consciously directs
itself to this point, and the famous "critical" tradition made
no mistake here. On this point too Spinoza anticipated Hegel,
but he went further. For Hegel, who criticized all theses of
subjectivity, nevertheless found a place for the Subject,
not only in the form of the "becoming-Subject of Substance"
(by which he "reproaches" Spinoza for "wrongly" taking
things no further than Substance), but in the *interiority* of
the *Telos* of the process without a subject, which by virtue
of the negation of the negation, realizes the designs and
destiny of the Idea. Thus Spinoza showed us the secret

alliance between Subject and Goal which "mystifies" the Hegelian dialectic.

I could go on. I will however deal with one last theme: that of the famous "*verum index sui et falsi*". I said that it seemed to us to allow a recurrent conception of the "break". But it did not only have that meaning. In affirming that "what is true is the sign of itself and of what is false", Spinoza avoided any problematic which depended on a "*criterion of truth*". If you claim to judge the truth of something by some "criterion", you face the problem of the criterion of this criterion—since it also must be true—and so on to infinity. Whether the criterion is external (relation of adequacy between mind and thing, in the Aristotelian tradition) or internal (Cartesian self-evidence), in either case the criterion can be rejected: for it only represents a form of Jurisdiction, a Judge to authenticate and guarantee the validity of what is True. And at the same time Spinoza avoids the temptation of talking about the Truth: as a good nominalist (nominalism, as Marx recognized, could then be the antechamber of materialism) Spinoza only talks about what is "true". In fact the idea of Truth and the idea of the Jurisdiction of a Criterion always go together, because the function of the criterion is to identify the Truth of what is true. Once he has set aside the (idealist) temptations of a theory of knowledge, Spinoza then says that "what is true" "identifies itself", not as a Presence but as a Product, in the double sense of the term "product" (*result* of the work of a process which "*discovers*" it), as it emerges in its own production. Now this position is not unrelated to the "criterion of practice", a major thesis of Marxist philosophy: for this Marxist "criterion" is not exterior but interior to practice, and since this practice is a process (Lenin insisted on this: practice is not an absolute "criterion"—only the process is conclusive) the criterion is no form of Jurisdiction; items of knowledge [*connaissances*] emerge in the process of their production.

There again, by the contrast between them, Spinoza allows us to perceive Hegel's mistake. Hegel certainly did rule out any criterion of truth, by considering what is true as interior to its process, but he restored the credentials of the Truth as Telos within the process itself, since each moment is only ever the "truth of" the moment which precedes it. When, in a provocative formula which took up Lenin's words ("Marx's doctrine is all-powerful because it is true") directed against the dominant pragmatism and every (idealist) idea of Jurisdiction, I "defined" knowledge as "*production*" and affirmed the *interiority* of the forms of scientificity to "theoretical practice", I based myself on Spinoza: not in order to provide *The* answer, but to counter the dominant idealism and, *via* Spinoza, to open a road where materialism might, if it runs the risk, find something other than words.

It is understandable that, behind these reasonings, we found other theses in Spinoza which supported them, and that we put these to use too, even at the cost of overdoing things.

Spinoza helped us to see that the concepts Subject/Goal constitute the "mystifying side" of the Hegelian dialectic: but is it enough to get rid of them in order to introduce the materialist dialectic of Marxism, by a simple process of subtraction and inversion? That is not at all sure, because, freed of these fetters, the new dialectic can revolve endlessly in the void of idealism, unless it is rooted in *new forms*, unknown to Hegel, and which can confer on it the status of materialism.

Now, what does Marx demonstrate in the *Poverty of Philosophy*, in the *Contribution to a Critique of Political Economy* and in *Capital*? Precisely that the functioning of the *materialist* dialectic is dependent on the apparatus of a kind of *Topography* [*Topique*]. I am alluding to the famous metaphor of the edifice, in which, in order to grasp the reality of a social formation, Marx *instals* an infrastructure (the economic "structure" or "base") and, above it, a super-structure. I am alluding to the theoretical problems posed by this apparatus: "the determination in the last instance (of the superstructure) by the economy (the infrastructure)", "the relative autonomy of (the elements of) the superstruc-ture", their "action and reaction on the infrastructure", the difference and the unity between determination and domination, etc. And I am alluding to the decisive problem, within the infrastructure for example, of the unity of the relations of production and productive forces *under the dominance of* the relations of production, therefore the problem of the *determination by relations* on the one hand (you find the trace of this problem everywhere in Marx: *cf.* the concepts of structure/elements, of position, function, support, etc.) and on the other hand the problem of *domination*.

Now, we are not talking here about a few formulae which might have slipped from Marx's pen by accident, but about a necessity, something which expresses a position essential to materialism and which must be taken seriously. For nowhere do you see Hegel thinking within the structure of a *Topography*. It is not that Hegel does not propose topographical distinctions: to take only one example, he does indeed talk about abstract right, subjective right (morality), and objective right (the family, civil society, the State), and talks about them as *spheres*. But Hegel only ever talks about spheres in order to describe them as "spheres within spheres", about circles in order to describe them as "circles within circles": he only advances topographical distinctions in order later to suspend them, to erase them and to transcend them (*Aufhebung*), since "their truth" always, for each of them, lies beyond itself. We know the consequences of this idealist retreat: it is abstract right which comes first! Morality is "the truth of" law! The family, civil society and the State are "the truth of" morality! And, within this last sphere (*Sittlichkeit*), civil society (let us say: Marx's infrastructure) is "the truth of" the family! And the State is "the truth of" civil society! The *Aufhebung* is at work here: *Aufhebung of every Topography*. But there is worse: the "spheres" which have been introduced are arranged in the order which allows the greatest possibility of this retreat. All the spheres of the *Philosophy of Right* are only figures of the law, the existence of Liberty. And, in order to "demonstrate" it, Hegel buries the economy between the family and the State, after abstract right and morality. This allows us to glimpse what might come of a dialectic abandoned to the absolute delirium of the negation of the negation: it is a dialectic which, "starting" from Being = Nothingness, itself produces, by the negation of the negation, all the figures in which it operates, of which it is the dialectic; it is a dialectic which produces its own "spheres" of existence; it is—to put it bluntly—a dialectic *which produces its own material substance*. A thesis which faithfully transposes and translates the fundamental thesis of bourgeois ideology: it is (the capitalist's) labour which has produced capital.

It is now possible to understand the materialist stamp of the Marxist Topography. The fact that the metaphor of the structure is a metaphor matters little: in philosophy you can only think through metaphors. But through this metaphor we come up against theoretical problems which have nothing metaphorical about them. By the use of his Topography, Marx introduces *real*, distinct spheres, which only fit together through the mediation of the *Aufhebung*: "below" is the economic infrastructure, "above" the super-structure, with its different determinations. The Hegelian order is overthrown: the State is always "up above", law is no longer either primary or omnipresent, and the economy is no longer squeezed between the family and the State, its "truth". The *position* of the infrastructure designates an unavoidable reality: the determination in the last instance by the economic. Because of this, the relation between infrastructure and superstructure no longer has anything to do with the Hegelian relation: "the truth of ...". The State is indeed always "up above", but not as "the truth of" the economy: in direct contradiction to a relation of "truth", it actually produces a relation of *mystification*, based in exploitation, which is made possible by force and by ideology.

The conclusion is obvious: *the position of the Marxist Topography protects the dialectic against the delirious idealist notion of producing its own material substance*: it imposes on it, on the contrary, a forced recognition of the material conditions of its own efficacy. These conditions are related to the definition of the sites (the "spheres"), to their limits, to their mode of determination in the "totality" of a social formation. If it wants to grasp these realities, the materialist dialectic cannot rest satisfied with the residual forms of the Hegelian dialectic. It needs other forms, which cannot be found in the Hegelian dialectic. It is here that Spinoza served us as a (sometimes direct, sometimes very indirect) reference: in his effort to grasp a "non-eminent" (that is, non-transcendent) not simply transitive (à la Descartes) nor expressive (à la Leibniz) causality, which would account for the action of the Whole on its parts, and of the parts on the Whole—an unbounded Whole, which is only the active relation between its parts: in this effort Spinoza served us, though indirectly, as a first and almost unique guide.

A Marxist cannot of course make the detour *via* Spinoza without paying for it. For the adventure is perilous, and whatever you do, you cannot find in Spinoza what Hegel gave to Marx: *contradiction*. To take only one example, this "theory of ideology" and this interpretation of the "First Level of Knowledge" as a concrete and historical world of men living (in) the materiality of the imaginary led me directly to the conception (to which *The German Ideology* can lend support): materiality/imaginary/inversion/subject: But I saw ideology as the universal element of historical existence: and I did not at that time go any further. Thus I disregarded the difference between the regions of ideology and the antagonistic class tendencies which run through them, divide them, regroup them and bring them into opposition. The absence of "contradiction" was taking its toll: the question of the class struggle in ideology did not appear. Through the gap created by this "theory" of ideology slipped theoreticism: science/ideology. And so on.

But in spite of everything, it seems to me that the benefit was not nil. We wanted to understand Marx's detour *via* Hegel. We made a detour *via* Spinoza: looking for arguments for materialism. We found some. And through this detour, unexpected if not unsuspected by many, we were able, if not to pose or to articulate, at least to "raise" (as you might raise an animal, unexpectedly disturbing it) some questions which otherwise might have remained dormant, sleeping the peaceful sleep of the eternally obvious, in the closed pages of *Capital*. While waiting for others either to show the futility of these questions or to answer them more correctly, we shall continue, you can bet, to be accused of structuralism . . .

5. On Tendencies in Philosophy

I spoke earlier about a theoreticist *error*. Now I want to speak of a theoreticist *tendency*. I used the first term in order not to shirk my duty or spare myself in any way. But the second, if I may say so, has even more damaging implications, because it is correct: an erroneous tendency, or more correctly still, a wrongly oriented, therefore deviant tendency. A *deviation*. For you can ultimately only talk about an error in philosophy, from a Marxist point of view, if you think of philosophy itself in the categories of rationalism (truth/error), that is to say according to non-Marxist philosophical theses. If I simply talked about my philosophical "error", without rectifying this expression by the use of the terms tendency and deviation, I would fall into the trap of the rationalist antithesis between truth and error, and would then be denouncing my past "error" in the name of a "truth" which I now possess: without knowing why I was made a present of it, and without regard to the very special dialectic which is at work in the practice of philosophy, which is not (a) science, but class struggle in theory.[22] Let us advance a thesis: strictly speaking all theoretical *errors* are scientific ones, in the recurrent relation which links a science to its own prehistory (which remains its contemporary and always accompanies it, its history's Alter Ego). In philosophy we are dealing with tendencies which confront each other on the existing theoretical "battlefield". These tendencies group themselves in the last instance around the antagonism between idealism and materialism, and they "exist" in the form of "philosophies" which realize the tendencies, their variations and their combinations, as a function of class theoretical positions, *in which it is the social practices* (political, ideological, scientific, etc.) *which are at stake*. Thus, in order to mark this distinction, you have to introduce a category which plays an all-important role in Marxist political practice and theoretical reflexion on philosophical theses and tendencies: the category of *correctness*. That

---

22. A formula which I proposed in my *Reply to John Lewis*.

is why I proposed (in my *Philosophy Course for Scientists*, 1967) the express use of this category to characterize the special "nature" of philosophical propositions, *theses* (or *positions*: a position which is *marked out*, thus *takes up position*, by *occupying* a *position* on the basis of and against other *positions*), saying: "Philosophy states propositions which are theses: a thesis is said to be *correct or not*". You can say the same of tendencies, which are the effect of an apparatus of theses. A tendency is correct or deviant (it follows a correct line or more or less departs from a correct line, even to the point of becoming antagonistic to it). Correctness does not fall from the sky: it has to be worked for, and may involve considerable effort, and it must be continually reworked: there must be *adjustment*. There is no doubt that philosophy also has a theoretical function, but the question is: of what kind and under what conditions? You would need an extensive treatment of the subject in order to answer this question. The point that I wanted to bring home, and which seems to me, as things are, decisive for Marxism, is not only the "mixed-up" character of the theoretical and practical functions of philosophy, but the *primacy of the practical function over the theoretical function* in philosophy itself. It was to mark the decisive importance of this position (Thesis) and to clarify the primacy of the practical function that I put forward the thesis: "Philosophy is, in the last instance, class struggle in theory".

Correct theses, correct tendency, deviation ... These categories allow us to give a quite different account than the rationalist one of what happens in a "philosophy". It is not a Whole, made up of homogeneous propositions submitted to the verdict: truth or error. It is a system of *positions* (theses), and, through these positions, itself occupies positions in the theoretical class struggle. It takes up these positions in the struggle, with reference to the enemy and against the enemy. But the enemy is also not a unified body: the philosophical battlefield is thus not a reproduction, in the form of opposed "systems", of the simple rationalist antithesis between truth and error. It is not a question of, on the one hand, a homogeneous good side, and on the other a bad side. The positions of the two sides are usually mixed up together—not all enemies are equally enemies, and in the heat of the struggle it is not always easy to identify in the crowd the *main* enemy, and to recognize that there also exist secondary enemies, which may be fighting for old positions (as if the front line had not changed), or for "partial" or misplaced stakes. It is therefore necessary to fight, if not everywhere at the same time, at least on several fronts, taking account *both* of the principal tendency *and* of the secondary tendencies, *both* of the principal stake *and* of the secondary stakes, while all the time "working" to occupy correct positions. All this will obviously not come about through the miracle of a consciousness capable of dealing with all problems with perfect clarity. There is no miracle. A Marxist philosopher able to intervene in the theoretical class struggle must start out from positions already recognized and established in the theoretical battles of the history of the Labour Movement—but he can only understand the existing state of the theoretical and ideological "terrain" if he comes to know it both theoretically and practically: in and through struggle. It may be that in the course of his endeavours, even when he starts out from already established positions in order to attack open or disguised enemies, he will take up positions which in the course of struggle are shown to be *deviant* positions, out of step with the correct line which he is aiming for. There is nothing astonishing in that. The essential thing is that he should then recognize his deviation and rectify his positions in order to make them more correct.

But let us go further. If it is true that philosophy, "class struggle in theory", is, in the last instance, this interposed conflict between tendencies (idealism and materialism) which Engels, Lenin and Mao spoke about, then since this struggle does not take place in the sky but on the theoretical ground, and since this ground changes its features in the course of history, and since at the same time the question of what is at stake also takes on new forms, you can therefore say that the idealist and materialist tendencies which confront one another in all philosophical struggles, on the field of battle, *are never realized in a pure form in any "philosophy"*. In every "philosophy", even when it represents as explicitly and "coherently" as possible one of the two great antagonistic tendencies, there exist manifest or latent elements of the *other* tendency. And how could it be otherwise, if the role of every philosophy is to try to besiege the enemy's positions, therefore to interiorize the conflict in order to master it? Now this mastery may escape precisely whoever is trying to establish it. For a simple reason: the fate of philosophical theses does not depend only on the position on which they stand—because the class struggle in theory is always secondary in relation to the class struggle in general, because *there is something outside of philosophy* which constitutes it as philosophy, even though philosophy itself certainly does not want to recognize the fact.

That is why both in order to talk about and in order to judge a philosophy it is correct to start out from Mao's categories on contradiction. Now Mao talks above all about politics, even in his philosophical texts—and in this he is correct, more so than might be imagined—and he gives reasons for believing what Engels and Lenin suggested, which is the theoretical foundation of the Leninist "materialist reading" not only of Hegel, the absolute idealist, but of *all* philosophers without exception (including Engels, Lenin and Mao themselves): that in every philosophy, in every philosophical position, you must consider *the tendency in its contradiction*, and within this contradiction the *principal* tendency and the *secondary* tendency of the contradiction, and within each tendency the principal aspect, the secondary aspect, and so on. But it is not a question of an infinite and formal Platonic division. What must be understood is how this division is fixed in a series of *meeting-points*, in which the political-theoretical conjuncture defines the *central meeting-point* ("the decisive link") and the secondary meeting-points; or, to change the metaphor: the principal "front" and the secondary "fronts", the main point of attack and defence, the secondary points of attack and defence. This is indeed, in its present form, very schematic, and perhaps even scholastic! "Distinguo", said Molière's philosopher, thus caricaturing *division* (a major operation in philosophical practice, which by its demarcations *realizes* a tendency in the struggle) by transforming it into simple *distinctions*, which establish *objects* and *essences*. Lenin's and Mao's "distinctions", however, are actually not distinctions, which determine a result, but divisions, the lines of which open up a path. On this basis, work can begin—the tools are of course always open to improvement—on a better understanding of what happens in "philosophy" and in "a" philosophy.

Why these general remarks? In order to be able to characterize more adequately than before the "tendency" of my first essays. As far as their *principal* tendency is concerned, and in spite of the severe criticism which I must make of them, I think that they do in their own way, with the available means and in a precise conjuncture, defend positions useful to Marxist theory and to the proletarian class struggle: against the most threatening forms of bourgeois ideology— humanism, historicism, pragmatism, evolutionism, philosophical idealism, etc. But as far as their *secondary*, theoreticist tendency is concerned, these same essays express a deviation harmful to Marxist positions and the class struggle.

But it is not enough to talk about a balance: on the one side/on the other. You must at the same time reassess the effect of the whole, that is, the effects of each tendency on the other and the global result. You can then talk about a *contradictory* unity (between the principal, basically correct tendency, and the secondary, deviant tendency). Within this unity the theoreticist tendency has not been without consequences for the theses of the principal tendency. The more politically-oriented of my critics saw this: the class struggle does not figure *in its own right* in *For Marx* and *Reading Capital*; it only makes an appearance when I talk about the practical and social function of ideology; and of course (this is certainly the biggest mistake I made in my essays on Marxist philosophy) there was no mention of class position in theory. But, on the other hand, one can also not ignore, within their contradiction, the effects of the principal (correct) tendency on the secondary (deviant) tendency. Certain of my theoreticist theses, modified by their relation to the principal tendency, and especially those drawn from Spinoza, also played a role in the struggle.

It is not my place to say what the result of this enterprise was, what problems were brought to light, which others were clarified, what categories and concepts were proposed which perhaps allowed us a better understanding of what is offered and reserved to us by the extraordinary theory bearing the name of Marx. But I think that I can say that a "front" was opened; and that even if it was not held and defended all along the line in the same manner, with equally correct arguments, it remains true that in its essentials (as far as the principal tendency was concerned) it was held on the basis of dialectical-materialist principles. My opponents did certainly recognize the weak points. And even if they were not able to take an "overall view" (for some of them this did not matter), they did turn to their advantage those details which could be so used, and the rest they invented. It was a fair fight. But, what is more important, certain of the theses which we attacked were forced to retreat: for example, the humanist and historicist theses, etc.

But now that I have learned the lesson of "practice", and knowing, as Lenin said, that it is more serious not to recognize an error than simply to commit it, I can look to the past, reassess my theses in the light of the contradiction which haunted them, and "sort things out".

There are theses which obviously must be got rid of, because, in their existing state, they are false (wrongly oriented) and therefore harmful. For example the definition of philosophy as "Theory of theoretical practice" seems to me quite indefensible, and must be done away with. And it is not enough to suppress a formula: it is a question of rectifying, within their theoretical apparatus, all the effects and echoes of its reverberation. In the same way, the category of "theoretical practice", which was very useful in another context, is nevertheless dangerous in its ambiguity, since it uses one and the same term to cover both scientific practice and philosophical practice, and thus induces the idea that philosophy can be (a) science: but in a context which does not cause the ambiguity to become speculative confusion, this category may still, on occasion, play a role, since it serves as a materialist reminder to "theory" of *practice*. As far as the antithesis science/ideology is concerned, I have said enough about it for it to be understood that in its *general*, rationalist-speculative form, it must be rejected, and "reworked" from another point of view, which must split it up into the elements of the complex process of the "production" of knowledge, where the class conflicts of the practical ideologies combine with the theoretical ideologies, the existing sciences and philosophy.

But there are other theses and categories which can, even in their old form, render theoretical and political services in struggle and in research, though they may sometimes have to be displaced, even if imperceptibly (Lenin's "shades of opinion"), and inserted into a more correct theoretical apparatus: a better adjusted one. I will not go through all the examples now: anyone who wishes may work out the proof. The whole point is that the guide marks of the theoretical class struggle must be taken seriously, so that it is easier to recognize and to know the class enemy—that is, on the existing theoretical terrain (which itself must be better grasped) the philosophical enemies—and possible to take up more correct theoretical class positions, in order to hold and defend a better adjusted front.

What was essentially lacking in my first essays was the class struggle and its effects in theory—to realize this is to allow certain of the categories which I began with to be replaced in (more) correct positions. An example, to return to it for a moment, is the famous "break". I want to keep it in service, using the same term, but displacing it, or rather assigning it a place on the firm ground of the front of dialectical materialism, instead of letting it float dangerously in the atmosphere of a perilously idealist rationalism. But what does it mean to talk about assigning it a place in a better adjusted apparatus? It means, above all, to recognize—which I failed to do—that if there is indeed something at stake here, in connexion with those specific and indisputable facts of which the break is the index, this break is itself not the last word in the affair. For not only must it be admitted that the break does not explain itself, since it actually only records the simple fact that certain symptoms and effects were produced by a certain theoretical event, the historical appearance of a new science; it must also be said that this event in theoretical history has to be explained by the conjunction of the material, technical, social, political and ideological conditions which determine it. And, among these conditions, the most important in certain cases, and indisputably in the case of Marx, is the intervention of *class theoretical positions*, or what could be called the intervention of the philosophical "instance".[23]

In the case of Marxist theory, the event which can be called a "break", as I defined it above, in fact seems to have been produced like a "fatherless child" by the *meeting* of what Lenin called the Three Main Sources, or, to use a more accurate term, by the *intersection* or *conjunction*, against the background of the class struggles of 1840–48 (in which the class struggle between bourgeoisie and proletariat was more important than the historical class struggle between the feudal class and the bourgeoisie), of *lines* of demarcation and of extremely complex theoretical and ideological *lineages*, which, aimlessly and each for itself, *criss-cross* in the resultant field of their intersection.

Now it is possible and necessary to distinguish as *dominant* in this contradictory process what we might call the *change in the class theoretical position* of the historical "individual" Marx-Engels. This change of class theoretical position took place, under the influence of the political class struggles and of their lessons, *in philosophy*. This claim is not at all strange if, as I suggest, philosophy really is, in the last instance, class struggle in theory.

I must insist on this point: in fact it takes me directly back to my first essays. At that time I said: the essential question is that of Marxist *philosophy*. I still think so. But, if I did see (in 1960–65) *what* the essential question was, I now see that I did not understand it very well ... I defined philosophy as "Theory of theoretical practice", thus con-

---

23. Again a precise example. I am indeed using the term *instance* intentionally. This again is a category which, until a better adapted one comes along, must be kept in use but put to work in its right place. Now recently a wind has been blowing, among Communist philosophers, strong enough to turn every instance upside-down ... But just because some use the term "instance" on every menu, whether it has any relevance or not, we do not need to follow them. For my part, I certainly did make a rather free use of "instances", because at the time I had nothing better; and I will now stop talking about the "economic instance", but will maintain the valuable term of instance for the Superstructure: the State, Law *and Philosophy*.

ferring on it, by the use of the single term "theory", the same status as a science. In *theoretically* overestimating philosophy, I underestimated it *politically*, as those who correctly accused me of not "bringing in" the class struggle were quick to point out. Another proof of this is the introduction, in *Lenin and Philosophy*, where I did rectify the essential point of my deviation in proposing a new definition of philosophy ("politics in theory"), of the system of "double, *equal* representation" at the level of the Sciences and of Politics, and the Thesis borrowed, not accidentally, from Hegel: philosophy *always* rises when dusk has fallen, in the historical period following a unique event—not the event of a political-ideological revolution, but the event of the birth or modification of the Sciences *themselves*. This was still an improvised solution, that is, a semi-compromise, which, while making some allowance for the events of the history of the sciences and for the philosophical reactions to them, did not really do them justice, because *a priori* it did them justice too well. If I now propose a different formula: "philosophy is, in the last instance, class struggle in theory", it is precisely in order to be able to give *both* the class struggle (the last instance) *and* the other social practices (among them scientific practice) their due in their "relation" to philosophy.

On this basis, new fields of research are opened up.

On the Evolution of the Young Marx

I

If I were asked to sum up in a few words the essential *Thesis* which I wanted to defend in my philosophical essays, I would say: Marx founded a new science, the science of History. I would add: this scientific discovery is a theoretical and political event unprecedented in human history. And I would specify: this event is irreversible.

A theoretical event. Before Marx, what one could call the "History Continent" was occupied by ideological conceptions derived from the religious, moral or legal-political sphere—in short, by philosophies of history. These claimed to offer a representation of what happens in societies and in history. In fact they only succeeded in masking, within distorting and misleading concepts, the mechanisms which really do govern societies and history. This mystification was not an accident: it was linked to their function. These conceptions were in fact only the theoretical detachment of practical ideologies (religion, morality, legal ideology, politics, etc.) whose essential function is to reproduce the relations of production (= of exploitation) in class societies. Marx "opened" the "History Continent" by breaking with these ideological conceptions. He opened it: by the principles of historical materialism, by *Capital* and his other works. He opened it: for, as Lenin says, Marx only laid the "corner-stones" of an immense domain which his successors continued to exploit, and the vast extent of the field and the new problems posed demand an unremitting effort.

A political event. For Marx's scientific discovery has been since the very beginning and has become more and more the object and the stake of a fierce and implacable class struggle. When he demonstrated that human history is the history of class societies, therefore of exploitation and of class domination, and thus finally of class struggle, when he demonstrated the mechanisms of exploitation and of capitalist domination, Marx collided directly with the interests of the ruling classes. Their ideologists let fly against him, and even now are still intensifying their attacks. But the exploited classes, and above all the workers, recognized "their" truth in Marx's scientific theory: they adopted it, and made it a weapon in their revolutionary class struggle. This recognition bears a name in history: it is the *Union* (or, as Lenin said, the Fusion) *of the Labour Movement and Marxist Theory*. This Encounter, this Union, this Fusion, have never taken place spontaneously or easily. For the Labour Movement, which existed long before the appearance and spread of Marxist theory, came under the influence of petty-bourgeois ideological conceptions, like utopian socialism, anarchism, etc. A great deal of work and a very long ideological and political struggle were needed before the Union could take place and acquire a historical existence. The very conditions of its realization and existence mean that this Union cannot be a once-and-for-all victory. It does not exist in isolation from the class struggle, and must be incessantly defended in the course of a bitter class struggle against the deviations and crises which threaten it: the evidence is the treachery, yesterday, of the Second International, and today the split in the International Communist Movement.

One fact is indisputable: for a hundred years the whole history of humanity has depended on the Union of the Labour Movement (and of the oppressed peoples) and Marxist Theory (which became Marxist-Leninist Theory). We only need to step back a little to see that, in different but convergent forms, this reality now easily dominates the scene of world history: the struggle of the proletariat and of the oppressed peoples against Imperialism. This fact is *irreversible*.

II

We could satisfy ourselves with these remarks. But if we

wish (whatever our place in this struggle) to advance in the exploration of the "History Continent", or (what, in one precise respect, comes to the same thing) to arrive at an active understanding of the forms of the present-day proletarian class struggle, we must go further. We must ask ourselves: under what conditions was Marx's scientific discovery possible?

This question may look like a detour. But it is not. It may look like a theoretical question. In fact it has political implications which are clearly vital.

III

When in my earlier essays I showed that Marx's scientific discovery represented a "break" [*coupure* or *rupture*] with previous ideological conceptions of history, what did I do? What did I do when I spoke of a "break" between science and ideology? What did I do when I spoke of ideology?

I developed a formal analysis, whose significance must now be indicated and whose limits must be traced.

Above all, I arrived at a *conclusion*. I took cognizance of a fact, of a theoretical event: the appearance of a scientific theory of History in a domain hitherto occupied by conceptions which I called ideological. Let us leave aside for a moment this description: *ideological*.

I showed that there existed an irreducible difference between Marx's theory and these conceptions. To prove it, I compared their conceptual content and their mode of functioning.

Their conceptual content: I showed that Marx had replaced the old basic concepts (which I called notions) of the philosophies of History with absolutely new, unheard-of concepts, not to be found in the old conceptions. Where the philosophies of History talked about man, the economic subject, need, the system of needs, civil society, alienation, theft, injustice, spirit, liberty—where they talked about "society" itself—Marx began to talk about the mode of production, social formation, infrastructure, superstructure, ideologies, classes, class struggle, etc. I concluded that there was no continuity (even in the case of Classical Political Economy) between the system of Marxist concepts and the system of pre-Marxist notions. This absence of a relation of continuity, this theoretical difference, this dialectical "leap", I called an "epistemological break" [*coupure* or *rupture*].

Their mode of functioning: I showed that *in practice* Marxist theory functioned quite differently from the old pre-Marxist conceptions. It seemed to me that the system of basic concepts of Marxist theory functioned like the "theory" of a science: as a "basic" conceptual apparatus, opened to the "infinitude" (Lenin) of its object, that is, designed ceaselessly to pose and confront new problems and ceaselessly to produce new pieces of knowledge. Let us say: it functioned as a (provisional) *truth*, *for* the (endless) conquest of new knowledge, itself capable (in certain conjunctures) of renewing this first truth. In comparison, it appeared that the basic theory of the old conceptions, far from functioning as a (provisional) *truth*, *for* the production of new pieces of knowledge, actually tried in practice to operate as the *truth of* History, as complete, definitive and absolute knowledge of History, in short as a closed system, excluding development because lacking an object in the scientific sense of the term, and thus only ever finding in reality its own mirror reflection. Here too I concluded that there was a radical difference between Marx's theory and earlier conceptions, and I talked about the "epistemological break" [*coupure* or *rupture*].

Finally, I called these earlier conceptions *ideological*, and understood the "epistemological break", the proof of which I had established, as a theoretical discontinuity between Marxist *science* on the one hand, and its *ideological* prehistory on the other. I should specify: not between science in general and ideology in general, but between Marxist science and *its own* ideological prehistory.

But what allowed me to say that the pre-Marxist conceptions were ideological? Or, what comes to the same thing, what sense did I give to the term *ideology*?

An ideological conception does not carry the inscription *ideology* on its forehead or on its heart, whatever sense you give to the word. On the contrary, it presents itself as the Truth. It can only be identified from outside, after the event: from the standpoint of the existence of a Marxist science of History. I repeat: not simply from the standpoint of the existence of Marxist science as science, but from the standpoint of Marxist science as the science of History.

In fact, every science, as soon as it arises in the history of theories and is shown to be a science, causes its own theoretical prehistory, with which it breaks, to appear as quite erroneous, false, untrue. That is how it treats it in practice: and this treatment is a moment in its history. Nevertheless there always exist philosophers who will draw edifying conclusions; who will draw out of this recurrent (retrospective) practice an idealist theory of the opposition between Truth and Error, between Knowledge and Ignorance, and even (provided that the term "ideology" is taken in a non-Marxist sense) between Science and Ideology, in general.

This effect of recurrence (retrospection) is also a factor in the case of Marxist science: when this science appears, it necessarily shows up *its own* prehistory as erroneous, but at the same time it also shows it up as *ideological* in the Marxist sense of the term. Better, it shows up its own prehistory as erroneous *because* ideological, and in practice treats it as such. Not only does it indicate error—it explains the historical reason for error. Thus it rules out the exploitation of the "break" between the science and its prehistory as an idealist antithesis of Truth and Error, of Knowledge and Ignorance.

On what principle does this difference, this unprecedented advantage rest? On the fact that the science founded by Marx is the science of the history of social formations. Because of this it gives, for the first time, a scientific content to the concept of *ideology*. Ideologies are not pure illusions (Error), but bodies of representations existing in institutions and practices: they figure in the superstructure, and are rooted in class struggle. If the science founded by Marx shows up the theoretical conceptions of its own prehistory as ideological, it is therefore not simply to denounce them as false: it is also to point out that they claim to be true, and were accepted and continue to be accepted as true—and to show why this is so. If the theoretical conceptions with which Marx broke (let us say, to simplify matters: the philosophies of history) deserve to be called ideological, it is because they were the *theoretical detachments* of practical *ideologies* which performed necessary functions in the reproduction of the relations of production of a given class society.

If this is true, then the "break" between Marxist science and its ideological prehistory refers us to something quite different from a theory of the difference between science and ideology, to something quite different from an epistemology. It refers us on the one hand to a theory of the superstructure, in which the State and Ideologies figure (I have tried to say a few words about this in the article on Ideological State Apparatuses). It refers us on the other hand to a theory of the material (production), social (division of labour, class struggle), ideological and philosophical conditions of the processes of production of knowledge. These two theories are based in the last instance on historical materialism.

But if this is true, Marx's scientific theory itself must answer the question of the conditions of its own "irruption" in the field of ideological conceptions with which it broke.

IV

The great Marxists (Marx above all, Engels, then Lenin) certainly felt that it was not enough to *note* the appearance of a new science, but that an analysis must also be provided, in conformity with the principles of Marxist science, of the conditions of its appearance. The first elements of this analysis can be found in Engels and Lenin, in the form of the "Three Sources" of Marxism: German philosophy, English political economy and French socialism.

But this old metaphor of "sources", which contains in itself idealist notions (origin, interiority of the current, etc.), must not lead us into error. What is quite remarkable about this "classical" theory is, first, that it attempts to understand Marx's discovery not in terms of individual or original genius, but in terms of a *conjunction* of different and independent theoretical elements (*Three* sources). It then presents this conjunction as having produced a fundamentally new effect in respect of the elements which entered into the conjunction: an example of a "leap" or "qualitative change", an essential category of the materialist dialectic.

But Engels and Lenin do not stop there. They do not defend a purely internal, purely "epistemological" conception of the appearance of Marxist science. They recall that these three theoretical elements exist against a historical background: a material, social and political history, dominated by decisive transformations in the forces and relations of production, by centuries of class struggle pitting the rising bourgeoisie against the feudal aristocracy, and finally dominated by the first great actions of the proletarian class struggle. In a word, they remind us that it is practical (economic, political, ideological) realities which are *represented* theoretically, in more or less abstract form, in German philosophy, English political economy and French socialism.

They are represented, but at the same time they are also *deformed*, mystified and masked, because these theoretical elements are by nature profoundly ideological. It is here that the decisive question arises.

In fact it is not enough to point out that the conjunction of these three theoretical elements caused Marxist science to appear. We must also ask *how* this ideological *conjunction* could produce a scientific *disjunction*, how this encounter could produce a "break". In other words, we must ask how and why, when this conjunction took place, Marxist thought was able to *leave ideology*: or, again, what the *displacement* was that produced such a prodigious transformation, what the change was that could bring to light what was hidden, overturn what was accepted, and discover an unknown necessity in the facts.

I want to propose the first elements of an answer to this question, by proposing the following thesis: it was by *moving* to take up absolutely new, proletarian class positions that Marx realized the possibilities of the theoretical conjunction from which the science of history was born.

V
This can be demonstrated by running through the main lines of the "moments" of the "evolution" of the young Marx's thought. Four years separate the liberal-radical

articles of the *Rheinische Zeitung* (1841) from the revolutionary break [*rupture*] of 1845, recorded in the *Theses on Feuerbach* and *The German Ideology*, in the famous phrases proclaiming the "settling of accounts with our erstwhile philosophical consciousness", and the arrival of a new philosophy which will no longer "interpret the world" but "change it". In these four years we see a young son of the Rhenish bourgeoisie move from bourgeois-radical political and philosophical positions to petty-bourgeois-humanist positions, then to communist-materialist positions (an unprecedented revolutionary materialism).

Let me specify the aspects of this "evolution".

We see the young Marx at the same time change the *object* of his thought (roughly, he moves from Law to the State, then to Political Economy), change his *philosophical* position (he moves from Hegel to Feuerbach, then to a revolutionary materialism), and change his *political* position (he moves from radical bourgeois liberalism to petty-bourgeois humanism, then to communism). Although these changes are not completely in phase, there are profound links between them. But they should not be fused into a single, formless unity, because they intervene at different levels, and each plays a distinct role in the process of transformation of the young Marx's thought.

We can say that, in this process, in which the *object* occupies the front of the stage, it is the (class) political position that occupies the determinant place; but it is the philosophical position that occupies the central place, because it guarantees the theoretical relation between the political position and the object of Marx's thought. This can be verified empirically in the history of the young Marx. It was indeed politics which allowed him to move from one object to another (schematically: from Press Laws to the State, then to Political Economy), but this move was realized and expressed each time in the form of a new philosophical position. On the one hand the philosophical position appears to be the theoretical expression of the political (and ideological) class position. On the other hand this translation of the political position into theory (in the form of a philosophical position) appears to be the condition of the theoretical relation to the object of thought.

If this is true, and if philosophy really does represent politics in theory, we can say that the philosophical position of the young Marx represents, in its variations, the *class theoretical conditions of* his thought. If this is true, then it is no surprise that the break of 1845, which ushered in a new science, is first expressed in the form of a philosophical break [*rupture*], of a "settling of accounts" with an erstwhile philosophical consciousness, and in terms of the proclamation of an unprecedented philosophical position.

This astonishing dialectic can be seen at work in the *1844 Manuscripts*. When you examine them closely, you appreciate the extent of the theoretical drama which Marx must have lived through in this text (he never published it, he never referred to it again). The crisis of the *Manuscripts* is summed up in the untenable contradiction between political and philosophical positions which confront one another in the treatment of the object: Political Economy. Politically, Marx wrote the *Manuscripts* as a Communist, and thus made the impossible theoretical gamble of attempting to use, in the service of his convictions, the notions, analyses and contradictions of the bourgeois economists, putting in the forefront what he calls "alienated labour", which he could not yet grasp as capitalist exploitation. Theoretically, he wrote these manuscripts on the basis of petty-bourgeois philosophical positions, making the impossible political gamble of introducing Hegel *into* Feuerbach, so as to be able to speak of labour *in* alienation, and of History *in* Man. The *Manuscripts* are the moving but implacable symptom of an unbearable crisis: the crisis which brings an object enclosed in its ideological limits up against incompatible political and theoretical class positions.

We find the solution of this crisis in the *Theses on Feuerbach* and in *The German Ideology*: or at least we find a claim that it is solved, the "germ" of a "new conception of the world" (Engels). The change which the *Theses* briefly indicate is a change, not in Marx's political position, but in his philosophical position. Marx finally abandons Feuerbach, breaks with the whole philosophical tradition of "interpreting the world", and advances into the unknown territory of a revolutionary materialism. This new position now expresses

Marx's political position in philosophy. In other words: Marx was taking a first step, but a decisive and irreversible one, towards proletarian class theoretical (philosophical) positions.

Here again it is politics which is the determinant element: the ever deeper engagement in the political struggles of the proletariat. Here again it is, from the theoretical point of view, philosophy which occupies the central place. It is as a consequence of this class theoretical position that Marx's treatment of his object, Political Economy, takes on a radically new character: breaking with all ideological conceptions to lay down and develop the principles of the science of History.

This is how I take the liberty of interpreting the theory of the "Three sources". The conjunction of the three theoretical elements (German philosophy, English political economy, French socialism) could only produce its effect (Marx's scientific discovery) by means of a *displacement* which led the young Marx not only onto proletarian class positions but also onto proletarian theoretical positions. Without the politics nothing would have happened; but without the philosophy, the politics would not have found its theoretical expression, indispensable to the scientific knowledge of its object.

I will add just a few words more. First to say that the new philosophical position announced in the *Theses* is only announced; it is not therefore given to us at a stroke or ready-made; it continues to be developed, silently or explicitly, in the later theoretical and political work of Marx and his successors, and more generally in the history of the Union between the Labour Movement and Marxist Theory. And this development is determined by the double effect of Marxist-Leninist science and practice.

Second, to point out that it is no surprise that the adoption of a proletarian philosophical position (even "in germ") is essential to the foundation of a science of History, that is, to an analysis of the mechanisms of class exploitation and domination. In every class society these mechanisms are covered-up-masked-mystified by an enormous coating of ideological representations, of which the philosophies of History, etc., are the theoretical form. For the mechanisms to become visible, it is necessary to *leave* these ideologies, that is, to "settle accounts" with the philosophical consciousness which is the basic theoretical expression of these ideologies. It is therefore necessary to abandon the theoretical position of the ruling classes, and take up a position from which these mechanisms can become visible: the proletarian standpoint. It is not enough to adopt a proletarian *political* position. This political position must be worked out into a theoretical (philosophical) position so that the causes and mechanisms of what is visible from the proletarian standpoint may be grasped and understood. Without this *displacement*, the science of History is unthinkable and impossible.

VI

I will add, finally, to come back to where I began, that this detour *via* the conditions of the appearance of the science of History is not a matter of scholasticism. On the contrary: it brings us back to earth. For what was demanded of the young Marx is still, and more than ever, demanded of us. More than ever, in order to "develop" Marxist theory, that is, in order to analyse the new capitalist-imperialist forms of exploitation and domination, more than ever, in order to make possible a correct Union between the Labour Movement and Marxist-Leninist Theory, we need to stand on proletarian positions in theory (in philosophy): to stand on such positions, which means to work them out, on the basis of proletarian *political* positions, by means of a radical critique of all the ideologies of the ruling class. Without revolutionary theory, said Lenin, there can be no revolutionary movement. We can add: without a proletarian position in theory (in philosophy), there can be no "development" of Marxist theory, and no correct Union between the Labour Movement and Marxist Theory.

3.
Is it Simple
to be a Marxist
in Philosophy?

The following text contains the main arguments with which Louis Althusser accompanied his submission, at the University of Picardy, of certain of his earlier writings[1] for the degree of doctorat d' Etat.

> "The dialectical form of exposition is only
> correct when it knows its limits."
> Marx, *A Contribution to the Critique of
> Political Economy*.

I think that I shall neither surprise nor upset anyone when I confess that I wrote none of these texts the little *Montesquieu*, the articles in *For Marx*, the two chapters in *Reading Capital*—with a view to presenting them as a university thesis. It is however true that 26 years ago, in 1949–50, I did place before Mr Hyppolite and Mr Jankélévitch a project for a *grande thèse* (as it used to be called) on politics and philosophy in the eighteenth century in France with a *petite thèse* on Jean-Jacques Rousseau's *Second Discourse*. And I never really abandoned this project, as my essay on Montesquieu shows. Why do I mention this point? Because it concerns the texts placed before you. I was already a Communist, and I was therefore trying to be a Marxist as well—that is, I was trying to the best of my ability to understand what Marxism *means*. Thus I intended this work on philosophy and politics in the eighteenth century as a necessary propaedeutic of an understanding of Marx's thought. In fact, I was already beginning to practice philosophy in a certain way, a way which I have never abandoned.

First of all I was beginning to make use of the eighteenth-century authors as a *theoretical detour*, a process which seems to me indispensable not only to the understanding of a philosophy but to its very existence. A philosophy does not make its appearance in the world as Minerva appeared to the society of Gods and men. It only exists in so far as it occupies a position, and it only occupies this position in so far as it has conquered it in the thick of an already occupied world.

1. *Montesquieu: Politics and History; Feuerbach's "Philosophical manifestoes"; For Marx;* the contribution to *Reading Capital* [*translator's note*].

It therefore only exists in so far as this conflict has made it something distinct, and this distinctive character can only be won and imposed in an indirect way, by a detour involving ceaseless study of other, existing positions. This detour is the form of the conflict which determines what side a philosophy takes in the battle and on the "Kampfplatz" (Kant), the battlefield which is philosophy. Because if the philosophy of philosophers is this perpetual war (to which Kant wanted to put an end by introducing the everlasting peace of his own philosophy), then no philosophy can exist within this theoretical relation of force except in so far as it marks itself off from its opponents and lays siege to that part of the positions which they have had to occupy in order to guarantee their power over the enemy whose impress they bear. If—as Hobbes says, speaking perhaps to empty benches, and with reference as much to philosophy as to the society of men—war is a generalized state, and leaves nowhere in the world for a shelter, and if it produces its own condition as its own result, which means that every war is essentially *preventive*, it is possible to understand that the war of philosophies, in which systems come into conflict, presupposes the preventive strike of positions against one another, and thus the necessary use by a philosophy of a detour *via* other philosophies in order to define and defend its own positions. If philosophy is, in the last instance, class struggle at the level of theory, as I have recently argued, then this struggle takes the form, proper to philosophy, of theoretical demarcation, detour and production of a distinctive position. To prove it, I need only refer, aside from the whole of philosophical history, to Marx himself, who was only able to define himself by reference to Hegel and by marking himself off from Hegel. And I think that, from afar, I have followed his example, by allowing myself to refer back to Spinoza in order to understand why Marx had to refer back to Hegel.

Of course this conception of philosophy as struggle, and, in the last instance, as class struggle in theory, implied a reversal of the traditional relation between philosophy and politics. So I went to work on a study of political philosophers and "ordinary" philosophers, from Machiavelli to Hegel, *via* Hobbes, Spinoza, Locke, Montesquieu, Rousseau and Kant. I claimed that it was necessary to get rid of the suspect division between philosophy and politics which at one and the same time treats the political figures as inferior, that is, as non-philosophers or Sunday-afternoon philosophers, and also implies that the political positions of philosophers must be sought *exclusively* in the texts in which they talk explicitly about politics. On the one hand I was of the opinion that every political thinker, even if he says almost nothing about philosophy, like Machiavelli, can nevertheless be considered a philosopher in a strong sense; and on the other hand I held that every philosopher, even if he says almost nothing about politics, like Descartes, can nevertheless be considered a political thinker in a strong sense, because the politics of philosophers—that is, the politics which make philosophies what they are—are something quite different from the political ideas of their authors. For if philosophy is in the last instance class struggle at the level of theory, the politics which constitute philosophy (like the philosophy which supports the thought of political thinkers) cannot be identified with such-and-such an episode of the political struggle, nor even with the political inclinations of the authors. The politics which constitute philosophy bear on and turn around a quite different question: *that of the ideological hegemony of the ruling class*, whether it is a question of organizing it, strengthening it, defending it or fighting against it. Here I am using formulae which I was not earlier in a position to put forward. But if I may say so, I was little by little discovering, as I challenged some accepted ideas, something resembling what I later called a "new practice of philosophy", and having discovered the need for this new practice, I straightaway started, for better or worse, to put it into practice—with the result, in any case, that it did later provide me with a special way of approaching Marx.

If I seemed to abandon this eighteenth-century theoretical propaedeutic, which in fact continued to inspire me, it was certainly not exclusively for personal reasons. What are called circumstances, those which I mention in the Preface to *For Marx*, what after the Twentieth Congress of the

CPSU was baptised by the name (without a concept) of the "personality cult", together with the rightist interpretations which then engulfed Marxism, celebrating or exploiting liberation or the hope of its coming in philosophies of man, of his freedom, of his designs, of transcendence, etc.— these circumstances obliged me to throw myself into the battle. Keeping everything in proportion, you might say that like the young Marx, writing for the *Rheinische Zeitung*, who was "forced to give an opinion on some practical questions" (the theft of wood or the Prussian censorship), I too was soon forced—on pain of being misunderstood on account of my silence—to "give an opinion" on some burning questions of Marxist theory. The occasion for me to do so was accidental; that is, it happened that in 1960 I had to write a simple review for the journal *La Pensée* of an international collection of articles on the young Marx. This review became a counter-attack, which did not simply take the accepted theses to task but attacked them from the flank; thus I displaced the ground of the debate and to this end proposed a certain number of theses which since that time I have continued to argue, to work on and then to rectify.

The reason that I recall these circumstances is that I want to make a second remark about the polemical or—to put it bluntly—the political character of my philosophical essays. Those essays which are now placed before you had to declare openly that struggle is at the heart of every philosophy. Of course, what I have just said should make it clear that they are not made up of politics in the raw, since they are philosophical, nor are they simply polemical, a war of words, since they come out of a reasoned argument, and because the whole meaning of the effort is to put forward and defend the simple idea that a Marxist cannot fight, in what he writes or in what he does, *without thinking out the struggle*, without thinking out the conditions, the mechanisms and the stakes of the battle in which he is engaged and which engages him. These texts are thus explicit interventions in a definite conjuncture: political interventions in the existing world of Marxist philosophy, directed at one and the same time against dogmatism and the rightist critique of dogmatism; and also philosophical interventions in politics, against economism and its humanist "appendix". But since they appealed to the history of the Labour Movement and to Marx, they could not be reduced to a simple commentary on the conjuncture. And I want to say this: whatever might be thought about its weaknesses and its limits, this philosophical intervention was the work of a member of the Communist Party, acting—even if I was at first isolated, even if I was not always listened to, even if I was then and still am criticized for what I said—within the Labour Movement and for it, thus the work of a militant trying to take politics seriously in order to think out its conditions, limits and effects within theory itself, trying in consequence to define the line and forms of intervention. It cannot be denied that such an initiative involved great efforts and risks. And since I am talking about risks, I may be allowed to talk about one of them (leaving the others undiscussed), the one which concerns the theoretical *position* of my essays.

Here it is. In the debate in which I became involved, I chose, with respect to *certain* politically and theoretically strategic points, to defend radical theses. These, literally stated, looked paradoxical and even theoretically provocative. Two or three examples, to illustrate this choice.

I argued and wrote that "theory is a practice", and proposed the category of theoretical practice, a scandalous proposal in some people's eyes. Now this thesis, like every thesis, has to be considered in terms of its effect in drawing a demarcation line, that is, in defining a position of opposition. Its first effect was, *in opposition to all forms of pragmatism*, to justify the thesis of the relative autonomy of theory and thus the right of Marxist theory not to be treated as a slave to tactical political decisions, but to be allowed to develop, in alliance with political and other practices, without betraying its own needs. But at the same time this thesis had another effect, *in opposition to the idealism of pure theory*, of stamping theory with the materialism of practice.

Another radical formulation: the internal character of the criteria of validation of theoretical practice. I was able to cite Lenin, who himself put forward this provocative thesis (among so many others): "Marx's theory is all-powerful because it is true" (it is not because it is verified by its successes and failures that it is true, but because it is true that it is verifiable by its successes and failures). But I brought in other arguments: that mathematics do not require the application of their theorems in physics and chemistry in order to prove them; that the experimental sciences do not require the technical application of their results in order to prove them. For demonstration and proof are the product of definite and specific material and theoretical apparatuses and procedures, internal to each science. There again it is the relative autonomy of theory which was at stake, not this time in opposition to theoretical idealism, but in opposition to the pragmatic and empiricist lack of discrimination which made it impossible to distinguish practices from one another, like the cows in the Hegelian night.

One last example: I argued the thesis of Marx's theoretical anti-humanism. A precise thesis, but one whose precise meaning some people did not want to understand, and which roused against me all the world's bourgeois and social-democratic ideology, even within the International Labour Movement. Why did I take up such radical positions? I shall not shelter behind the argument of manifest ignorance, which can still be useful, but at the proper time. I want first of all to defend the principle of taking up these radical positions. Because obviously they were met with cries of dogmatism, speculation, scorn for practice, for the concrete, for man, etc. This indignation was not without a certain piquancy.

For my part, since I was not unaware of the relation which I mentioned above between philosophy and politics, I remembered Machiavelli, whose rule of Method, rarely stated but always practised, was that one must think *in extremes*, which means within a position from which one states border-line theses, or, to make the thought possible, one occupies the place of the impossible. What does Machiavelli do? In order to change something in his country's history, therefore in the minds of the readers whom he wants to provoke into thought and so into volition, Machiavelli explains, off-stage as it were, that one must rely on one's own strength, that is in fact *not rely on anything*, neither on an existing State nor on an existing Prince, but on the non-existent impossibility: a new Prince in a new Principality.

I found an echo of and a basis for this argument in Lenin. He of course, a few years after *What is to be Done?*, in response to certain criticisms which had been made of his formulae, replied in the form of the theory of the bending of the stick. When a stick is bent in the wrong direction, said Lenin, it is necessary if you want to put matters right—that is, if you want to straighten it and keep it straight—to grasp it and bend it durably in the opposite direction. This simple formula seems to me to contain a whole theory of the effectiveness of speaking the truth, a theory deeply rooted in Marxist practice. Contrary to the whole rationalist tradition, which only requires a straight, true idea in order to correct a bent, false idea, Marxism considers that ideas only have a historical existence in so far as they are taken up and incorporated in the materiality of social relations. Behind the relations between simple ideas there thus stand relations of force, which place certain ideas in power (those which can be schematically called the ruling ideology) and hold other ideas in submission (which can be called the oppressed ideology), until the relation of force is changed. It follows that if you want to change historically existing ideas, even in the apparently abstract domain called philosophy, you cannot content yourself with simply preaching the naked truth, and waiting for its anatomical obviousness to "enlighten" minds, as our eighteenth-century ancestors used to say: you are forced, since you want to force a change in ideas, to recognize the force which is keeping them bent, by applying a counter-force capable of destroying this power and bending the stick in the opposite direction so as to put the ideas right.

All this outlines the logic of a social process whose scope is obviously wider than any written text. But in a written text like *What is to be Done?* the only form which this relation of forces can take is its presence, its recognition and its anticipation in certain radical formulae, which cause the relation of force between the new ideas and the dominant ideas to be felt in the very statement of the theses themselves. If I might, in my own modest way, allow myself to be inspired and empowered by these examples, I would say: yes, I did consciously confront and deal with the relation between ideas as a relation of force, and yes, I did consciously "think in extremes" about some points which I considered important and bend the stick in the opposite direction. Not for the pleasure of provocation, but to alert my readers to the existence of this relation of forces, to provoke them in this connexion and to produce definite effects, not in function of some belief in the omnipotence of theory, for which I have been reproached by certain "headmasters" of the school of philosophy, but on the contrary in the materialist knowledge of the weakness of theory left to itself, that is, in the consciousness of the conditions of force which theory must recognize and to which it must defer if it is to have a chance of transforming itself into a real power.

As a proof of what I have been saying, I would be happy, when the opportunity offers itself, to argue the point that this relation of force, counter-bending and bending, this *extremism* in the formulation of theses, belongs quite properly to philosophy, and that even if they did not admit as much, as Lenin did in passing and from behind the shelter of a common maxim, the great philosophers always practised it, whether they hid this fact behind an idealist disclaimer or brought it out into the full light of day in their treatment of the "scandals" of materialism.

It remains true that in bending the stick in the opposite direction, you run a risk: of bending it too little, or too much, the risk which every philosopher takes. Because in this situation, in which social forces and interests are at stake, but can never be untangled with absolute certainty, there is no court of final appeal. If you intervene too abruptly you run the risk of not immediately finding the mark; if you bend the stick too little or too much you run the risk of finding yourself being pulled back into error. This, as you perhaps know, is what I publicly admitted to have happened to some extent in my own case, when I recognized in 1967 and explained more recently in the *Elements of Self-criticism* that my writings of 1965, which have been laid before you, were impaired by a theoreticist tendency and just a little compromised by a flirt with structuralist terminology. But to be able to explain these failings I needed the perspective of time—not just a ten years interval, but the experience of the effects caused by my writings, of further work and of self-criticism. It has been written: you need to understand. I would add: especially to understand what you yourself have written.

Before discussing the detailed argument of my essays, a word about their very general objective.

This objective can be made out from the titles of my books: *For Marx*, *Reading Capital*. For these titles are slogans. I think that I can speak here for figures of my generation, who have lived through Nazism and fascism, the Popular Front, the Spanish War, the War and the Resistance, and the Stalin period. Caught up in the great class struggles of contemporary history, we had engaged ourselves in the struggles of the Labour Movement and wanted to become Marxists. Now it was not easy to be a Marxist and to find one's feet within Marxist theory, even after the Twentieth Congress, since the dogmatism of the preceding period lived on, now in conjunction with its counterpoint, all that "Marxist" philosophical twaddle about man. And since this twaddle was based on the letter of the works of the young Marx, it was necessary to return to Marx in order to throw a little light on ideas clouded over by the trials of history. I do not want to lay stress on the political importance of this operation; it did however have something original about it, for which I have never been forgiven, in the fact that it criticized dogmatism not from the right-wing positions of humanist ideology, but from the left-wing positions of theoretical anti-humanism, anti-empiricism and anti-economism. I was not alone in the operation: as I later found out, others—not only della Volpe in Italy but also certain young Soviet thinkers whose writings have not been widely published—had also, in their own manner, set out on the same path. We were attempting to give back to Marxist theory, which had been treated by dogmatism and by Marxist humanism as the first available ideology, something of its status as a theory, a revolutionary theory. Marx had expressed the hope, in the Preface to *Capital*, for "a reader who is willing ... to think for himself". In order to try to understand what Marx had thought, the very least that we had to do was to return to Marx and "think for ourselves" about what he had thought.

Thus, in opposition to the subversion to which Marx's thought had been subjected, it seemed to me indispensable to lay stress on one simple idea: the unprecedented and revolutionary character of this thought. *Unprecedented*, because Marx had—in a work of conceptual elaboration which begins with *The German Ideology* and culminates in *Capital*—founded what we might call, as a first approximation, the science of history. *Revolutionary*, because this scientific discovery which armed the proletariat in its struggle caused a complete upset in philosophy: not only by causing philosophy to revise its categories in order to bring them into line with the new science and its effects, but also and above all by giving philosophy the means, in the term of an understanding of its real relation to the class struggle, of taking responsibility for and transforming its own practice.

It is this innovation, this radical difference between Marx and his predecessors, that I wanted not only to bring out but also to clarify and if possible to explain, because I considered it to be politically and theoretically *vital* for the Labour Movement and its allies and still do consider it vital *for this difference to be grasped*. To this end I had to establish myself at the level of the new philosophy, produced by Marx in the course of his scientific revolution, and in a movement of thought close to Spinoza and sanctioned by Marx to try to grasp this difference on the basis of the newly acquired truth. But to the same end I had to grasp the philosophy capable of grasping the difference, that is, I had to obtain a clear view of Marx's own philosophy. Now everyone knows that the mature Marx left us nothing in this line except the extraordinary 1857 Introduction to *A Contribution to the Critique of Political Economy* and the intention, which he never realized, of writing a dozen pages on the dialectic. No doubt Marx's philosophy is, as Lenin said, contained in *Capital*, but in a practical state, just as it is also contained in the great struggles of the Labour Movement. I decided that it had to be extracted, and basing myself on the available fragments and examples, I tried to give it a form resembling its concept. That is why the question of Marxist philosophy naturally occupied the centre of my attention. I did not make it the centre of the world, I did not raise philosophy to the level of command, but I had to make this philosophical detour in order to grapple with the radical character of Marx's work.

This conviction has always been with me. I would now formulate it differently than in *For Marx* and *Reading Capital*, but I consider that I made no mistake in locating philosophy as the place from which Marx can be understood, because that is where his *position* is summed up.

The "Last Instance..."

I now suggest to you that my essays should be approached by three rough paths which travel across them and intersect.

I will first take the path of the "last instance".

We know that Marx and Engels argued the thesis of the determination by the economy *in the last instance*. This little phrase, which seems like nothing at all, in fact upsets the whole ruling conception of society and of history. Not enough attention has been paid to the figure or metaphor in which Marx presents his conception of a society in the Preface to the 1859 *Contribution*. This figure is that of a *topography*, that is, of a spatial apparatus which assigns positions in space to given realities.

The Marxist topography presents society in terms of the metaphor of an edifice whose upper floors rest, as the logic of an edifice would have it, on its foundation. The foundation is in German *die Basis* or *die Struktur*, which is traditionally translated as *base* or more often *infrastructure*: it is the economy, the unity of the productive forces and relations of production under the dominance of the relations of production. From the base of the ground floor rise the upper floor or floors of the *Überbau*, in translation the legal-political and ideological superstructure.

A simple image, it will be said, representing realities. Agreed: but it also *distinguished these realities*, which is very important, for example by placing positive law, which Hegel includes within civil society, in the category of the superstructure, and thus distinguishing something very different from simple realities: their *efficacy* and its *dialectic*.

When Marx says that the base or infrastructure is determinant in the last instance, he implies that what it determines is the superstructure.

For example: "The specific economic form, in which unpaid surplus-labour is pumped out of direct producers, determines the relationship of rulers and ruled, as it grows directly out of production itself and in turn, reacts upon it as a determining element".[2]

But the determination which Marx is thinking of here is *only* determination *in the last instance*. As Engels wrote (in a letter to Bloch): "According to the materialist conception of history, the *ultimately* determining element in history is the production and reproduction of real life. More than this neither Marx nor I have ever asserted. Hence if somebody twists this into saying that the economic element is the *only* determining one, he transforms that proposition into a meaningless, abstract, senseless phrase."[3]

In the determination of the topography, the last *instance* really is the *last* instance. If it is. *the last one*, as in the legal

2. Marx continues: "Upon this, however, is founded the entire formation [*Gestaltung*] of the economic community which grows up out of the production relations themselves, thereby simultaneously its own specific political form [*Gestalt*]. It is always the direct relationship of the owners of the conditions of production to the direct producers—a relation always naturally corresponding to a definite stage in the development of the methods [*Art und Weise*] of labour and thereby its social productivity—which reveals the innermost secret [*innerste Geheimnis*], the hidden basis [*Grundlage*] of the entire social structure [*Konstruktion*], and with it the political form of the relation of sovereignty and dependence, in short, the corresponding specific form of the State." (*Capital*, vol. III, p. 772; Moscow edition, 1962.)

3. Engels continues: "The economic situation is the basis, but the various elements of the superstructure: political forms of the class struggle and its results, to wit: constitutions established by the victorious class after a successful battle, etc., juridical forms, and even then the reflexes of all these actual struggles in the brains of the participants, political, juristic, philosophical theories, religious views and their further development into systems of dogmas, also exercise their influence upon the course of the historical struggles and in many cases preponderate in determining their *form*."

image which it invokes (court of the last instance), that is because there are *others*, those which figure in the legal-political and ideological superstructure. The mention of the last instance in determination thus plays a double role: it divides Marx sharply off from all mechanistic explanations, and opens up within determination the functioning of different instances, the functioning of a real difference in which the dialectic is inscribed. The topography thus signifies that the determination in the last instance by the economic base can only be grasped within a differentiated, therefore complex and articulated whole (the *"Gliederung"*), in which the determination in the last instance fixes the real difference of the other instances, their relative autonomy and their own mode of reacting on the base itself.

Before drawing the consequences, I would like to underline the decisive theoretical importance of this category of the *"last instance"*, too often considered as a philosophical approximation or popularization. To argue for the determination in the last instance *by the economy* is to mark oneself off from all idealist philosophies of history, it is to adopt a materialist position. But to talk about the determination by the economy *in the last instance* is to mark oneself off from every mechanistic conception of determinism and to adopt a dialectical position. However, when you are working in Hegel's shadow you must be on your guard against the idealist temptations involved in the dialectic. And Marx is on his guard, because when he inscribes the dialectic within the functioning of the instance of a topography, he effectively protects himself from the illusion of a dialectic capable of producing its own material content in the spontaneous movement of its self-development. In submitting the dialectic to the constraints of the topography, Marx is submitting it to the real conditions of its operation, he is protecting it from speculative folly, he is forcing it into a materialist mould, forcing it to recognize that its own figures are prescribed by the material character of its own conditions. That this inscription and this prescription are not in themselves sufficient to provide us with the figures of the materialist dialectic in person, I agree, but they do save us from at least one temptation: that of seeking these figures ready-made in Hegel.

In this manner we come back to the themes developed in my essays, whose object was to differentiate between Marx and Hegel. I have stated elsewhere what debt Marx owed to Hegel, and also why he was constantly forced to make the detour *via* Hegel in order to find his own way forward.[4]

Yes, Marx was close to Hegel, but above all *for reasons which are not mentioned*, for reasons which go back further than the dialectic, for reasons which relate to Hegel's critical position in respect to the theoretical presuppositions of classical bourgeois philosophy, from Descartes to Kant. To sum it up in a word: Marx was close to Hegel in his insistence on rejecting every philosophy of the Origin and of the Subject, whether rationalist, empiricist or transcendental; in his critique of the cogito, of the sensualist-empiricist subject and of the transcendental subject, thus in his critique of the idea of a theory of knowledge. Marx was close to Hegel in his critique of the legal subject and of the social contract, in his critique of the moral subject, in short of every philosophical ideology of the Subject, which whatever the variation involved gave classical bourgeois philosophy the means of *guaranteeing* its ideas, practices and goals by not simply reproducing but philosophically elaborating the notions of the dominant legal ideology. And if you consider the grouping of these critical themes, you have to admit that Marx was close to Hegel just in respect to those features which Hegel had openly borrowed from Spinoza, because all this can be found in the *Ethics* and the *Tractatus Theologico-politicus*. These deep-rooted affinities are normally passed over in pious silence; they nevertheless constitute, from Epicurus to Spinoza and Hegel, the premises of Marx's materialism. They are hardly ever mentioned, for the simple reason that Marx himself did not mention them, and so the whole of the Marx-Hegel relationship is made to hang on the dialectic, because this Marx did talk about! As if he would not be the first to agree that you must never judge someone on the basis of his own self-conscious image,

4. *Cf.* "Marx's Relation to Hegel" (in *Politics and History*, New Left Books, 1972) and the *Elements of Self-criticism*.

but on the basis of the whole process which, behind this consciousness, produces it.

I hope I shall be excused for laying so much stress on this point, but it is the key to the solution of very many problems, real or imaginary, concerning Marx's relation to Hegel, and within Marx concerning *the relation of the dialectic to materialism*. In fact I believe that the question of the Marxist dialectic cannot be properly posed unless the dialectic is *subjected to the primacy of materialism*, and a study is made of what forms this dialectic must take in order to be the dialectic of *this* materialism. From this point of view it is easy to understand how the idea of the dialectic could have imposed itself on a philosophy like that of Hegel, not only because the dramatic turmoil of the French Revolution and its after-effects provided the hard lesson, but also because the dialectic was the only means of thinking within a philosophy which had very good reasons for originally refusing (even if it later transformed and reintroduced them) the use and guarantee of the categories of Origin and Subject. Of course, Hegel did not apply himself to the search for the dialectic only after rejecting Origin and Subject. In a single movement he created the dialectic which he needed to differentiate himself from the classical philosophies, and, to force it to serve his ends, he "mystified the dialectic", to use Marx's words. But that does not mean that the Hegelian mystification itself is not witness to a relation constant since the time of Epicurus, and perhaps before him, *between materialism*, which can only play its role by drawing a demarcation line between itself and every philosophy of the Origin, whether of Being, of the Subject or of Meaning, *and the dialectic*. To make the matter clearer in a few words: when you reject the radical origin of things, whatever the figure used, you need to create quite different categories from the classical ones in order to get a grasp on those notions—essence, cause or liberty— whose authority is drawn from this origin. When you reject the category of origin as a philosophical issuing bank, you have to refuse its currency too, and put other categories into circulation: those of the dialectic. That is in outline the profound relation linking the premises of the materialism to be found in Epicurus, Spinoza and Hegel, which governs not only everything about the dialectic but also the dialectic itself.

It is this which seems to me important, much more than the "conclusions without premises" which are the only judgements made by Marx on Hegel and where he raises *only and for its own sake* the question of the dialectic. He does this, of course, in order to recognize in Hegel the merit of having—I quote—"been the first to express the general movement of the dialectic", which is correct and certainly a rather reserved statement, but also in order to argue, this time without any reservations, that Hegel had "mystified" it, and that Marx's own dialectic was not only not that of Hegel, but "its exact opposite". But we also know that according to Marx it was enough, in order to demystify the Hegelian dialectic, to invert it. I have argued enough in the past about the fact that this idea of inversion did not do the job and was only a metaphor for a real materialist transformation of the figures of the dialectic, about which Marx promised us a dozen pages which he never wrote. This silence was surely not accidental. It was doubtless a consequence of the need to trace a line back from the conclusions to the materialist premises of the dialectic, and on the basis of these premises to think out, in the strong sense, the new categories which they imply and which can be found in operation in *Capital* and in Lenin's writings, but which do not always or do not yet clearly bear their name.

I became involved in this problem when I started to look for the difference, in their very proximity, between Marx and Hegel. It is quite obvious that if Marx borrowed from Hegel the word and the idea of the dialectic, he nevertheless could not possibly have accepted this doubly mystified dialectic—mystified not only in the idealist attempt to produce its own material content, but also and above all in the figures which realize the miracle of its self-incarnation: negation and the negation of the negation, or *Aufhebung*. Because if the Hegelian dialectic rejects every Origin, which is what is said at the beginning of the *Logic*, where Being is immediately identified with Nothingness, it projects this into the End of a Telos which in return creates, within its own process, its own Origin and its own Subject. There is

no assignable Origin in Hegel, but that is because the whole
process, which is fulfilled in the final totality, is indefinitely,
in all the moments which anticipate its end, its own Origin.
There is no Subject in Hegel, but that is because the becoming-
Subject of substance, as an accomplished process of the
negation of the negation, is the Subject of the process itself.
If Marx took over the idea of the dialectic from Hegel, he
not only "inverted" it in order to rid it of the pretension
or fantasy of self-production, but also had to transform its
figures so that they should cease to produce the implied
effects. Lenin made the point again and again during the
years 1918–23 that if socialism does not succeed in transforming petty commodity production, then, as long as it is
allowed to exist, petty commodity production will continue
to give rise to capitalism. One might say, in the same manner:
as long as Marxism does not succeed in transforming the
figures of the dialectic mystified by Hegel, these figures will
continue to give rise to Hegelian, mystified effects. Now this
transformation was not to be found in my head, nor only
in the future, but out in the open in the texts of Marx and
Lenin and the practice of the proletarian class struggle.

I was therefore simply trying to formulate conceptually
what already existed in the practical state.

That, to approach the matter from this direction, is why
I claimed that Marx did not have the same idea of the nature
of a social formation as Hegel, and I believed that I could
demonstrate this difference by saying that Hegel thought
of society as a *totality*, while Marx thought of it as a complex
whole, structured in dominance. If I may be allowed to be
a little provocative, it seems to me that we can leave to Hegel
the category of *totality*, and claim for Marx the category of
the *whole*. It might be said that this is a verbal quibble, but I
do not think that this is entirely true. If I preferred to reserve
for Marx the category of the whole rather than that of the
totality, it is because within the totality a double temptation
is always present: that of considering it as a pervasive essence
which exhaustively embraces all of its manifestations, and—
what comes to the same thing—that of discovering in it,
as in a circle or a sphere (a metaphor which makes us think
of Hegel once again), a centre which would be its essence.

On this point I believed that I had found an important difference between Marx and Hegel. For Hegel, society, like history, is made up of circles within circles, of spheres within spheres. Dominating his whole conception is the idea of the expressive totality, in which all the elements are total parts, each expressing the internal unity of the totality which is only ever, in all its complexity, the objectification-alienation of a simple principle. And in fact, when you read the *Rechtsphilosophie*, you find that Hegel is deploying, in the dialectic of the Objective Spirit which produces them, the spheres of abstract law, of *Moralität* and *Sittlichkeit*, so that each produces the other through the negation of the negation so as to find their truth in the State. There are many differences between them, but since their relation is always one of "truth", these differences are always affirmed only to be denied and transcended in other differences, and this is possible because in each difference there is already present the in-itself of a future for-itself. And when you read the Introduction to the *Philosophy of History*, you find the same process, one might even say the same procedure: each moment of the development of the Idea exists in its States, which realize a simple principle—the beauty of individuality for ancient Greece, the legal spirit for Rome, etc. And borrowing from Montesquieu the idea that in a historical totality all concrete determinations, whether economic, political, moral or even military, express one single principle, Hegel conceives history in terms of the category of the expressive totality.

For Marx, the differences are real, and they are not only differences in spheres of activity, practices and objects: they are differences in *efficacy*. The last instance operates here in such a way that it explodes the peaceful fiction of the circle or the sphere. It is not an accident that Marx abandons the metaphor of the circle for that of the edifice. A circle is closed, and the corresponding notion of totality presupposes that one can grasp all the phenomena, exhaustively, and then reassemble them within the simple unity of its centre. Marx on the other hand presents us with an edifice, a foundation, and one or two upper floors—exactly how many is not stated. Nor does he say that everything must fall into these categories, that everything is either infrastructure or superstructure. You could even argue for the idea, essential to *Capital*, that the Marxist theory of societies and of history implies a whole theory of their incidental costs and their failures. Marx only says that you must distinguish, that the distinctions are real, irreducible, that in the order of determination the share of the base and that of the superstructure are unequal, and that this inequality or unevenness in dominance is constitutive of the unity of the whole, which therefore can no longer be the expressive unity of a simple principle all of whose elements would be the phenomena.

That is why I talked about *a whole*, to make it clear that in the Marxist conception of a social formation everything holds together, that the independence of an element is only ever the form of its dependence, and that the interplay of the differences is regulated by the unity of a determination in the last instance; but that is why I did not talk about a *totality*, because the Marxist whole is complex and uneven, and stamped with this unevenness by the determination in the last instance. It is this interplay, this unevenness, which allow us to understand that something real can happen in a social formation and that through the political class struggle it is possible to get a hold on real history. I made the point in passing: no politics have ever been seen in the world which were inspired by Hegel. For where can you get a hold on the circle when you are caught in the circle? Formally, the Marxist topography gives an answer when it says: *this* is what is determinant in the last instance—the economy, therefore the economic class struggle, extended into the political class struggle for the seizure of State power—and *this* is how the class struggle in the base is linked (or is not linked) to the class struggle in the superstructure. But that is not all. In pointing this out, the Marxist topography refers any questioner to his place in the historical process: *this* is the place which you occupy, *and this* is where you must move to in order to change things. Archimedes only wanted a single fixed point in order to lift up the world. The Marxist topography names the place where you must fight because that is where the fight will take place for the transformation of the world. But this place is no longer a point, nor is it fixed—it is an articulated system of positions governed by the determination in the last instance.

All this remains formal, no-one will deny it, in the Preface to the *Contribution* to which I have alluded. But the *Communist Manifesto* called things by their names and *Capital* repeated them. *Capital* is full of examples of the topographical figure. It is through the use of this figure that theoretical determination can become practical decision, because it arranges things in such a way that the workers, who Marx was talking to, can seize them. The concept which is grasped (*Begriff*) becomes in Marx the theoretical-practical apparatus of a topography, a means of practically grasping the world.

It is easy to see that, in this new whole, the dialectic at work is not at all Hegelian. I tried to show this in connexion with the question of contradiction, by pointing out that if you take seriously the nature of the Marxist whole and its unevenness, you must come to the conclusion that this unevenness is necessarily reflected in the form of the *overdetermination* or of the *underdetermination* of contradiction. Of course, it is not a question of treating overdetermination or underdetermination in terms of the addition or subtraction of a quantum of determination, a quantum added or subtracted from a pre-existing contradiction, that is, one leading a *de jure* existence somewhere. Overdetermination or underdetermination are not exceptions in respect to a pure contradiction. Just as Marx says that man can only be alone within society, just as Marx says that the existence of simple economic categories is an exceptional product of history, in the same way a contradiction in the pure state can only exist as a determinate product of the impure contradiction.

The effect of this thesis is quite simply to change the reference points from which we look at contradiction. And, in particular, it warns us against the idea of what I have called simple contradiction, or more exactly contradiction in the logical sense of the term, whose terms are two equal entities each simply bearing one of the contrary signs + or −, A or not-A. If I might now go a little further than I did in my first essays, but in the same direction, I should say that contradiction, as you find it in *Capital*, presents the surprising characteristic of being *uneven*, of bringing contrary terms into operation which you cannot obtain just by giving the second a sign obtained by negating that of the first. This is because they are caught up in a *relation of unevenness* which continuously reproduces its conditions of existence just on account of this contradiction. I am talking for example about the contradiction within which the capitalist mode of production exists and which, tendentially, condemns it to death, the contradiction of the capitalist *relation of production*, the contradiction which divides classes into classes, in which two quite unequal classes confront each other: the capitalist class and the working class. Because the working class is not the opposite of the capitalist class, it is not the capitalist class negated, deprived of its capital and its powers—and the capitalist class is not the working class plus something else, namely riches and power. They do not share the same history, they do not share the same world, they do not lead the same class struggle, and yet they do come into confrontation, and this certainly is a contradiction since the *relation of confrontation reproduces the conditions of confrontation* instead of transcending them in a beautiful Hegelian exaltation and reconciliation.

I think that if you keep in sight this special characteristic of Marxist contradiction, that it is *uneven*, you will come up with some interesting conclusions, not only about *Capital* but also about the question of the struggle of the working class, of the sometimes dramatic contradictions of the Labour Movement and of the contradictions of socialism. For if you want to understand this unevenness, you will have to follow Marx and Engels in taking seriously the conditions which make the contradiction uneven, that is, the material and structural conditions of what I have called the structured whole in dominance, and here you will get a glimpse into the theoretical foundations of the Leninist thesis of uneven development. Because in Marx all development is uneven, and here again it is not a question of additions to or subtractions from a so-called even development, but of an essential characteristic. Every development is uneven, because it is contradiction which drives development, and because contradiction is uneven. That is why, alluding to the *Discourse on the Origin of Inequality* by Rousseau, who was the principal theoretician of alienation before Hegel, I once added as a sub-title to my article "On the Materialist Dialectic" the phrase: "On the Unevenness of Origins", signifying by the plural, *origins*, that there is no Origin in the philosophical sense of the term, and that every beginning is marked with unevenness.

I have only sketched out a few themes, simply to indicate the critical importance of the thesis of the last instance for understanding Marx. And it is of course true that every interpretation of Marxist theory involves not only theoretical stakes but also political and historical. These theses on the last instance, on the structured whole in dominance, on the unevenness of contradiction, had an immediate principal objective, which governed the way in which they were expressed: that of recognizing and indicating the place and the role of theory in the Marxist Labour Movement, not just by taking note of Lenin's famous slogan, "Without revolutionary theory there can be no revolutionary movement", but by going into detail in order to free theory from confusions, mystifications and manipulations. But beyond this primary objective, my theses had other, more important aims, bearing on the temptations faced by the Labour Movement: the temptation of a messianic or critical idealism of the dialectic, which has haunted intellectuals in revolt from the time of the young Lukács and even of the old and new Young Hegelians; the temptation of what I called the poor man's Hegelianism, the evolutionism which has always, in the Labour Movement, taken the form of economism. In both cases, the dialectic functions in the old manner of pre-Marxist philosophy as a philosophical guarantee of the coming of revolution and of socialism. In both cases, materialism is either juggled away (in the case of the first hypothesis) or else reduced to the mechanical and abstract materiality of the productive forces (in the case of the second hypothesis). In all cases the practice of this dialectic runs up against the implacable test of the facts: the revolution did not take place in nineteenth-century Britain nor in early twentieth-century Germany; it did not take place in the advanced countries at all, but elsewhere, in Russia, then later in China and Cuba, etc. How can we understand this displacement of the principal contradiction of imperialism onto the

weakest link, and correlatively how can we understand the
stagnation in the class struggle in those countries where it
appeared to be triumphant, without the Leninist category of
uneven development, which refers us back to the unevenness
of contradiction and its over- and underdetermination?
I am deliberately stressing underdetermination, because
while certain people easily accepted a simple supplement
to determination, they could not accept the idea of underdetermination, that is, of a threshold of determination which,
if it is not crossed, causes revolutions to miscarry, revolutionary movements to stagnate or disappear, and
imperialism to rot while still developing, etc. If Marxism
is capable of registering these facts, but not capable
of understanding them, if it cannot grasp, in the strong
sense, the "obvious" truth that the revolutions which
we know are either premature or miscarried, but from within
a theory which dispenses with the normative notions of
prematurity and of miscarriage, that is, with a normative
standpoint, then it is clear that something is wrong on the
side of the dialectic, and that it remains caught up in a certain
idea which has not yet definitively settled accounts with Hegel.

That is why I think that, in order to see more clearly what
makes Marx different, one must put into its proper perspective
the immediate formulation in which he expressed his relation
to the Hegelian dialectic. To do so, one must first consider
how Marx's materialism is expressed, because the question
of the dialectic depends on this. And there does exist a rather
good way of dealing with this problem, which I have just
tried to follow: that which uses the category of determination
in the last instance.

On The Process Of Knowledge

I now want, much more briefly, to take another path across
my essays in order to look at another group of theses developed there on the question of "knowledge".

I cannot hide the fact that in this matter I depended heavily
on Spinoza. I said a moment ago that Marx was close to
Hegel in his critique of the idea of a theory of knowledge.
But this Hegelian critique is already present in Spinoza.
What does Spinoza in fact mean when he writes, in a famous

phrase, "*Habemus enim ideam veram* ..."? That we have a true idea? No: the weight of the phrase lies on the "*enim*". It is *in fact* because and only because we have a true idea that we can produce others, according to its norm. And it is *in fact* because and only because we have a true idea that we can know that it is true, because it is "*index sui*". Where does this true idea come from? That is quite a different question. But it is a fact that we do have it (*habemus*), and whatever it may be that produces this result, it governs everything that can be said about it and derived from it. Thus Spinoza *in advance* makes every theory of knowledge, which reasons about the *justification* of knowledge, dependent on the *fact* of the knowledge which we already possess. And so every question of the Origin, Subject and Justification of knowledge, which lie at the root of all theories of knowledge, is rejected. But that does not prevent Spinoza from talking about knowledge: not in order to understand its Origin, Subject and Justification, but in order to determine the process and its moments, the famous "three levels", which moreover appear very strange when you look at them close up, because the first is properly the lived world, and the last is specially suited to grasping the "singular essence"— or what Hegel would in his language call the "universal concrete"—of the Jewish people, which is heretically treated in the *Theologico-Political Treatise*.

I am sorry if some people consider, apparently out of theoretical opportunism, that I thus fall into a heresy, but I would say that Marx—not only the Marx of the 1857 *Introduction*, which in fact opposes Hegel through Spinoza, but the Marx of *Capital*, together with Lenin—is in fact on close terms with Spinoza's positions. For while they too reject every theory of the Origin, Subject and Justification of knowledge, *they too talk* about knowledge. And the fact that Lenin claims for Marxism the expression "theory of knowledge" is not an embarrassment when you realize that he defines it as ... the dialectic. In fact Marx and Lenin talk about knowledge in very general terms, to describe the general aspects of its process. One must be suspicious of those passages in which Marx states such generalities. There is at least one case, among others, with respect to which he did explain himself: that of "*production*". At one and the same time he outlines the general characteristics of production and yet argues that general production and, *a fortiori*, production in general do not exist, because only particular modes of production exist within concrete social formations. This is one way of saying that everything takes place within the concrete structure of particular processes, but that in order to be able to grasp what is happening you need the help of that minimum of non-existent generality without which it would be impossible to perceive and understand what does exist. Well, I think that the 1857 *Introduction* is in this vein. I think that it introduces neither a "theory of knowledge" nor its surrogate, an epistemology: I think that it only expresses that minimum of generality without which it would be impossible to perceive and understand the concrete processes of knowledge. But just like the general concept of production, the general concept of knowledge is there only to disappear in the concrete analysis of concrete processes: in the complex history of the processes of knowledge.

In the whole of this affair I based myself as closely as possible on Marx's 1857 *Introduction*, and if I used it to produce some necessary effects of theoretical provocation, I think that I did nevertheless remain faithful to it.

I was directly and literally inspired by Marx, who several times uses the concept of the "*production*" of knowledge, to argue my central thesis: the idea of knowledge as *production*. I obviously also had in mind an echo of Spinozist "production", and I drew on the double sense of a word which beckoned both to labour, practice, and to the display of truth. But essentially—and in order to provoke the reader— I held closely, I would even say mechanically, to the Marxist concept of production, which literally suggests a process and the application of tools to a raw material. I even outbid Marx by presenting a general concept of "practice", which reproduced the concept of the labour process to be found in *Capital*, and, referring back to theoretical practice, I used and no doubt forced a little Marx's text in order to arrive at the distinction between the three generalities,[5] the first

5. *Cf. For Marx*, "On the Materialist Dialectic"; English edition, pp. 183–190 [*translator's note*].

of which functioned as the theoretical raw material, the second as the instruments of theoretical labour, and the third as the concrete-in-thought or knowledge. I admit that Spinoza was involved in this affair, too, because of his "three levels of knowledge", and the central role of the second: scientific abstraction.

What interested me above all else in Marx's text was his radical double opposition to empiricism, and to Hegel. In opposition to empiricism, Marx argued that knowledge does not proceed from the concrete to the abstract but from the abstract to the concrete, and that all this takes place, I quote, "*in thought*", while the real object, which gives rise to this whole process, exists outside of thought. In opposition to Hegel, Marx argued that this movement from the abstract to the concrete was not a manner of producing reality but of coming to know it. And what fascinated me in all this argument was that *one had to begin with the abstract*. Now Marx wrote that knowledge is "*a product of thinking, of comprehension ... a product of the assimilation and transformation (ein Produkt der Verarbeitung) of perceptions and images into concepts*", and also that "it would seem to be the proper thing *to start with the real and concrete elements ... e.g.* to start in the sphere of economy with population ... Closer consideration shows, however, that this is wrong. *Population is an abstraction.*"[6] I concluded that perceptions and images (*Anschauung* und *Vorstellung*) were treated by Marx as abstractions. And I attributed to this abstraction the status of the concrete or of experience as you find it in Spinoza's first level of knowledge, that is, in my language, the status of the ideological. Of course I did not say that Generalities II, working on Generalities I, only work on ideological material, because they could also be working on abstractions which are already scientifically elaborated, or on both together. But there did remain this border-line case of a purely ideological raw material, a hypothesis which allowed me to introduce the science/ideology antithesis, and the epistemological break, which Spinoza, long before Bachelard,

6. Introduction to *A Contribution to the Critique of Political Economy*, Moscow, 1971, p. 205 [*translator's note*].

inserted between his first and second levels of knowledge, and thus I produced a certain number of ideological effects which, as I have pointed out in my *Elements of Self-criticism*, were not free of all theoreticism.

But, of course, since I suffer from what Rousseau called something like "the weakness of believing in the power of consequences", I did not stop there, but drew an important distinction: that between *the real object and the object of knowledge*. This distinction is contained in the very phrases in which Marx deals with the process of knowledge. As a materialist, he argues that knowledge is knowledge of a real object (Marx says: a real subject), which (I quote) "remains, after as before, outside the intellect and independent of it".[7] And, a little later, in reference to the subject of investigation, society, he writes (I quote) that it "must always be envisaged therefore as the pre-condition of comprehension". Marx therefore poses, as a pre-condition of the whole process of knowledge of a real object, the existence of this real object outside of thought. But this exteriority of the real object is affirmed at the same time as he affirms the specific character of the process of knowledge, which is "the product of the assimilation and transformation" of perceptions and images into concepts. And, at the end of the process, the thought-concrete, the thought-totality, which is its result, presents itself as knowledge of the real-concrete, of the real object. The distinction between the real object and the process of knowledge is indubitably present in Marx's text, as is the reference to the work of elaboration and the diversity of its moments, and the distinction between the thought-concrete and the real object, of which it gives us knowledge.

I used this text not in order to construct a "theory of knowledge" but in order to stir something within the world of the blindly obvious, into which a certain kind of Marxist philosophy retreats in order to protect itself from its enemies. I suggested that if all the knowledge which we possess really is knowledge of a real object which remains "after as before" independent of the intellect, there was perhaps some point

7. *Op. cit.*, p. 207, translation modified [*translator's note*].

in thinking about the interval separating this *"before"* from the *"after"*, an interval which is the process of knowledge itself, and in recognizing that this process, defined by the "work of elaboration" of successive forms, was inscribed precisely, from beginning to end, in a transformation which bears not on the real object,[8] but only on its stand-ins, first of all on the perceptions and images, then on the concepts which come out of them. Thus I arrived at my thesis: if the process of knowledge does not transform the real object, but only transforms its perception into concepts and then into a thought-concrete, and if all this process takes place, as Marx repeatedly points out, *"in thought"*, *and not in the real object*, this means that, with regard to the real object, in order to know it, "thought" operates on the transitional forms which designate the real object in the process of transformation in order finally to produce a concept of it, the thought-concrete. I referred to the set of these forms (including the last one) produced by this operation in terms of the category "object of knowledge". In the movement which causes the spontaneous perceptions and images to become the concept of the real object, each form does indeed relate to the real object, but without becoming confused with it. But neither can the thought-concrete which is finally produced be confused with the real, and Marx attacks Hegel precisely for allowing this confusion to take place. Once again Spinoza came to mind, and the memory of his haunting words: the idea of a circle is not the circle, the concept of a dog does not bark—in short, you must not confuse the real thing and its concept.

Of course, if this necessary distinction is not solidly supported, it may lead to nominalism, even to idealism. It is generally agreed that Spinoza fell into nominalism. But he did in any case take measures to protect himself from idealism, both in developing his theory of a substance with infinite attributes, and in arguing for the parallelism of the

8. "That is, so long as the intellect adopts a purely speculative, purely theoretical attitude" (Marx). He distinguishes between the theoretical attitude (*knowledge* of the real object) and the practical attitude (*transformation* of the real object).

two attributes *extension* and *thought*. Marx protects himself
in another way, more securely, by the use of the thesis of
the *primacy of the real object over the object of knowledge*,
and by the *primacy of this first thesis over the second: the
distinction between the real object and the object of knowledge*.
Here you have that minimum of generality, that is, in the
case in question, of materialist theses, which, by drawing
a line between themselves and idealism, open up a free
space for the investigation of the concrete processes of the
production of knowledge. And finally, for whoever wants
to make the comparison, this thesis of the distinction between
real object and object of knowledge "functions" in a very
similar manner to Lenin's distinction between absolute
truth and relative truth, and to a very similar purpose.

Lenin wrote: "You will say that this distinction between
relative and absolute truth is indefinite. And I shall reply:
it is sufficiently 'indefinite' *to prevent science from becoming
a dogma in the bad sense of the term*, from becoming dead,
frozen, ossified; but at the same time it is sufficiently 'definite'
to enable us to *draw a dividing-line in the most emphatic
and irrevocable manner* between ourselves and fideism and
agnosticism, between ourselves and philosophical idealism
and the sophistry of the followers of Hume and Kant."[9]
Which means, to put it bluntly: our thesis is precise enough
not to fall into idealism, precise enough to draw a line between
itself and idealism, that is, correct enough in its generality
to prevent the living freedom of science from being buried
under its own results.

The same is true, keeping everything in proportion, of
my thesis on the difference between the real object and the
object of knowledge. The stakes were considerable. It was
a question of preventing the science produced by Marx
from being treated "as a dogma in the bad sense of the term",
it was a question of bringing *to life* the prodigious work
of criticism and elaboration carried out by Marx, without
which he would never have been able—to put it in his way,
which remains classical—to discover behind the appearance

9. *Materialism and Empirio-criticism*, Moscow, 1967, p. 123 [*translator's
note*].

of things, and in diametrical opposition to this appearance, their unrecognized "intimate relations". It was a question of getting people to understand and to appreciate the unprecedented break which Marx had to make with the accepted world of appearances, that is, with the overwhelmingly "obvious truths" of the dominant bourgeois ideology. And since we were ourselves involved in the matter, it was a question of turning this truth into a living and active truth for us, because we had to break with other "obvious truths", sometimes couched in Marx's own vocabulary, whose meaning the dominant ideology or deviations in the Labour Movement had distorted. It was a question of recalling that if, as Lenin said, "the living soul of Marxism is the concrete analysis of a concrete situation", then knowledge of the concrete does not come at the beginning of the analysis, it comes *at the end*, and the analysis is only possible on the basis of Marx's concepts, and not on the basis of the immediate, "obvious" evidence of the concrete—which one cannot do without, but which cannot really be understood from the marks which it bears on its face.

Finally—and this was not the least important aspect—it was a question of recalling with Marx that knowledge of reality changes something in reality, because it *adds* to it precisely the fact that *it* is known, though everything makes it appear as if this *addition* cancelled itself out in its result. Since knowledge *of* reality belongs in advance to reality, since it is knowledge *of nothing but* reality, it adds something to it only on the paradoxical condition of adding *nothing* to it,[10] and once produced it reverts to it without need of sanction, and disappears in it. The process of knowledge adds to reality at each step its own knowledge of that reality, but at each step reality puts it in its pocket, because this knowledge is its own. *The distinction between object of knowledge and real object presents the paradox that it is affirmed only to be annulled. But it is not a nullity*: because in order to be annulled it must be constantly affirmed. That is normal, it is the infinite cycle of all knowledge, which

10. *Cf*. Engels: "Knowledge of nature just as it is, *without any foreign addition*". *Cf*. also the Leninist theory of reflection.

adds something to reality—precisely, knowledge of reality—only to give it back, and the cycle is only a cycle, and therefore living, *as long as it reproduces itself*, because only the production of new knowledge keeps old knowledge alive. These things happen more or less as in Marx's text, which says: living labour must "add new value to materials" in order that the value of the "dead labour" contained in the means of production should be preserved and transferred to the product, since (I quote) it is "by the simple addition of a certain quantity of labour that ... the original values of the means of production are preserved in the product" (*Capital*, Part III, ch. VIII, "Constant Capital and Variable Capital").

What is at stake with regard to these theses? Let us take Marxist science and suppose that political conditions are such that no-one works on it any more, no-one is adding any new knowledge. Then the old knowledge that reality has pocketed is there, within it, in the form of enormous and dead "obvious" facts, like machines without workers, no longer even machines but things. We could no longer in this case be sure, as Lenin puts it, of preventing science "from becoming a dogma in the bad sense of the term, from becoming dead, frozen, ossified". Which is another way of saying that Marxism itself risks repeating truths which are no longer any more than the names of things, when the world is demanding new knowledge, about imperialism *and* the State *and* ideologies *and* socialism *and* the Labour Movement itself. It is a way of recalling Lenin's astonishing remark, that Marx *only laid the foundation stones* of a theory which we must at all costs develop in every direction. It is a way of saying: Marxist theory can fall behind history, and even behind itself, if ever it believes that it has arrived.

Marx and Theoretical Humanism

I now want, very briefly, to follow one last path across my essays, in order to test out another provocative thesis: that of Marx's theoretical anti-humanism. I would say that, just for the pleasure of watching the ideological fireworks with which it was met, I would have had to invent this thesis if I had not already put it forward.

It is a serious thesis, as long as it is seriously read, and above all as long as serious attention is paid to one of the two words which make it up, and not the diabolical one, but the word "*theoretical*". I said and repeated that the concept or category of man did not play a theoretical role in Marx. But unfortunately this term "theoretical" was ignored by those who did not want to understand it.

Let us try to understand it.

And, to that end, let me first say a word about Feuerbach, some of whose texts I translated. No-one will deny that Feuerbach's philosophy is openly a theoretical humanism. Feuerbach says: every new philosophy announces itself under a new name. The philosophy of modern times, my philosophy, he says, announces itself under the name "Man". And in fact man, the human essence, is the central principle of the whole of Feuerbach's philosophy. It is not that Feuerbach is not interested in nature, because he does talk about the sun and the planets, and also about plants, dragonflies and dogs, and even about elephants in order to point out that they have no religion. But he is first of all preparing his ground, if I may put it in that way, when he talks about nature, when he calmly tells us that each species has its own world, which is only the manifestation of its essence. This world is made up of objects, and among them there exists one object *par excellence* in which the essence of the species is accomplished and perfected: its essential object. Thus each planet has the sun as an essential object, which is also the essential object of the planet, etc.

Now that the ground is prepared, we can turn our attention to man. He is the centre of his world as he is at the centre of the horizon that bounds it, of his *Umwelt*. There is nothing in his life which is not *his*: or rather, nothing which is not *him*, because all the objects of his world are only his objects in so far as they are the realization and projection of his essence. The objects of his perception are only his manner of perceiving them, the objects of his thought are only his manner of thinking them, and the objects of his feelings are only his manner of feeling them. All his objects are essential in so far as what they give him is only ever his own essence. Man is always in man, man never leaves the sphere of man, because—in a simple little phrase which the young Marx took over from Feuerbach, and which provoked some scholarly discussion among the participants in last summer's Hegel Congress in Moscow—the world is the world of man and man is the world of man. The sun and the stars, the dragon-flies, perception, intelligence and passion are only so many transitions on the road to the decisive truths: man's specific characteristic, unlike the stars and the animals, is to have his own species, the essence of his species, his whole generic essence as the object, and in an object which owes nothing to nature or religion. By the mechanism of objectification and inversion, the generic essence of man is given to man, unrecognizable in person, in the form of an exterior object, of another world, in religion. In religion, man contemplates his own powers, his productive forces as powers of an absolute other before whom he trembles and kneels down to implore pity. And this is perfectly practical, because out of it came all the rituals of religious worship, even the objective existence of miracles, which really do take place in this imaginary world since they are only, in Feuerbach's words (and I quote), "the realization of a desire" (*Wunscherfüllung*). The absolute object which is man thus comes up against the absolute in God, but does not realize that what he comes up against *is himself*. The whole of this philosophy, which does not limit itself to religion, but also deals with art, ideology, philosophy, and in addition—a fact which is too little known—with politics, society, and even history, thus rests on the identity of essence between subject and object, and this identity is explained by the power of man's essence to project itself in the self-realization which constitutes its objects, and in the alienation which separates object from subject, makes the object exterior to the subject, reifies it, and inverts the essential relation, since scandalously enough the Subject finds itself dominated by itself, in the form of an Object, God or the State, etc., which is however nothing but itself.

It must not be forgotten that this discourse, of which I can only sketch the premises here, had a certain grandeur, since it called for the inversion produced by religious or political alienation to be itself inverted; in other words, it called for an inversion of the imaginary domination of the attributes of the human subject; it called on man finally to claim back possession of his essence, alienated in his domination by God and the State; it called on man finally— no longer in the imaginary world of religion, in the "heaven of the State", or in the alienated abstraction of Hegelian philosophy, but on the earth, here and now, in real society— to realize his true human essence which is the human community, "communism".

Man at the centre of his world, in the philosophical sense of the term, the originating essence and the end of his world— that is what we can call a theoretical humanism in the strong sense.

It will be agreed, I think, that Marx, having originally espoused Feuerbach's problematic of the generic essence of man and of alienation, later broke with him, and also that this break with Feuerbach's theoretical humanism was a radical event in the history of Marx's thought.

But I would like to go further. For Feuerbach is a strange philosophical personality with this peculiarity (if I may be allowed the expression) of "blowing the gaff". Feuerbach is a *confessed* theoretical humanist. But behind him stands a whole row of philosophical precursors who, while they were not so brave as to confess it so openly, were working on a philosophy of man, even if in a less transparent form. Far be it from me to denigrate this great humanist tradition whose historical merit was to have struggled against feudalism, against the Church, and against their ideologists, and to have given man a status and dignity. But far be it from us, I think, to deny the fact that this humanist ideology, which produced great works and great thinkers, is inseparably linked to the rising bourgeoisie, whose aspirations it expressed, translating and transposing the demands of a commercial and capitalist economy sanctioned by a new system of law, the old Roman law revised as bourgeois commercial law. Man as a free subject, free man as a subject of his actions and his thoughts, is first of all man free to possess, to sell and to buy, the subject of law.

I will cut matters short and put forward the claim here that, with some untimely exceptions, the great tradition of classical philosophy has reproduced in the categories of its systems *both* the right of man to know, out of which it has made the subject of its theories of knowledge, from the *cogito* to the empiricist and the transcendental subject; *and* the right of man to act, out of which it has made the economic, moral and political subject. I believe, but obviously cannot prove it here, that I have the right to claim the following: in the form of the different subjects in which it is both divided up and disguised, the category of man, of the human essence, or of the human species, plays an essential *theoretical* role in the classical pre-Marxist philosophies. And when I talk about the *theoretical* role which a category plays, I mean that it is intimately bound up with the other categories, that it cannot be cut out of the set without altering the functioning of the whole. I think I can say that, with a few exceptions, the great classical philosophy represents, in implicit form, an indisputably humanist tradition. And if in his own way Feuerbach "blows the gaff", if he puts the human essence squarely at the centre of the whole thing, it is because he thinks that he can escape from the constraint which caused the classical philosophies to hide man behind a division into several subjects. This division, let us say into two subjects, in order to simplify matters, which makes man a subject of knowledge and a subject of action, is a characteristic mark of classical philosophy and prevents it from coming out with Feuerbach's fantastic declaration. Feuerbach himself thinks that he can overcome this division: for the plurality of subjects he substitutes the plurality of attributes in the human subject, and he thinks that he can settle another politically important problem, the distinction between individual and species, in terms of sexuality, which suppresses the individual because it requires that there should always be at least two of them, which already makes a species. I think that it becomes obvious from the manner in which Feuerbach proceeds that even before him the main concern of philosophy was man. The difference was that man was divided up between several subjects, and between the individual and the species.

It follows that Marx's theoretical anti-humanism is much more than a settling of accounts with Feuerbach: it is directed at one and the same time *both* against the existing philosophies of society and history *and* against the classical tradition of philosophy, and thus through them against the whole of bourgeois ideology.

I would say that Marx's theoretical anti-humanism is above all a *philosophical* anti-humanism. If what I have just said has any truth in it, you only have to compare it with what I said earlier about Marx's affinities with Spinoza and Hegel in their opposition to philosophies of the Origin and the Subject to see the implications. And in fact if you examine the texts which might be considered the authentic texts of Marxist philosophy, you do not find the category of man or any of its past or possible disguises. The materialist and dialectical theses which make up the whole of what little Marxist philosophy exists can give rise to all kinds of interpretations. But I do not see how they can allow any humanist interpretation: on the contrary, they are designed to exclude it, as one variety of idealism among others, and to invite us to think in a *quite different* manner.

But we still have not finished, because we still have to understand the theoretical anti-humanism of historical materialism, that is, the elimination of the concept of man as a central concept by the Marxist theory of social formations and of history.

Perhaps we ought first of all to deal with two objections. In fact, we certainly ought to try, because they come up again and again. The first concludes that any Marxist theory conceived in the above manner ends by despising men and paralysing their revolutionary struggle. But *Capital* is full of the sufferings of the exploited, from the period of primitive accumulation to that of triumphant capitalism, and it is written for the purpose of helping to free them from class servitude. This however does not prevent Marx but on the contrary *obliges* him to abstract from concrete individuals and to treat them theoretically as simple "supports" of relations, and this in the same work, *Capital*, which analyses the mechanisms of their exploitation. The second objection opposes to Marx's theoretical anti-humanism the existence of humanist ideologies which, even if they do in general serve the hegemony of the bourgeoisie, may also, in certain circumstances and within certain social strata, and even in a religious form, express the revolt of the masses against exploitation and oppression. But this raises no difficulty, as soon as you realize that Marxism recognizes the existence of ideologies and judges them in terms of the role which they play in the class struggle.

What is at stake here is something quite different: the *theoretical* pretensions of the humanist conception to explain society and history, starting out from the human essence, from the free human subject, the subject of needs, of labour, of desire, the subject of moral and political action. I maintain that Marx was only able to found the science of history and to write *Capital* because he broke with the *theoretical* pretensions of all such varieties of humanism.

In opposition to the whole of bourgeois ideology, Marx declares: "A society is not composed of individuals" (*Grundrisse*), and: "My analytic method does not start from Man but from the economically given period of society" (*Notes on Wagner's Textbook*). And against the humanist and Marxist socialists who had proclaimed in the *Gotha Programme* that "labour is the source of all wealth and all culture", he argues: "The bourgeois have very good grounds for falsely ascribing supernatural creative power to labour". Can one imagine a more distinct break?

The effects can be seen in *Capital*. Marx shows that what in the last instance determines a social formation, and allows us to grasp it, is not any chimerical human essence or human nature, nor man, nor even "men", but a *relation*, the production relation, which is inseparable from the Base, the infrastructure. And, in opposition to all humanist idealism, Marx shows that this relation is not a relation between men, a relation between persons, nor an intersubjective or psychological or anthropological relation, but a double relation: a relation between groups of men concerning the relation between these groups of men and things, the means of production. It is one of the greatest possible theoretical mystifications that you can imagine to think that social relations can be reduced to relations between men, or even between groups of men: because this is to suppose that social relations are relations which only involve *men*, whereas actually they also involve *things*, the means of production, derived from material nature. The production relation is, says Marx, a relation of distribution: it distributes men among classes at the same time and according as it attributes the means of production to a class. The classes are born out of the antagonism in this distribution which is also an attribution. Naturally, human individuals are parties to this relation, therefore active, but first of all in so far as they are held within it. It is because they are parties to it, as to a freely agreed contract, that they are held within it, and it is because they are held within it that they are parties to it. It is very important to understand why Marx considers men in this case only as "supports" of a relation, or "bearers" of a function in the production process, determined by the production relation. It is not at all because he reduces men in their concrete life to simple bearers of functions: he considers them as such in this respect because the capitalist production relation reduces them to this simple function within the infrastructure, in production, that is, in exploitation. In effect, the man of production, considered as an agent of production, *is only that* for the capitalist mode of production; he is determined as a simple "support" of a relation, as a simple "bearer of functions", completely anonymous and interchangeable, for if he is a worker he may be thrown into the street, and if he is a capitalist he may make a fortune or go bankrupt. In all cases he must submit to the law of a production relation, which is a relation of exploitation, therefore an antagonistic class relation; he must submit to the law of this relation and its effects. If you do not submit the individual concrete determinations of proletarians and capitalists, their "liberty" or their personality to a theoretical "reduction", then you will understand nothing of the terrible practical "reduction" to which the capitalist production relation submits individuals, which treats them only as bearers of economic functions and nothing else.

But to treat individuals as simple bearers of economic functions has consequences for the individuals. It is not Marx the theoretician who treats them as such, but the capitalist production relation! To treat individuals as bearers of interchangeable functions is, within capitalist exploitation, which is the fundamental capitalist class struggle, *to mark them* irreparably in their flesh and blood, to reduce them to nothing but appendices of the machine, to cast their wives and children into the hell of the factory, to extend their working day to the maximum, to give them just enough to reproduce themselves, and to create that gigantic reserve army from which other anonymous bearers can be drawn in order to put pressure on those who are in employment, who are lucky enough to have work.

But at the same time it is to create the conditions for an organization of struggle of the working class. For it is the development of the capitalist class struggle, that is, of capitalist exploitation, which itself creates these conditions. Marx continually insisted on the fact that it was the capitalist organization of production which *forcibly taught the working class the lesson of class struggle*, not only in concentrating masses of workers in the place of work, not only in mixing them together, but also and above all in imposing on them a terrible discipline of labour and daily life, all of which the workers suffer only to turn it back in common actions against their masters.

But in order for all this to happen, the workers must be party to and held within *other relations*.

The capitalist social formation, indeed, cannot be reduced to the capitalist production relation alone, therefore to its infrastructure. Class exploitation cannot continue, that is, reproduce the conditions of its existence, without the aid of the superstructure, without the legal-political and ideological relations, which in the last instance are determined by the production relation. Marx did not enter into this analysis, except in the form of a few brief remarks. But from everything that he said we can conclude that these relations too treat concrete human individuals as "bearers" of relations, as "supports" of functions, to which men are only parties because they are held within them. Thus, legal relations abstract from the real man in order to treat him as a simple "bearer of the legal relation", as a simple subject of law, capable of owning property, even if the only property which he possesses is that of his naked labour power. Thus too political relations abstract from the living man in order to treat him as a simple "support of the political relation", as a free citizen, even if his vote only reinforces his servitude. And thus too the ideological relations abstract from the living man in order to treat him as a simple subject either subjected to or rebelling against the ruling ideas. But all these relations, each of which uses the real man as its support, nevertheless determine and brand men in their flesh and blood, just as the production relation does. And since the production relation is a relation of class struggle, it is the class struggle which in the last instance determines the superstructural relations, their contradiction, and the overdetermination with which they mark the infrastructure.

And just as the capitalist class struggle creates, within production, the conditions of the workers' class struggle, so you can see that the legal, political and ideological relations can contribute to its organization and consciousness, through the very constraints which they impose. For the proletarian class struggle really did learn politics within the framework of bourgeois relations, and *via* the bourgeois class struggle itself. Everyone knows very well that the bourgeoisie was only able to overthrow the old régime, its production relation and its State, by engaging the popular masses in its struggle, and everyone knows that the bourgeoisie was only able to defeat the great landowners by enrolling the workers in its political battle, afterwards of course massacring them. Through its law and its ideology as well as through its bullets and its prisons, the bourgeoisie educated them in the political and ideological class struggle, among other ways by forcing them to understand that the proletarian class struggle had nothing to do with the bourgeois class struggle, and to shake off the yoke of its ideology.

It is here that the last instance, and the contradictory effects which it produces within the "edifice", intervenes to account for the dialectic of these paradoxical phenomena, which Marx grasps not with the help of the ridiculous concept of man, but with quite different concepts: production relation, class struggle, legal, political and ideological relations. Theoretically, the functioning of the last instance allows us to account for the difference and unevenness between the

forms of the class struggle, from the economic struggle to the
political and ideological struggle, and thus for the interplay
existing between these struggles and for the contradictions
existing in this struggle.

Marx's theoretical anti-humanism, as it operates within
historical materialism, thus means a refusal to root the
explanation of social formations and their history in a
concept of man with theoretical pretensions, that is, a concept
of man as an *originating subject*, one in whom originate
his needs (*homo oeconomicus*), his thoughts (*homo rationalis*),
and his acts and struggles (*homo moralis, juridicus* and
politicus). For when you begin with man, you cannot avoid
the idealist temptation of believing in the omnipotence of
liberty or of creative labour—that is, you simply submit,
in all "freedom", to the omnipotence of the ruling bourgeois
ideology, whose function is to mask and to impose, in the
illusory shape of man's power of freedom, another power,
much more real and much more powerful, that of capitalism.
If Marx does not start with man, if he refuses to derive
society and history theoretically from the concept of man,
it is in order to break with this mystification which only
expresses an ideological relation of force, based in the capitalist production relation. Marx therefore starts out from the
structural cause producing this effect of bourgeois ideology
which maintains the illusion that you should start with man:
Marx starts with the given economic formation, and in the
particular case of *Capital*, with the capitalist production
relation, and the relations which it determines in the last
instance in the superstructure. And each time he shows that
these relations determine and brand men, and how they
brand them in their concrete life, and how, through the
system of class struggles, living men are determined by the
system of these relations. In the 1857 *Introduction* Marx
said: the concrete is a synthesis of many determinations.
We might paraphrase him and say: men in the concrete
sense are determined by a synthesis of the many determinations of the relations in which they are held and to which
they are parties. If Marx does not start out from man, which
is an empty idea, that is, one weighed down with bourgeois
ideology, it is in order finally to reach living men; if he

makes a detour *via* these relations of which living men are the "bearers", it is in order finally to be able to grasp the laws which govern both their lives and their concrete struggles.

We should note that at no time does this detour *via* relations estrange Marx from living men, because at each moment of the process of knowledge, that is, at each moment in his analysis, Marx shows how each relation—from the capitalist production relation, determinant in the last instance, to the legal-political and ideological relations—brands men in their concrete life, which is governed by the forms and effects of the class struggle. Each of Marx's abstractions corresponds to the "abstraction" imposed on men by these relations, and this terribly concrete "abstraction" is what makes men into exploited workers or exploiting capitalists. We should also note that the final term of this process of thought, the "thought-concrete", to which it leads, is that synthesis of many determinations which defines concrete reality.

Marx thus placed himself on class positions, and he had in view the *mass* phenomena of the class struggle. He wanted to aid the working class to understand the mechanisms of capitalist society and to discover the relations and laws within which it lives, in order to reinforce and orient its struggle. He had no other object than the class struggle; his aim was to help the working class to make revolution and thus finally, under communism, to suppress the class struggle and classes.

The only more or less serious objection which can be made to the thesis of Marx's theoretical anti-humanism is, I must be honest enough to admit it, related to those texts which, in *Capital*, return to the theme of alienation. I say purposely: the *theme*, because I do not think that the passages in which this theme is taken up have a *theoretical* significance. I am suggesting that alienation appears there not as a really considered concept but as a substitute for realities which had not yet been thought out sufficiently for Marx to be able to refer to them: the forms, still on the horizon, of organization and struggle of the working class. The theme of alienation in *Capital* could thus be said to function as a substitute for a concept or concepts not yet formed, because the objective historical conditions had not yet produced their object. If this hypothesis is correct, it becomes possible to understand that the Commune, in answering Marx's expectations, rendered the theme of alienation superfluous, as did the whole of Lenin's political practice. In fact alienation disappears from Marx's thought after the Commune, and never appears in Lenin's immense work.

But this problem does not just concern Marxist theory; it also involves the historical forms of its fusion with the Labour Movement. This problem faces us openly today: we shall have to examine it.

Something New

The following remarks constitute Althusser's contribution to the public discussion in L'Humanite *on the draft resolution presented to the 21st—Extraordinary—Congress of the French Communist Party, held in October 1974. The resolution as finally adopted by the Congress can be read in* Cahiers du communisme, *no. 11, November 1974.*

By instinct, Communists have understood that the resolution put forward for consideration by the 21st Congress contains something new, which could be important.

It is obviously not a question of a change in line. But, within the same line, the Resolution provides more exact formulations, and rectifications and innovations.

1. The political line is defined with a new precision. The objective of the present class struggle is, in the short term, "democratic change", a "new democracy" which will apply the "democratic reforms" contained in the Common Programme, around which the Union of the Left has been sealed. The motor of democratic change will be the "Union of the French People", who can be "gathered together" into a "large majority". The present struggles prove that this union is "under way".

Where are the innovations? Essentially they concern two points:

(a) Who will be in power in the "new democracy"? Not the United Left alone, but the "alliance of all parties and organizations interested in democratic change". Of course the Union of the Left will remain the heart of this Broad Alliance.

(b) Just as the 20th Congress put the accent on "Popular Union", the Resolution puts the accent on the "Union of the French People".

But, first of all, why this extra notion? Does it not duplicate the notion of the Broad Alliance? The Resolution is not very clear on this important point (*cf.* paragraph 24, chapter IV).

What difference is there in principle between the Union of the Left and Popular Union? Between the Broad Alliance and the Union of the French People? The difference which exists between a union concluded *between organizations* and a union forged *among the masses*. The first is a minority, the second can be a "large majority".

There is of course a dialectic operating between the political union of organizations and union among the masses. When the Union of the Left was concluded, its effects were felt far beyond the ranks of the supporters of the Left, among the masses. The same will be true of the Broad Alliance, when it is concluded. But—*and this is the decisive point*—what is it that has made possible, necessary and inevitable the union between the French Communist Party, which has been fighting for it for years, the Socialist Party and the Left Radicals? The unprecedented development, in May 1968 and since, of the class struggle of the masses of the people, therefore the union of the masses in action.

The development of the union of the masses in the class struggle: thus the agreement between organizations; thus the further development of the union of the masses; thus the broadening of the alliance between organizations, etc. That is the dialectic of the movement, *in which it is the union of the masses in the class struggle which plays the determinant role*.

One must therefore clearly distinguish between the alliance between organizations and the Union of the French People, so as to be able to grasp their dialectic, and also so as not to give the term "majority" a purely electoral sense. Because, once the elections are won, the alliance in power will only be able to govern against the monopolies if it can depend on the power of a people united in the class struggle to come.

By definition, the Union of the French People can only be realized at the base. How? "Around the reforms proposed by the Common Programme." But what are the means to this end? The explanations given by the militants of the Party and of the other allied organizations, and their diffusion. Discussions, therefore. Now all this is true. But more is needed: Marxists know that at the level of the masses ideas are only really exchanged in action and through action.

One must therefore be explicit. The Union of the French People is the union of working people, democrats and patriots *around the working class*; it is a union, *at the grass roots*, of the masses of the people in protest and struggle: workers, peasants, employees, artisans, tradesmen, intellectuals, women, soldiers, etc. The union of political, trades union and other *organizations* is both the effect and the condition of the struggle: but *it is the Union of the French People which is the decisive motor of the struggle*.

This union is under way. But it must *continually* gain strength and especially cohesion if it is to win victory. It is not enough to count on "the crisis" and the general discontent, nor to pile up "sectional" actions. To think that these actions are going to "converge" by themselves would be to fall into the illusion of spontaneism. This discontent and these actions have to be *welded together* in a common political will. Now what is capable of really bringing and welding these actions and protests together? The working class and its organizations, and in the front rank of these, the Party. That is why the Union of the French People can only be constructed around the working class.

I should like the Resolution to say: (1) the Union of the French People is the decisive motor of the coming political transformations; (2) the Union of the French People must be welded together around the working class; (3) the Union of the French People will be welded together by the action of the masses and action among the masses: the role of the Party is essential in this.

These clarifications are all the more necessary because the Resolution makes an innovation in comparison to the 20th Congress by talking about the Union of the *French*

People. Why? The idea here is to unite around the working class not only democrats but also patriots (*e.g.* the Gaullists) who are concerned about France's independence and future. An "electoral manoeuvre", it will be said. A way of gaining votes to cross the famous "barrier".

Communists will never fall into electoral cretinism. They know that electoral relations of force *can* (here it is the case) obscure the relations of class forces.

When the Resolution defines the French people which it is calling on to unite—"the whole people, with the sole exception of the feudal barons of big business"—it tells the truth, but in the form of a *slogan*.

It is true that objectively, and in the long run, only the monopolists and their agents (plus: world imperialism) have a real interest in the maintenance of the dictatorship of the monopolies in France.

But it is equally true that if this fraction of monopolists has been able to maintain itself in power up to the present day, it is because it has been able and clever enough to re-present "the general interest of the bourgeoisie as a class" (Marx), and it could only do this because it had a *mass base*: not only in the bourgeoisie, but also in the petty bourgeoisie and even in a part of the working class. Thus the electoral "barrier" which has caused so many surprises.

What "obstacle" did the electoral drive of the left come up against? Precisely *the present frontier of the mass class base of the bourgeoisie*, dominated by its monopolist fraction.

To reduce this "barrier" to nothing but prejudice, or simply to the anti-communist offensive (that is, to "ideas") is idealism. There is of course "tradition": but this is constituted and maintained by *concrete links*, not only ideological (ideology is something different from just "ideas") but also *material*, between the ruling class and its mass base. These relations are complicated, but always precise and vary-ing according to social category. The monopolists are not stupid: they know how to use existing relations, to let events develop or to intervene with such-and-such a measure to pre-serve these relations, through which they "hold on to" the different elements of their mass base (just two examples in a hundred: they know how to close their eyes to tax frauds among a certain social category; they "hold on to" some working people by the DPO, etc.).

To win these elements for the Union of the French People, propaganda (= ideas), though indispensable, is not enough. In each case you must study the material and ideological nature of these relations. *Only thus* can you find the correct response, therefore the correct forms of explanation, propaganda and action. Only thus can you wage a correct ideological struggle, relevant to the masses where they are, as they are: otherwise you will miss the mark. Have the difficulties which *L'Humanité* is facing also been looked at from this point of view?

In fact the need is for the Popular Union to *become* the Union of the French People, *by winning over the majority of the mass base* of the bourgeoisie. Here too you cannot count on any miracles of spontaneity, even stimulated by the crisis (in the past crises have opened the way to fascism). The need is for a political victory, the result of political action, whose centre is the working class and whose means are its organizations of class struggle. If this victory is brought off, then, and only then, will the enemies of the French people be reduced to the monopolists and their agents alone. That is why the definition of the French people by the Resolution has the truth of a slogan, which needs both detailed concrete analysis and action if it is to become real.

2. The Resolution contains *theoretical rectifications*, which, politically, all tend in the same direction.

It is no longer a question of defining "advanced democracy" in terms of the notorious formula: "Replace the logic of of profit" (capitalism?) "by the logic of needs" (what?). The 20th Congress had already toned this formula down, but it kept the essential terms. At that time Paul Laurent said: the "logic of needs" alludes rather to communism ("From each according to his ability, to each according to his needs"— Marx; a formula which moreover defines communism by its relations of distribution and not by its relations of production)—"its use should not be extended". In fact, since advanced democracy is not even socialism, what was this vague allusion to communism doing there?

It is true that the Resolution still talks, for some reason, about a "policy for man" and a "policy of reason" (*sic*). But it rectifies itself in several places: what matters is to satisfy *popular demands*. In using this latter kind of language it is possible to avoid falling into utopianism, that is, into political idealism, and raising excessive hopes, thus causing disappointments—and to avoid the temptation of trying to outbid everyone in spiritualism (*cf.* an article in *La Nouvelle Critique*, February 1973, on the Common Programme, centred on the "needs of the human person"!).

The Resolution does not repeat the old formula of an *"advanced democracy opening the road to socialism"*. On the contrary, it puts the accent on "new democracy", "democratic change". In fact, democracy cannot be qualified by any adjective (authentic, true, advanced) which measures a given real democracy against an "essence" of democracy—but only by one which measures it against its class content: in our case, *democracy for the people*. Likewise, the Resolution puts the accent on "limited democratic reforms". That does not mean that socialism is forgotten! Nor that a policy of reforms necessarily falls into reformism. Communists know that every victory in the class struggle is, in the more or less long term, a *step forward* towards socialism. It is not a question of a tactical manoeuvre, aimed at *others*: "Socialism frightens them? Then we shall keep quiet about socialism! And let us guarantee that this is not the thin end of the wedge!" On the contrary, it is a question of rejecting utopianism and its dangers.

Because it is true, and for us first of all, that there is no "thin end of the wedge". That means: you cannot programme revolution, whether peaceful or otherwise. Lenin said so often enough: it is not enough that revolution (the transition to socialism) should be "on the agenda". The "situation" must also be "revolutionary", which presupposes the accumulation and welding together of a considerable number of national and international contradictions. Finally, the "subjective conditions" (the organizations of class struggle of the masses) must be abreast of the objective conditions.

None of this can be programmed. None of it resembles the "thin end of a wedge". But there is a definite political consequence: you need a mass political line, strong enough and flexible enough to prepare the Party, even when the revolution is still far off, not only to cope with the "revolutionary situation" when it is opened up, but first of all, right now, to prepare it, to help it mature—without knowing in advance either when or how it will prevent itself.

The danger of the utopian-idealist formulae which the Resolution abandons or rightly rectifies can be seen. These formulae may deliver militants and the Party over to the illusion of the spontaneity of history, or to the idealism of the omnipotence of "ideas"—and divert them from their revolutionary task, which before the revolution does not consist in phrasemongering about Revolution, its antechambers and open doors, but in really preparing oneself to make it when the time is right.

As regards reformism, the matter is clear: a policy is reformist when it negotiates reforms which hinder revolution; it is revolutionary when it fights for reforms which prepare revolution.

I think that the Resolution should lead to the rectification or re-examination of a certain number of other utopian idealist formulae (*e.g.*, on the State, Law, and "State Monopoly Capitalism") which in recent years have flourished in the shadow of the slogans which the Resolution has correctly given up.

3. A few words, finally, on the Party.

All the measures proposed lead in the same direction. It is a question of making the Party into a vanguard party which is a *mass party*: through a bold recruitment policy, the promotion of the young militants linked most closely with the masses (the best in the factory, "the most popular"), and the appeal to the initiative of all militants.

These measures outline the image of a great mass party, armed with Marxist-Leninist theory, and cleared of the remains of dogmatism and sectarianism.

The watchword has been given: we are talking about a "New Party" or, to put it schematically, the accent is no longer placed *on the cadres* (*cf.* Stalin: "The cadres decide everything") but *on the masses*.

It necessarily follows that a heavier responsibility falls to the base of the Party: to the branches. The reason is simple: it is through its base, the branches, that the Party can become a mass party, applying a mass line in mass actions. A party must have many members before it can become a mass party, but that by itself is not enough: what makes it a mass party are its links with the masses, the mass actions in which it takes part, and above all the mass actions in which it can take the initiative "one step ahead of the masses, and one step only" (Lenin).

In these last years some Party militants have had to jump into a moving train, or have even got left on the platform. Why? Because they did not understand in time what was happening among the masses; they did not pay sufficient attention to their needs and reactions, nor did they make a detailed analysis of these, in order to give them shape, by proposing suitable united actions. The appeal to initiative, like G. Marchais' appeal to "get thinking", is addressed to every militant, but above all to the Party branches.

There can be no mass line (the Union of the French People) without a mass party: but there can be no mass party without clear initiative from "the base of the Party" (article XV of the *Statutes*), the *branches*, which are at the heart of the masses.

I therefore propose that the Resolution should specify, after paragraph 14, chapter V:

"In order properly to fulfil its vanguard role, the Party must thus become a great mass Party, capable of applying the mass line of the Union of the French People. The Party must greatly increase its membership: but to do that, and because it does so, it must be linked to the masses, to their responses and aspirations, in order to give these a shape and to initiate necessary actions, 'one step ahead of the masses, and one step only' (Lenin). This mass line places a heavier responsibility on the Party base, on the branches, and especially on the factory branches, because they are at the heart of the masses."

Louis Althusser
(Paris—V)

Bibliography

1. Works by Louis Althusser

1. *Montesquieu: la politique et l'histoire;* Paris, 1959.
2. Translator's note in L. Feuerbach, *Manifestes Philosophiques;* Paris, 1960.
3. "Philosophie et sciences humaines", *Revue de l'enseignement philosophique*, no. 5, June-July 1963.
4. Problèmes étudiants", in *La Nouvelle Critique*, no. 152, January 1964.
5. Presentation of the article of P. Macherey, "La Philosophie de la science de G. Canguilhem", in *La Pensée*, no. 113, January–February 1964.
6. "Freud et Lacan", in *La Nouvelle Critique*, nos. 161–162, December 1964–January 1965.
7. *Pour Marx;* Paris, 1965. Contains:
    i. Préface: aujourd'hui.
    ii. Les *Manifestes Philosophiques* [From *La Nouvelle Critique*, December 1960].
    iii. Sur le jeune Marx [*La Pensée*, March–April 1961].
    iv. Contradiction et surdétermination [*La Pensée*, December 1962].
    v. Notes sur un théâtre matérialiste [*Esprit*, December 1962].
    vi. Sur la dialectique matérialiste [*Cahiers de l'I.S.E.A.*, June 1964].
    vii. Marxisme et humanisme [*Cahiers de l'I.S.E.A.*, June 1964].
    viii. Note complémentaire sur l'humanisme 'réel' [*La Nouvelle Critique*, March 1965].
8. *Lire le Capital;* Paris, 1965 (with E. Balibar, J. Rancière, P. Macherey and R. Establet). Contains:
    i. Du *Capital* à la philosophie de Marx.
    ii. L'objet du *Capital*.
    A second edition appeared in four volumes, in 1968 and 1973.
9. "Matérialisme historique et matérialisme dialectique", in *Cahiers Marxistes-Léninistes*, no. 11, 1966.
10. "Sur le *Contrat Social* (les décalages)", in *Cahiers pour l'analyse*, no. 8, 1966.
11. "Sur le travail théorique: difficultés et ressources", in *La Pensée*, no. 132, April 1967.
12. Preface to the second (Spanish) edition of *Pour Marx: La Revolución téorica de Marx;* Mexico-Buenos Aires, 1967.

13. *Cours de philosophie pour scientifiques* (mimeographed); 1967.
14. *Lénine et la philosophie;* Paris, 1969.
15. "La Philosophie comme arme de la révolution", in *La Pensee*, no. 138, March–April 1968. [First appeared, in shortened form, in *L'Unità*, 1.2.1968.]
16. "Comment lire *Le Capital?*", in *L'Humanité*, 23.3.1969.
17. "Avertissement aux lecteurs du Livre I du *Capital*", in K. Marx, *Le Capital*, Garnier-Flammarion edition; Paris, 1969.
18. Letters, in M-A. Macciocchi, *Lettere dall' interno del P.C.I. a Louis Althusser;* Milan, 1969. [English edition: London, NLB 1973.]
19. "A propos de l'article de Michel Verret sur Mai Etudiant", in *La Pensée*, no. 145, 1969.
20. "To my English Readers"; Preface to the English edition of *Pour Marx: For Marx;* London, 1969.
21. "Idéologie et appareils idéologiques d'Etat (notes pour une recherche)", in *La Pensée*, June 1970, no. 151.
22. *Reading Capital*; London 1970. [English translation of the second edition of ref. 8, containing only the contributions of Althusser and Balibar].
23. *Lenin and Philosophy and Other Essays;* London, 1971. English translation of refs. 6, 14, 24 (except "Sur le rapport de Marx à Hegel"), 17, 21, together with:
    i. A letter on Art in Reply to André Daspre [From *La Nouvelle Critique*, April 1966].
    ii. Cremonini, Painter of the Abstract [From *Démocratie Nouvelle*, August 1966].
24. *Lénine et la philosophie* (2nd edition, 1972). Second edition also includes:
    i. "Sur le rapport de Marx à Hegel" [Intervention in J. Hyppolite's seminar, 23.1.1968].
    ii. "Lénine devant Hegel" (1969).
25. "Une erreur politique", in *France Nouvelle*, July 25 and August 1, 1972.
26. "Reply to John Lewis (Self-Criticism)", in *Marxism Today*, October and November 1972.
27. *Politics and History;* London, 1972. Contains:
    i. Montesquieu: Politics and History [Ref. 1].
    ii. Rousseau: the Social Contract [Ref. 10].
    iii. Marx's Relation to Hegel [Ref. 24 (i)].
28. "The Condition of Marx's Scientific Discovery", in *Theoretical Practice*, nos. 7–8, January 1973.
29. Intervention in the discussion on "Les communistes, les intellectuels et la culture", Fête de l'*Humanité;* in *France Nouvelle*, 18.9.1973.
30. Four unpublished texts in Saül Karsz, *Théorie et Politique:* Louis Althusser (Paris, 1974):
    i. Projet de préface pour un recueil de textes (1968).
    ii. Texte ronéotypé (1970).
    iii. A propos de *Lénine et la Philosophie* et de l'article "Comment lire *Le Capital?*".
    iv. Préface à la seconde édition en espagnol du livre de Marta Harnecker, *Los Conceptos elementales del materialismo histórico;* Mexico-Buenos Aires, 1971.

31. *Eléments d'autocritique;* Paris, 1974.
32. *Philosophie et philosophie spontanée des savants;* Paris, 1974. [Amended version of ref. 13.]

2. Works on Louis Althusser

1. M. Dufrenne, *Pour l'homme;* Paris, 1966.
2. Central Committee of the French Communist Party: "Débats sur les problèmes idéologiques et culturels"; report of interventions made during the Central Committee meeting held at Argenteuil in March 1966, in *Cahiers du Communisme*, nos. 5–6, May–June 1966.
3. J.-L. Nancy, "Marx et la philosophie", in *Esprit*, no. 349, 1966.
4. R. Paris, "En deçà du marxisme", *Les Temps Modernes*, no. 240, 1966.
5. N. Poulantzas, "Vers une théorie marxiste", *Les Temps Modernes, ibid.*
6. J. Pouillon, "Du côté de chez Marx", *Les Temps Modernes, ibid.*
7. G. Thibert, "Pour lire Althusser", in *Quatrième Internationale*, no. 30, March 1967.
8. A. Badiou, "Le (re) commencement du matérialisme dialectique", in *Critique,* no. 240, 1967.
9. J. Conilh, "Lecture de Marx", in *Esprit*, no. 360, 1967.
10. A. Glucksmann, "Un Structuralisme ventriloque", in *Les Temps Modernes*, no. 250, 1967. [See ref. 26 below.]
11. H. Lefebvre, "Sur une interprétation du marxisme", in *L'Homme et la Société*, 1967, no. 4.
12. C. Luporini, "Réflexions sur Louis Althusser", in *L'Homme et la Société*, 1967, no. 4 [Introduction to the Italian edition of *Pour Marx.*]
13. E. Bottigelli, "En lisant Althusser", in *Raison Présente*, 1967, no. 2.
14. L. Sève, "Méthode structurale et méthode dialectique", *La Pensée*, no. 135, December 1967.
15. J.-A. Gianotti, "Contra Althusser", in *Teoria e pratica*, Sao Paulo, 1968, no. 3.
16. J. Hyppolite, "Le 'scientifique' et l' 'idéologique' dans une perspective marxiste", in *Diogène*, no. 64, 1968.
17. P. Vilar, B. Fraenkel, R. Paris, S. Pullberg, F. Châtelet, J.-C. Forquin, *Dialectique marxiste et Pensée structurale* (seminar on Althusser), in *Cahiers du Centre d'Etudes Socialistes*, 1968.
18. F. George, "Lire Althusser", in *Les Temps Modernes*, no. 275, 1969.
19. C. Glucksmann, "A propos d'Althusser: la pratique léniniste de la philosophie", in *La Nouvelle Critique*, no. 23, 1969.
20. V. Korać, "The Phenomenon of 'Theoretical Anti-humanism'", in *Praxis*, nos. 3–4, 1969.
21. H. Lefebvre, "Les paradoxes d'Althusser", in *L'Homme et la Société*, no. 13, 1969.
22. E. Mandel, "Althusser 'corrects' Marx", *International*, September 1970.
23. S. Karsz, J. Pouillon [ref. 6], A. Badiou [ref. 8], E. De Ipola, J. Rancière [ref. 30], *Lectura de Althusser;* Buenos Aires, 1970.
24. B. Oelgart, *Idéologues et idéologies de la nouvelle gauche;* Paris, 1970.
25. L. Kolakowski, "Althusser's Marx", in *Socialist Register*, 1971.
26. A. Glucksmann, "A Ventriloquist Structuralism", in *New Left Review*, no. 72, March-April 1972. [Translation of ref. 10 above.]

27. G. Lock, "Louis Althusser: Philosophy and Leninism", in *Marxism Today*, June 1972.

28. A. Brossat, "Les Epigones", in *Critiques de l'Economie Politique*, October-December 1972, no. 9.

29. M. Lowy, "Objectivité et point de vue de classe dans les sciences sociales", in *Critiques de l'Economie Politique*, October-December 1972, no. 9.

30. J. Rancière, "Sur la théorie de l'idéologie: la politique d'Althusser", in *L'Homme et la Société*, no. 27, 1972. [See also ref. 47.]

31. N. Geras, "Althusserian Marxism", in *New Left Review*, no. 71, January-February 1972.

32. B. Sichère, "Sur la lutte idéologique", in *Tel Quel*, no. 52, Winter 1972.

33. M. Glabermann, "Lenin versus Althusser", in *Radical America*, 1972, vol. 3, no. 5. (Special number on Althusser).

34. J.-P. Fargier and others, "Pratiques artistiques et luttes de classes: une conception de la philosophie", in *Cinéthique*, Winter 1972, nos. 13–14.

35. *Ibid.*, nos. 15–16, "De la 'nouvelle' pratique philosophique".

36. J. Lewis, "The Althusser Case", in *Marxism Today*, January and February 1972.

37. P. Vilar, "Histoire marxiste, histoire en construction. Essai de dialogue avec Althusser", in *Annales*, 1973, no. 1.

38. M. Cranston, "The Ideology of Althusser", in *Problems of Communism* [United States Information Service journal], March-April 1973.

39. M. Cornforth, "The Althusser-Lewis Debate", in *Marxism Today*, May 1973.

40. P. Vilar, "Marxist History, a History in the Making: Towards a dialogue with Althusser", in *New Left Review*, no. 80, July-August 1973. [Translation of ref. 35.]

41. J. Metzger, "Après avoir lu le dernier livre de L. Althusser" [*Réponse à John Lewis*], in *France Nouvelle*, 16 October 1973.

42. P. Nemo, "Althusser est-il maoïste?", in *Le Nouvel Observateur*, 6.8.1973.

43. E. Terray, "Le Livre de L. Althusser [*Réponse à John Lewis*], un événement politique", in *Le Monde*, 17.8.1973.

44. J. Rancière, "La nouvelle orthodoxie de L. Althusser", *Le Monde*, 12.9.1973.

45. J. Colombel, "Althusser, le PCF et les trompettes de la renommée", in *Politique Hebdo*, 1.10.1973.

46. A. Gilles, "Maître Althusser et la politique", in *Communisme*, no. 6, September-October 1973.

47. A. Lipietz, "D'Althusser à Mao?", in *Les Temps Modernes*, November 1973.

48. G. Lock, "Real Problems and Real Answers", *The Times Higher Education Supplement*, 4.1.1974.

49. S. Karsz, *Théorie et politique: Louis Althusser;* Paris, 1974.

50. J. Rancière, "On the Theory of Ideology (the Politics of Althusser)", in *Radical Philosophy*, no. 7 (Spring 1974).

51. N.-E. Thévenin, "Sur *Réponse a John Lewis* ou les yeux et la mémoire", in *La Nouvelle Critique*, no. 73, April 1974.

52. H. Jour, "Louis Althusser révisionniste 'de gauche'?"; in *Prolétariat*, no. 5, 2ᵉ trimestre 1974.
53. M. Glucksmann, *Structuralist Analysis in Contemporary Social Thought* [on Althusser and Lévi-Strauss]; London, 1974.
54. J.-M. Vincent and others, *Contre Althusser;* Paris 1974.
55. J. Rancière, *La Leçon d'Althusser;* Paris, 1974.
56. Henry Veltmeyer, "Towards an Assessment of the Structuralist Interrogation of Marx: Claude Lévi-Strauss and Louis Althusser", in *Science and Society*, Winter 1974–75.
57. Joseph Gabel, "Marxisme hongrois, 'hungaro-marxisme', Ecole de Budapest (Contribution à une sociologie de la connaissance du courant althusserien)", in *L'Homme et la Société*, January-June 1975, no. 35–36.
58. Pierre Riboulet, "Quelques remarques à propos de la lutte des classes dans l'idéologie", in *L'Homme et la Société, ibid.*

Index

Angelov, S., 3
Aquinas, Thomas, 44
Archimedes, 183
Aristotle, 43, 60, 134, 137
Aron, Raymond, 115n
Augustine, 44

Bachelard, Gaston, 61, 114, 121, 122n, 124n, 190
Balibar, Étienne, vii, 12n, 14, 17n, 19n, 24n, 29n, 62n
Bentham, Jeremy, 85
Bernstein, Eduard, 73, 85
Bettelheim, Charles, 6, 23, 24, 25
Boas, Franz, 128
Brunschvicg, Léon, 132
Brus, Wlodzimierz, 20n
Bukharin, Nikolai, 112

Canguilhem, Georges, 124n
Carr, Edward Hallett, 9
Chang Chung-shih, 27n
Communist Party of China, 25–27
Communist Party of France, 2–3, 25, 75, 78, 208ff.
Communist Party of Great Britain, 39, 45, 77
Communist Party of the Soviet Union, 5, 15, 36, 74–5, 79, 82–3, 92, 168, 173
Cranston, Maurice, 4–5
Croce, Benedetto, 115n

Della Volpe, Galvano, 173
Descartes, René, 4, 61, 97, 119, 136–7, 141, 167, 178
Dietzgen, Joseph, 36
Dühring, Eugen, 73

Ellman, Michael, 25–6

Engels, Friedrich, 37, 38, 39, 64–5, 70, 73, 98, 109n, 114, 116, 144, 145, 149, 156–7, 159, 175, 176, 185, 194n
Epicurus, 178, 179

Feuerbach, Ludwig, 61, 66, 69, 97–8, 109n, 158, 159, 196–200
Fichte, Johann Gottlieb, 61, 69
Franklin, Benjamin, 43
Freud, Sigmund, 60

Galilei, Galilco, 60
Garaudy, Roger, 2, 6, 76, 83
Geras, Norman, 3
Glucksmann, André, 3
Glucksmann, Christine, 2n
Gramsci, Antonio, 37, 65, 94, 110n

Hegel, Georg Wilhelm Friedrich, 4, 36, 42, 44, 54, 61, 68–70, 85, 112, 113n, 123n, 128, 130, 133–41, 145, 150, 158, 159, 166, 170, 176, 178–88, 190, 192, 198
Hitler, Adolf, 16
Hobbes, Thomas, 166, 167
Hugo, Victor, 99
Hume, David, 193
Husserl, Edmund, 4, 96–7
Hyppolite, Jean, 165

Jankélévitch, M., 165

Kalinin, Mikhail, 9
Kant, Immanuel, 4, 61, 69, 73, 85, 96–8, 166–7, 178, 193
Karsz, Saül, vii
Kautsky, Karl, 14, 91, 112
Khrushchev, Nikita, 5, 20, 32, 79
Klugmann, James, vii

Kolakowski, Leszek, 3–4, 6
Korac, Veljko, 3
Korsch, Karl, 6n, 115n

Lassalle, Ferdinand, 63
Laurent, Paul, 212
Lecourt, Dominique, 133n
Leibniz, Gottfried Wilhelm, 141
Lenin, Vladimir Ilyich, 8, 12n, 17, 18,
    22–3, 28–30, 36–9, 50, 54, 60, 61n,
    64–5, 66n, 67, 73–4, 75n, 83, 85,
    87–90, 92, 95, 96, 98, 107, 110n, 112,
    113n, 114–7, 122, 123n, 133, 137–8,
    144, 145, 147–9, 151–2, 154, 156–7,
    161, 169–72, 180–1, 185–8, 193–4,
    195, 207, 213, 215
Lévi-Strauss, Claude, 128–9
Lévy, Bernard-Henry, 5
Lewis, John, vii, 2, 5, 6, 7, 21, 34–99
    (*passim*), 102, 105, 107, 109n
Locke, John, 167
Lukács, Georg, 6n, 115n, 186
Luxemburg, Rosa, 112
Lysenko, Trofim, 78, 120n

Machiavelli, Niccolò, 136, 166–7,
    170–1
Mandel, Ernest, 6
Mao Tse-tung, 5, 26–7, 37, 50, 58, 65,
    110n, 112, 114, 117, 144, 145–6
Marchais, Georges, 215
Marcuse, Herbert, 6, 118n
Marx, Karl, 10, 11, 17, 18, 19n, 38–41,
    43, 47, 49n, 50–4, 56, 59, 60–76,
    83–4, 85n, 86, 94, 97–9, 102, 104–5,
    107–18, 119–21, 123, 126, 128–30,
    133–4, 136–41, 147, 149, 151–61,
    165, 168–70, 173–207, 211, 212
McLellan, David, 4
Mepham, John, 3
Mészaros, István, 4
Metzer, Joe, 3
Milhau, Jacques, 2
Molière, Jean-Baptiste, 145
Montesquieu, Charles de Secondat,
    165, 167, 182

Nan Ching, 27n
Napoleon III, 99

Pannekoek, Anton, 115n
Pascal, Blaise, 112
Plato, 36, 44, 119, 145
Plekhanov, Georgy, 91
Poulantzas, Nicos, 24n
Proudhon, Pierre-Joseph, 66, 73, 99,
    111, 123n

Rancière, Jacques, 3n, 6
Reich, Wilhelm, 118n
Ricardo, David, 113n
Rochet, Waldeck, 2
Rousseau, Jean-Jacques, 59, 165, 167,
    185, 191

Sakharova, T. A., 3
Sartre, Jean-Paul, 43–5, 59–61, 97–9
Saussure, Ferdinand de, 128
Sève, Lucien, 2, 96
Shakhty trial, 9
Sollers, Philippe, 5
Spartacus, 46
Spinoza, Baruch, 122, 126, 132–41,
    146, 166, 167, 174, 178, 179, 187–93,
    200
Stalin, Josef Vissarionovich, 3, 5, 6, 7,
    13–16, 18–20, 22–4, 26–8, 31–2, 36,
    37, 75, 78, 79–83, 89, 91, 92, 126n,
    173, 214
Stirner, Max, 115n, 116, 118n
Sweezy, Paul, 20–1

Thales, 110n
Tran Duc Thao, 97
Trotsky, Leon, 23, 29, 79n, 81n, 82–3

Vico, Giambattista, 41, 55
Vincent, Jean-Marie, 6n

Wagner, Adolph, 112
Weitling, Wilhelm, 113
Weydemeyer, Joseph, 49n

Althusser, Louis.
    Essays in self-criticism / Louis
Althusser; translated by Grahame
Lock. -- London : NLB ; Atlantic
Highlands, N.J. : Humanities Press,
1976.
    viii, 224 p. ; 22 cm.
    CONTENTS: Reply to John Lewis: Not
on "The critique of the personality
cult". Remark on the category
"Process without a subject or goal (s
"--Elements of self-criticism: On th
evolution of the young Marx.--Is it
simple to be a Marxist in philosophy
"Something new".
    Bibliography: p. [217]-221.
                    (Cont. on next card